REAL ESTATE
APPRAISAL EXAM

REAL ESTATE APPRAISAL EXAM

NEW YORK

Library of Congress Cataloging-in-Publication Data:
Real estate appraisal exam.—1st ed.
   p. cm.
  ISBN: 978-1-57685-587-4 (alk. paper)
1. Real property—Valuation—Examinations, questions, etc.
I. LearningExpress (Organization)
HD1387.R363 2007
333.33'2076—dc22

2007000762

Printed in the United States of America

9 8 7 6 5 4 3 2 1

First Edition

ISBN: 978-1-57685-587-4

Regarding the Information in This Book
We attempt to verify the information presented in our books prior to publication. It is always a good idea, however, to double-check such important information as minimum requirements, application and testing procedures, and deadlines with your state's real estate licensing agency, as such information can change from time to time.

For more information or to place an order, contact LearningExpress at:
  55 Broadway
  8th Floor
  New York, NY 10006

Or visit us at:
  www.learnatest.com

Contributors ▶

Robert S. Abelson, PhD, is an Appraiser Qualifications Board (AQB) certified Uniform Standards of Professional Appraisal Practice (USPAP) instructor and has been teaching real estate appraisal courses since 1999. He is an active member of the California Real Estate Educators Association. Dr. Abelson is a co-revision author of the California Community Colleges' *Real Estate Appraisal Instructor and Student Study Guides* and has served as a review editor for other real estate publishers. He is an active California certified general appraiser and has been appraising commercial and residential properties throughout Southern California since 1993.

Timothy A. Griffith, MS, ASA, is the president of Griffith & Associates, a real estate appraisal and consulting firm located in Secaucus, New Jersey, and has been involved in the field of real estate since 1985. He also serves as an adjunct lecturer of real estate valuation at Baruch College (CUNY) and as an instructor at Bergen Community College. Mr. Griffith has a master of science degree in real estate valuation and analysis from New York University, is an AQB certified USPAP instructor, and is the former governor of Region 15 for the American Society of Appraisers.

Elaine Israel is a writer who lives and works in New York City.

Joseph S. Rabianski, PhD, CRE, has taught appraisal, investment, finance, and market analysis over his 35-year career in real estate. He also takes on consulting assignments in these areas. He has coauthored five books and published more than 90 articles on real estate–related topics in academic and professional journals.

Steve Williamson owns Real Estate Education Specialists in Orlando, Florida. He is an author of real estate–related textbooks, a speaker, and has been a real estate appraisal course instructor for the past 25 years. He obtained his real estate broker license in 1979 and was one of the first state-certified general real estate appraiser course instructors in Florida.

Contents ▶

REAL ESTATE
APPRAISAL EXAM

1 ▶ The Real Estate Appraisal Exams

CHAPTER SUMMARY

Congratulations! You are about to take the next step in your real estate appraisal career. This chapter provides an overview of the Appraisal Foundation's Appraiser Qualifications Board's (AQB) National Uniform Exam Content Outlines as well as how this book can help you succeed on whatever exam you take!

WHATEVER LEVEL OF appraisal licensing or certification exam you are planning to take, this book can help you get a top score. It will show you how to put all the pieces of test preparation together. Not only that, this book includes four complete practice exams covering the topics mandated in the AQB's current National Uniform Exam Content Outlines; two exams for those seeking to become a state-licensed real estate appraiser or state-certified residential appraiser, and two exams for those seeking to earn their certification as a general appraiser. It also includes a real estate math review, a real estate glossary, and access to two online exams to practice your exam on the computer.

▶ Your Upcoming Real Estate Appraisal Exam

To respond to the failure of an extensive number of savings and loan institutions in the 1980s, Congress enacted legislation in 1989 called the Financial Institutions Reform, Recovery, and Enforcement Act (FIRREA). FIRREA included a provision mandating that a state-licensed or state-certified real estate appraiser must be used for any federally related real estate transaction.

This law also required that state regulatory and licensing agencies use the expertise of the private sector as a source for the setting of the qualifications and standards for real property appraisers. The Appraisal Foundation was authorized to provide this expertise, and continues to do so today. Although the educational and professional requirements for licensure, certification, and recertification vary by state, there is a uniform minimum criteria set by the AQB, to which every state must adhere. Effective January 1, 2008, these minimum criteria are changing drastically, and it is strongly encouraged that every candidate for licensure or certification contact the Appraisal Foundation (www.appraisalfoundation.org), as well his or her particular state's appraiser regulatory agency for all details that are available. Every appraiser candidate should consult the AQB's *Student Appraiser Guide* to understand what the changes to the core curriculum will be and how it will affect him or her. Simply Google "Student Appraiser Guide" for the link to the document on the Appraisal Foundation's website.

Remember, while the AQB provides each state and territory with the minimum requirements, every candidate for licensure or certification must look to his or her individual state for the exact specifics regarding the classifications that are utilized and the requirements that are necessary to obtain them. A contact list of regulatory agencies can be found on page 3 of this chapter.

As you are probably well aware, the final step to gaining any level of licensure or certification as an appraiser is taking the exam. Some states administer their own examination for licensure and certification; other states use the services of an independent testing company. These examinations can either be pencil-and-paper tests or administered on a computer. They are usually between 100 and 125 questions, depending on the level of licensure or certification that you are testing for, and the tests usually have a time limit between one and three hours. Whatever your state's particular case, every one of these exams must minimally adhere to the AQB's National Uniform Exam Content Outlines. These outlines detail the essential domains to be tested, as well as what percentage of the exam each of these essential domains should comprise. The current outlines require the testing of knowledge of 15 domains*:

- Influences on Real Estate Value
- Legal Considerations
- Types of Value
- Economic Principles
- Real Estate Markets and Analysis
- Valuation Process
- Property Description
- Highest and Best Use Analysis
- Appraisal Statistical Concepts (Math and Statistics)
- Sales Comparison Approach
- Site Value
- Cost Approach

*Please note that the practice exams in this book were developed using the current standards; however, the practice examinations available to you online were developed using the outline that will go into effect in 2008.

- Income Approach
- Valuation of Partial Interest
- Appraisal Standards and Ethics (USPAP)

New examination content outlines have been developed that will become effective January 1, 2008, concurrent with the 2008 criteria changes. This new outline omits the "Valuation Process" domain and stipulates for significantly more questions in "Real Estate Markets and Analysis," "Sales Comparison Approach," "Appraisal Statistical Concepts," and "Appraisal Standards and Ethics." Also of interest to test takers is that, in an effort to make the state testing more uniform across the nation and its territories, the AQB is currently developing new uniform state appraiser examinations that will also become effective on January 1, 2008. States may opt to use these examinations or their equivalents in lieu of developing new examinations or hiring independent testing agencies to do so.

▶ About Licensing and Certification Requirements and Exams

As we have already stressed, the most accurate and up-to-date information about your particular exam is available through your state's appraisal regulatory agency. That is why it is essential to contact your state's organization before the exam. For your convenience, here's a list of the contact information for each state's regulatory board.

At the time of publication, the following information was correct. Please understand that websites and/or other contact information may have since changed.

▶ State Real Estate Appraiser Regulatory Boards

ALABAMA
Alabama Real Estate Appraisers Board
P.O. Box 304355
Montgomery, AL 36130-4355
334-242-8747
www.reab.state.al.us

ARIZONA
Arizona Board of Appraisal
1400 W. Washington, Suite 360
Phoenix, AZ 85007
602-542-1539
www.appraisal.state.az.us

ALASKA
Board of Certified Real Estate Appraisers
333 Willoughby Avenue, 9th Floor
P.O. Box 110806
Juneau, AK 99811-0806
907-465-5470
www.commerce.state.ak.us/occ

ARKANSAS
Arkansas Appraiser Licensing
and Certification Board
101 E. Capitol Street, Suite 430
Little Rock, AR 72201
501-296-1843
www.state.ar.us/alcb

CALIFORNIA
Office of Real Estate Appraisers
1102 Q Street, Suite 4100
Sacramento, CA 95814
916-552-9000
www.orea.ca.gov

COLORADO
Division of Real Estate
1560 Broadway, Suite 925
Denver, CO 80202
303-894-2166
www.dora.state.co.us/real-estate

CONNECTICUT
Real Estate Appraisal Commission
State Office Building, Room 110
165 Capitol Avenue
Hartford, CT 06106
860-713-6150
www.ct.gov

DELAWARE
Council on Real Estate Appraisers
Cannon Building, Suite 203
861 Silver Lake Boulevard
Dover, DE 19904
302-744-4505
www.dpr.delaware.gov

DISTRICT OF COLUMBIA
Department of Consumer & Regulatory
Affairs/Occupational & Professional
Licensing Administration
941 N. Capitol Street NE, Room 7200
Washington, D.C. 20002
202-442-4320
http://dcra.dc.gov/dcra/site/default.asp

FLORIDA
Department of Business and Professional Regulation
400 W. Robinson Street, Suite N-801
Orlando, FL 32801
850-487-1395
www.state.fl.us/dbpr/re/index.shtml

GEORGIA
Georgia Real Estate Commission and Appraisers
Board
International Tower
229 Peachtree Street, NE, Suite 1000
Atlanta, GA 30303-1605
404-656-3916
www.grec.state.ga.us/index.html

HAWAII
Hawaii Real Estate Appraiser Advisory Committee
P.O. Box 3469
Honolulu, HI 96801
808-586-2701
www.hawaii.gov/dcca/pvl

IDAHO
Idaho Real Estate Appraiser Board
Bureau of Occupational Licenses
Owyhee Plaza
1109 Main Street, Suite 220
Boise, ID 83702-5642
208-334-3233
www.ibol.idaho.gov

ILLINOIS
Illinois Office of Banks and Real Estate
310 S. Michigan Avenue, Suite 2130
Chicago, IL 60604
312-793-3000
www.obre.state.il.us

INDIANA
Real Estate Appraiser Licensure
and Certification Board
Indiana Professional Licensing Agency
Indiana Government Center—South
402 W. Washington Street, Room W072
Indianapolis, IN 46204
317-234-3009
www.in.gov/pla/bandc/appraiser

IOWA
Iowa Real Estate Appraiser Examining Board
1920 SE Hulsizer Road
Ankeny, IA 50021-3941
515-281-4126
www.state.ia.us/iapp

KANSAS
Kansas Real Estate Appraisal Board
1100 SW Wannamaker Road, Suite 104
Topeka, KS 66604
785-271-3373
www.accesskansas.org/kreab

KENTUCKY
Kentucky Real Estate Appraisers Board
2624 Research Park Drive, Suite 204
Lexington, KY 40511
859-543-8943
www.kreab.ky.gov

LOUISIANA
Louisiana Real Estate Appraisers Board
5222 Summa Court
Baton Rouge, LA 70809
225-765-0191
www.reab.state.la.us/

MAINE
Maine Board of Real Estate Appraisers
35 State House Station
Augusta, ME 04333-0035
207-624-8603
www.maineprofessionalreg.org

MARYLAND
Maryland Real Estate
Appraisers Commission
500 N. Calvert Street
Baltimore, MD 21202
410-230-6165
www.dllr.state.md.us

MASSACHUSETTS
Board of Registration of
Real Estate Appraisers
239 Causeway Street, Suite 500
Boston, MA 02114
617-727-3055
www.mass.gov/dpl/boards/ra

MICHIGAN
Michigan Board of Real Estate Appraisers
Licensing Division
P.O. Box 30018
Lansing, MI 48909
517-241-9288
www.michigan.gov/appraisers

MINNESOTA
Minnesota Department of Commerce
85 7th Place East, Suite 500
St. Paul, MN 55101
651-296-4026
www.commerce.state.mn.us

MISSISSIPPI
Mississippi Appraiser Board
P.O. Box 12685
Jackson, MS 39236
601-932-9191
www.mrec.state.ms.us/default.asp?siteid=2

MISSOURI
Missouri Real Estate Appraisers Commission
3605 Missouri Boulevard
P.O. Box 1335
Jefferson City, MO 65102-1335
573-751-0038
www.pr.mo.gov/appraisers.asp

MONTANA
Board of Real Estate Appraisers
301 S. Park Avenue, 4th Floor
P.O. Box 200513
Helena, MT 59620-0513
406-841-2323
http://mt.gov/bsd/license/
bsd_boards/rea_boards/board_page.asp

NEBRASKA
Nebraska Real Property Appraiser Board
P.O. Box 68509
Lincoln, NE 68509
402-471-9015
www.appraiser.ne.gov

NEVADA
Nevada Real Estate Division
2501 E. Sahara Avenue, Suite 102
Las Vegas, NV 89104-4137
702-486-4033
www.red.state.nv.us

NEW HAMPSHIRE
New Hampshire Real Estate Appraiser Board
State House Annex, Room 426
25 Capitol Street
Concord, NH 03301-6312
603-271-6186
www.nh.gov/nhreab

NEW JERSEY
Board of Real Estate Appraisers
Division of Consumer Affairs
P.O. Box 45032
Newark, NJ 07101
973-504-6480
www.state.nj.us/lps/ca/nonmed.htm

NEW MEXICO
New Mexico Real Estate Appraisers Board
2550 Cerrillos Road
Santa Fe, NM 87505
505-476-4639
www.rld.state.nm.us

NEW YORK
Department of State
New York State Board of
Real Estate Appraisers
84 Holland Avenue
Albany, NY 12208
518-474-4429
www.dos.state.ny.us

NORTH CAROLINA
North Carolina Appraisal Board
5830 Six Forks Road
Raleigh, NC 27609
919-870-4854
www.ncappraisalboard.org

NORTH DAKOTA
Real Estate Appraiser Qualifications and Ethics Board
P.O. Box 1336
Bismarck, ND 58502-1336
701-222-1051
www.governor.state.nd.us/boards/
boards_query.asp?Board_ID=92

OHIO
Ohio Real Estate Appraiser Board
Division of Real Estate and Professional Licensing
Ohio Department of Commerce
77 S. High Street, 20th Floor
Columbus, OH 43215-6133
614-466-4100
www.com.state.oh.us

OKLAHOMA
Oklahoma Real Estate Appraiser Board
P.O. Box 53408
Oklahoma City, OK 73152-3408
405-521-6636
www.oid.state.ok.us

OREGON
Appraiser Certification and Licensure Board
1860 Hawthorne Avenue NE, Suite 200
Salem, OR 97301
503-485-2555
www.oregonaclb.org

PENNSYLVANIA
Pennsylvania State Board of Certified Real Estate Appraisers
2601 N. Third Street
P.O. Box 2649
Harrisburg, PA 17105-2649
717-783-4866
www.dos.state.pa.us/real

RHODE ISLAND
Rhode Island Real Estate Appraisers Board
Department of Business Regulation
Appraisal Section
233 Richmond Street, Suite 230
Providence, RI 02903
401-222-2255
www.dbr.state.ri.us

SOUTH CAROLINA
South Carolina Real Estate Appraisers Board
P.O. Box 11847
Columbia, SC 29211-1847
803-896-4400
www.llr.state.sc.us

SOUTH DAKOTA
South Dakota Department of Revenue and Regulation
445 E. Capitol Avenue
Pierre, SD 57501-3185
605-773-4608
www.state.sd.us/appraisers

TENNESSEE
Tennessee Real Estate Appraiser Commission
500 James Robertson Parkway, 6th Floor
Nashville, TN 37243
615-741-1831
www.state.tn.us/commerce/boards/treac

TEXAS
Texas Appraiser Licensing and Certification Board
P.O. Box 12188
Austin, TX 78711-2188
512-465-3950
www.talcb.state.tx.us

UTAH

Utah Division of Real Estate

Department of Commerce

P.O. Box 146711

Salt Lake City, UT 84114-6711

801-530-6747

www.commerce.utah.gov/dre

VERMONT

Vermont Board of Real Estate Appraisers

81 River Street

Montpelier, VT 05609-1104

802-828-3228

www.vtprofessionals.org/opr1/appraisers

VIRGINIA

Department of Professional

and Occupational Regulation

3600 W. Broad Street, 5th Floor

Richmond, VA 23230-4817

804-367-2039

www.dpor.virginia.gov/dporweb/

apr_main.cfm

WASHINGTON

Business and Professions Division—Real Estate

Appraiser Section

P.O. Box 9015

Olympia, WA 98507-9015

360-664-6504

www.dol.wa.gov/business/appraisers/

applicense.html

WEST VIRGINIA

Licensing and Certification Board

2110 Kanawha Boulevard, Suite 101

Charleston, WV 25311

304-558-3919

www.wvappraiserboard.org

WISCONSIN

Wisconsin Department of Regulation

and Licensing

P.O. Box 8935

Madison, WI 53708-8935

608-266-2112

http://drl.wi.gov/index.htm

WYOMING

Certified Real Estate Appraiser Board

2020 Carey Avenue, Suite 702

Cheyenne, WY 82002-0180

307-777-7141

http://realestate.state.wy.us

► U.S. Territories Real Estate Appraisers Boards

AMERICAN SAMOA
American Samoa Government
P.O. Box 7
Pago Pago, AS 96799
684-633-4163
www.asg-gov.net

PUERTO RICO
Puerto Rico Board of Examiners of Real Estate
Appraisers
P.O. Box 9023271
San Juan, PR 00902-3271
787-722-4816

GUAM
Government of Guam
Department of Revenue and Taxation
P.O. Box 23607
Barrigada, GU 96913
671-635-1840
www.guampay.com

VIRGIN ISLANDS
Department of Licensing and Consumer Affairs
Number 1 Sub Base, Room 205
Charlotte Amalie, St. Thomas USVI 00801
340-639-7488
www.dlca.gov.vi

MARIANA ISLANDS
Board of Professional Licensing
Commonwealth of Northern Mariana Islands
P.O. Box 502078
Saipan, MP 96950
670-234-5897
www.ncees.org/licensure/licensing_boards/nmi.php

► The Right Questions

Once you've found your state's regulatory board, it's important to know the right questions to ask. To find out everything you need to know about your exam, use the following checklist of questions.

- Which exam is given in my state?
- How many questions are there?
- Is the exam multiple choice?
- Is the exam handwritten or is it given on the computer?
- How do I register?
- How much does the exam cost?
- How long will the exam take to complete?
- Can I use a calculator on the exam?

- If I can use a calculator, what kind of calculators are permitted?
- Where is the exam given?
- What day is the exam given?
- Can I reschedule my exam?
- What time is the exam?
- What do I have to bring to the exam?
- What is not allowed at the test centers?
- If the exam is given on the computer, will I be allowed to practice on a computer before the exam begins?
- How is the exam scored?
- What is the passing score?
- When will I receive my score report?
- What happens if I do not pass the exam?
- Can I retake the exam?
- If I have special needs, how do I arrange for them?

If you are already working for an appraisal company, your colleagues can be a good source of information about the tests. And of course, your appraisal course instructors and the administration of your school may also be able to provide guidance.

▶ How This Book Can Help You

The process of preparing for an appraisal exam is an overwhelming task, but this book guides you through several manageable steps. After finishing this chapter, move on to Chapter 2, which explains how to set up an individualized study plan and presents specific study strategies that you can use during your study sessions. You will learn the steps to take in order to maximize your chances for scoring high on your exam. You will also find when to take sample exams so you can check your scores and still have enough time to focus on the areas in which you need more work. In addition, you will increase your understanding and retention of the real estate material you are studying by using many study strategies, not just one or two.

While you are reading Chapter 2, take the time to create an individualized study plan that will fit your needs and schedule. This is a crucial step in the test-preparation process. After you finish reading Chapter 2, spend some time using each different study strategy that was explained.

Chapter 3 contains the first practice exam designed for those sitting for a state-licensed real estate appraiser or state-certified residential appraiser exam. Chapter 4 contains the first practice exam designed for those sitting for the certified general appraiser exam. You should take your first applicable practice exam before you begin studying. That way, you will be able to find your strengths and weaknesses and you will be able to focus your studying on the exact topics that are giving you the most trouble.

After you finish the first practice exam, you will find a "Real Estate Appraisal Refresher Course" (Chapter 5). This review briefly covers the domains stipulated in the AQB's National Uniform Exam Content Outlines. Because you already know which domains on the first exam gave you trouble, you can focus on those topics.

After the refresher course comes the "Real Estate Math Review" (Chapter 6). This contains a basic review of arithmetic, algebra, geometry, and word problems, as well as the particular subtopics found in the "Appraisal Statistical Concepts" domain that you will encounter on your test.

Do you need help with real estate terms? Chapter 7, "Real Estate Glossary," has the most commonly tested and used real estate and real estate appraisal terms. This glossary will help you prepare not only for your exam, but also for your career.

Once you have reviewed the course, the math, and the glossary, it's time for more practice exams. There are two more practice exams in this book. After every exam, you should review the topics that still give you the most trouble and study accordingly. For more study tips, read Chapter 2.

2 ▶ The LearningExpress Test Preparation System

CHAPTER SUMMARY

Taking the real estate appraisal exam can be tough. It demands a lot of preparation if you want to achieve a top score. The next step in your career as an appraiser depends on your passing the exam. The Learning-Express Test Preparation System, developed exclusively for Learning-Express by leading test experts, gives you the discipline and attitude you need to be a winner.

F ACT: TAKING A real estate appraisal licensing or certification exam is not easy, and neither is getting ready for it. The next step in your career as a real estate appraiser depends on getting a passing score, but there are all sorts of pitfalls that can keep you from doing your best on this exam. Here are some of the obstacles that can stand in the way of your success:

- being unfamiliar with the format of the exam
- being paralyzed by test anxiety
- leaving your preparation to the last minute
- not preparing at all!
- not knowing vital test-taking skills: how to pace yourself through the exam, how to use the process of elimination, and when to guess
- not being in tip-top mental and physical shape
- arriving late at the test site, having to work on an empty stomach, or being uncomfortable during the exam because the room is too hot or too cold

What's the common denominator in all these test-taking pitfalls? One word: control. Who's in control, you or the exam?

Here's some good news: The LearningExpress Test Preparation System puts you in control. In nine easy-to-follow steps, you will learn everything you need to make sure that you are in charge of your preparation and your performance on the exam. Other test takers may let the test get the better of them; other test takers may be unprepared or out of shape, but not you. You will have taken all the steps you need to take to get a high score on the real estate appraisal exam.

Here's how the LearningExpress Test Preparation System works: Nine easy steps lead you through everything you need to know and do to get ready to master your exam. Each step discussed in this chapter includes both reading about the step and one or more activities. It's important that you do the activities along with the reading, or you won't be getting the full benefit of the system. Each step tells you approximately how much time that step will take you to complete.

Step 1: Get Information	50 minutes
Step 2: Conquer Test Anxiety	20 minutes
Step 3: Make a Plan	30 minutes
Step 4: Learn to Manage Your Time	10 minutes
Step 5: Learn to Use the Process of Elimination	20 minutes
Step 6: Know When to Guess	20 minutes
Step 7: Reach Your Peak Performance Zone	10 minutes
Step 8: Get Your Act Together	10 minutes
Step 9: Do It!	10 minutes
Total	**3 hours**

We estimate that working through the entire system will take you approximately three hours, although it's perfectly okay if you work faster or slower. If you take an afternoon or evening, you can work through the whole LearningExpress Test Preparation System in one sitting. Otherwise, you can break it up and do just one or two steps a day for the next several days. It's up to you—remember, you are in control.

▶ Step 1: Get Information

Time to complete: 50 minutes
Activity: Read Chapter 1, The Real Estate Appraisal Exams

Knowledge is power. The first step in the LearningExpress Test Preparation System is finding out everything you can about your real estate appraisal exam. Once you have the information, the other steps in the LearningExpress Test Preparation System will show you what to do with it.

Part A: Straight Talk about the Real Estate Appraisal Exams

Why do you have to take this exam, anyway? You have already been through your pre-license courses for certification; why should you have to go through a rigorous exam? It's simply an attempt on the part of your state to be sure that you have the knowledge and skills necessary for the level of licensure or certification that you are seeking. Every profession that requires practitioners to exercise financial and fiduciary responsibility to clients also requires practitioners to be licensed—and licensure requires an exam. Real estate is no exception.

It's important for you to remember that your score on the exam does not determine how smart you are, or even whether you will make a good real estate appraiser. There are all kinds of skills an exam like this can't test: whether you have the drive and determination to be a top appraiser, whether you will faithfully exercise your responsibilities to your clients, or whether you can be trusted with confidential information about people's finances. Those kinds of things are hard to evaluate, while a test is easy to evaluate.

However, this is not to say that the exam is not important. The knowledge tested on the exam is essential knowledge that you will need to do your job. Your ability to enter the profession you've trained for depends on your passing this exam. And that's why you are here—using the LearningExpress Test Preparation System to achieve control over the exam.

Part B: What's on the Test

If you haven't already done so, stop here and read Chapter 1 of this book, which gives you an overview of the real estate appraisal exams. Then, go to the Appraisal Foundation's website (www.appraisalfoundation.org) and to your state's appraiser regulatory board's website and read the most up-to-date information about your exam directly from the test developers.

▶ Step 2: Conquer Test Anxiety

Time to complete: 20 minutes
Activity: Take the Test Anxiety Quiz

Having complete information about the exam is the first step in gaining control of the exam. Next, you have to overcome one of the biggest obstacles to test success: test anxiety. Test anxiety not only impairs your performance on the exam itself, but also keeps you from preparing. In Step 2, you will learn stress management techniques that will help you succeed on your exam. Learn these strategies now, and practice them as you work through the exams in this book, so they will be second nature to you by exam day.

Combating Test Anxiety

The first thing you need to know is that a little test anxiety is a good thing. Everyone gets nervous before a big exam—and if that nervousness motivates you to prepare thoroughly, so much the better. It's said that Sir Laurence Olivier, one of the foremost British actors of the twentieth century, felt ill before every performance. His stage fright didn't impair his performance; in fact, it probably gave him a little extra edge—just the kind of edge you need to do well, whether on a stage or in an examination room.

Above is the Test Anxiety Quiz. Stop and answer the questions to find out whether your level of test anxiety is something you should worry about.

Stress Management before the Test

If you feel your level of anxiety getting the best of you in the weeks before the test, here is what you need to do to bring the level down again.

- **Get prepared.** There's nothing like knowing what to expect and being prepared for it to put you in control of test anxiety. That's why you are reading this book. Use it faithfully, and remind yourself that you are better prepared than most people who are taking the test.

- **Practice self-confidence.** A positive attitude is a great way to combat test anxiety. This is no time to be humble or shy. Stand in front of the mirror and say to your reflection, "I am prepared. I am full of self-confidence. I am going to ace this test. I know I can do it." Say it into a tape recorder and play it back once a day. If you hear it often enough, you will believe it.

- **Fight negative messages.** Every time someone starts telling you how hard the exam is or how it's almost impossible to get a high score, start saying your self-confidence messages. Don't listen to the negative messages. Turn on your tape recorder and listen to your self-confidence messages.
- **Visualize.** Imagine yourself as a certified real estate appraiser. Think of yourself talking with clients, appraising properties, and best of all, receiving first payment for your services. Visualizing success can help make it happen—and it reminds you of why you are doing all this work in preparing for the exam.
- **Exercise.** Physical activity helps calm your body down and focus your mind. Besides, being in good physical shape can actually help you do well on the exam. Go for a run, lift weights, go swimming—and do it regularly.

Stress Management on Test Day

There are several ways you can bring down your level of test anxiety on test day. They will work best if you practice them in the weeks before the test, so you know which ones work best for you.

- **Deep breathing.** Take a deep breath while you count to five. Hold it for a count of one, and then let it out for a count of five. Repeat several times.
- **Move your body.** Try rolling your head in a circle. Rotate your shoulders. Shake your hands from the wrist. Many people find these movements very relaxing.
- **Visualize again.** Think of the place where you are most relaxed: lying on the beach in the sun, walking through the park, or whatever. Now close your eyes and imagine you are actually there. If you practice in advance, you will find that you need only a few seconds of this exercise to experience a significant increase in your sense of well-being.

When anxiety threatens to overwhelm you during the exam, there are still things you can do to manage the stress level.

- **Repeat your self-confidence messages.** You should have them memorized by now. Say them silently to yourself, and believe them!
- **Visualize one more time.** This time, visualize yourself moving smoothly and quickly through the test, answering every question right and finishing just before time is up. Like most visualization techniques, this one works best if you have practiced it ahead of time.
- **Find an easy question.** Find an easy question, and answer it. Getting even one question finished gets you in the test-taking groove.
- **Take a mental break.** Everyone loses concentration once in a while during a long test. It's normal, so you shouldn't worry about it. Instead, accept what has happened. Say to yourself, "Hey, I lost it there for a minute. My brain was taking a break." Put down your pencil, close your eyes, and do some deep breathing for a few seconds. Then you will be ready to go back to work.

Try these techniques ahead of time, and decide which ones work best for you!

▶ Step 3: Make a Plan

Time to complete: 30 minutes
Activity: Construct a study plan

One of the most important things you can do to get control of yourself and your exam is to make a study plan. Too many people fail to prepare simply because they fail to plan. Spending hours on the day before the exam poring over sample test questions not only raises your level of test anxiety, but it is simply no substitute for careful preparation and practice over time.

Don't fall into the cram trap. Take control of your preparation time by mapping out a study schedule. On the following pages are two sample schedules, based on the amount of time you have before you take your real estate appraisal exam. If you are the kind of person who needs deadlines and assignments to motivate you for a project, here they are. If you are the kind of person who doesn't like to follow other people's plans, you can use the suggested schedules here to construct your own.

Even more important than making a plan is making a commitment. You can't review everything you learned in your real estate appraisal courses in one night. You have to set aside some time every day for study and practice. Try for at least 20 minutes a day. Twenty minutes daily will do you much more good than two hours on Saturday.

Don't put off your study until the day before the exam. Start now. A few minutes a day, with half an hour or more on weekends, can make a big difference in your score.

Schedule A: The 30-Day Plan

If you have at least a month before your exam, you have plenty of time to prepare—as long as you don't waste it! If you have less than a month, turn to Schedule B.

Time	Preparation
Days 1–4	Skim over the written materials from your training program, particularly noting 1) areas you expect to be emphasized on the exam and 2) areas you don't remember well. On Day 4, concentrate on those areas.
Day 5	Take your first practice exam.
Day 6	Score the first practice exam. Use the "For Review" section at the end of the test to see which topics you need to review most. Identify two areas that you will concentrate on before you take the second practice exam.
Days 7–10	Study the two areas you identified as your weak points. Don't forget, there is the real estate appraisal refresher course in Chapter 5, the real estate math review in Chapter 6, and the real estate glossary in Chapter 7. Use these chapters to improve your score on the next practice test.
Day 11	Take your second practice exam.
Day 12	Score the second practice exam. Identify one area to concentrate on if you want take a third practice exam different from the one you're studying for.
Days 13–18	Study the one area you identified for review. Again, use the appraisal refresher course, math review, and glossary for help.
Day 19	Take the third practice exam online.
Days 20–21	Once again, identify one area to review, based on your score on the third practice exam. Study the one area you identified for review. Use the appraisal refresher course, math review, and glossary for help.
Days 22–25	Take an overview of all your training materials, consolidating your strengths and improving on your weaknesses.
Days 26–27	Review all the areas that have given you the most trouble in the three practice exams you have taken so far.
Day 28	Take another practice exam online. Note how much you have improved!
Day 29	Review one or two weak areas by studying the appraisal refresher course, math review, and glossary.
Day before the exam	Relax. Do something unrelated to the exam and go to bed at a reasonable hour.

Schedule B: The Ten-Day Plan

If you have two weeks or less before you take the exam, use this ten-day schedule to help you make the most of your time.

Time	Preparation
Day 1	Take your first practice exam and score it using the answer key. Use the "For Review" section to see which topics you need to review most.
Day 2	Review one area that gave you trouble on the first practice exam. Use the real estate appraisal refresher course in Chapter 5, the real estate math review in Chapter 6, and the real estate glossary in Chapter 7 for extra practice in these areas.
Day 3	Review another area that gave you trouble on the first practice exam. Again, use the refresher course, math review, and glossary for extra practice.
Day 4	Take your second practice exam and score it.
Day 5	If your score on the second practice exam doesn't show improvement on the two areas you studied, review them. If you did improve in those areas, choose a new weak area to study today.
Day 6	Take the third practice exam online.
Day 7	Choose your weakest area from the third practice exam to review. Use the refresher course, math review, and glossary for extra practice.
Day 8	Review any areas that you have not yet reviewed in this schedule.
Days 9 and 10	Use your last study days to brush up on any areas that are still giving you trouble. Use the refresher course, math review, and glossary.
Day before the exam	Relax. Do something unrelated to the exam and go to bed at a reasonable hour.

▶ Step 4: Learn to Manage Your Time

Time to complete: Ten minutes to read, many hours of practice!
Activity: Practice these strategies as you take the sample tests in this book

Steps 4, 5, and 6 of the LearningExpress Test Preparation System put you in charge of your exam by showing you test-taking strategies that work. Practice these strategies as you take the sample tests in this book, and then you will be ready to use them on test day.

First, you will take control of your time on the exam. It's a terrible feeling to find that there are five minutes left when you are only three-quarters of the way through the test. Here are some tips to keep that from happening to you.

- **Follow directions.** Some real estate appraisal exams are given on the computer. If a tutorial is offered, you should take the tutorial before the exam. Read the directions carefully and ask questions before the exam begins if there's anything you don't understand.
- **Pace yourself.** If there is a timer on the screen as you take the exam, keep an eye on it. This will help you pace yourself. For example, when one-quarter of the time has elapsed, you should be one-quarter of the way through the test. If you are falling behind, pick up the pace a bit. If you do not take your exam on a computer, use your watch or the clock in the testing room to keep track of the time you have left.
- **Keep moving.** Don't waste time on one question. If you don't know the answer, skip the question and move on. You can always go back to it later.
- **Don't rush.** Although you should keep moving, rushing won't help. Try to keep calm and work methodically and quickly.

▶ Step 5: Learn to Use the Process of Elimination

Time to complete: 20 minutes
Activity: Complete the worksheet on Using the Process of Elimination

After time management, the next most important tool for taking control of your exam is using the process of elimination wisely. It's standard test-taking wisdom that you should always read all the answer choices before choosing your answer. This helps you find the right answer by eliminating wrong answer choices. Sure enough, that standard wisdom applies to your exam, too.

Let's say you are facing a question like this one:

Alicia died, leaving her residence in town and a separate parcel of undeveloped rural land to her brother Brian and her sister Carrie, with Brian owning one-quarter interest and Carrie owning three-quarters interest. How do Brian and Carrie hold title?
a. as tenants in survivorship
b. as tenants in common
c. as joint tenants
d. as tenants by the entirety

You should always use the process of elimination on a question like this, even if the correct answer jumps out at you. Sometimes, the answer that jumps out isn't correct after all. Let's assume, for the purpose of this exercise, that you are a little rusty on property ownership terminology, so you need to use a little intuition to make up for what you don't remember. Proceed through the answer choices in order.

So you start with choice **a**. This one is pretty easy to eliminate; this tenancy doesn't have to do with survivorship. Because some real estate appraisal exams are given on a computer, you won't be able to cross out answer choices; instead, make a mental note that choice **a** is incorrect.

Choice **b** seems reasonable; it's a kind of ownership that two people can share. Even if you don't remember much about tenancy in common, you could tell it's about having something "in common." Make a mental note, "Good answer, I might use this one."

Choice **c** is also a possibility. Joint tenants also share something in common. If you happen to remember that joint tenancy always involves equal ownership rights, you mentally eliminate this choice. If you don't, make a mental note, "Good answer" or "Well, maybe," depending on how attractive this answer looks to you.

Choice **d** strikes you as a little less likely. Tenancy by the entirety doesn't necessarily have to do with two people sharing ownership. This doesn't sound right, and you have already got a better answer picked out in choice **b**. If you are feeling sure of yourself, you can mentally eliminate this choice.

If you're pressed for time, you should choose answer **b**. If you have the time to be extra careful, you could compare your answer choices again. Then, choose one and move on.

If you are taking a test on paper, like the practice exams in this book, it's good to have a system for marking good, bad, and maybe answers. We're recommending this one:

X = bad
✓ = good
? = maybe

If you don't like these marks, devise your own system. Just make sure you do it long before test day—while you're working through the practice exams in this book—so you won't have to worry about it during the exam.

Even when you think you are absolutely clueless about a question, you can often use the process of elimination to get rid of one answer choice. If so, you are better prepared to make an educated guess, as you will see in Step 6. More often, the process of elimination allows you to get down to only two possibly right answers. Then you are in a strong position to guess. And sometimes, even though you don't know the right answer, you find it simply by getting rid of the wrong ones, as you did in this example.

Try using your powers of elimination on the questions on the Using the Process of Elimination worksheet. The questions aren't about real estate appraisal work; they're just designed to show you how the process of elimination works. The answer explanations for this worksheet show one possible way you might use the process to arrive at the correct answer.

The process of elimination is your tool for the next step, which is knowing when to guess.

Use the process of elimination to answer the following questions.

1. Ilsa is as old as Meghan will be in five years. The difference between Ed's age and Meghan's age is twice the difference between Ilsa's age and Meghan's age. Ed is 29. How old is Ilsa?

    a. 4
    b. 10
    c. 19
    d. 24

2. "All drivers of commercial vehicles must carry a valid commercial driver's license whenever operating a commercial vehicle." According to this sentence, which of the following people need NOT carry a commercial driver's license?

    a. a truck driver idling his engine while waiting to be directed to a loading dock
    b. a bus operator backing her bus out of the way of another bus in the bus lot
    c. a taxi driver driving his personal car to the grocery store
    d. a limousine driver taking the limousine to her home after dropping off her last passenger of the evening

3. Smoking tobacco has been linked to

    a. increased risk of stroke and heart attack.
    b. all forms of respiratory disease.
    c. increasing mortality rates over the past ten years.
    d. juvenile delinquency.

4. Which of the following words is spelled correctly?

    a. incorrigible
    b. outragous
    c. domestickated
    d. understandible

Answers

Here are the answers, as well as some suggestions as to how you might have used the process of elimination to find them.

1. **d.** You should have eliminated choice **a** right away. Ilsa can't be four years old if Meghan is going to be Ilsa's age in five years. The best way to eliminate other answer choices is to try plugging them in to the information given in the problem. For instance, for choice **b**, if Ilsa is 10, then Meghan must be 5. The difference in their ages is 5. The difference between Ed's age, 29, and Meghan's age, 5, is 24. Does 24 = 2 times 5? No. Then choice **b** is wrong. You could eliminate answer **c** in the same way and be left with choice **d**.

2. c. Note the word *not* in the question, and go through the choice one by one. Is the truck driver in choice **a** "operating a commercial vehicle"? Yes, idling counts as "operating," so he needs to have a commercial driver's license. Likewise, the bus operator in choice **b** is operating a commercial vehicle; the question doesn't say the operator has to be on the street. The limo driver in choice **d** is operating a commercial vehicle, even if it doesn't have a passenger in it. However, the cabbie in choice **c** is *not* operating a commercial vehicle, but his own private car.

3. a. You could eliminate choice **b** simply because of the presence of the word *all*. Such absolutes hardly ever appear in correct answer choices. Choice **c** looks attractive until you think a little about what you know—aren't *fewer* people smoking these days, rather than more? So how could smoking be responsible for a higher mortality rate? (If you didn't know that *mortality rate* means the rate at which people die, you might keep this choice as a possibility, but you would still be able to eliminate two answers and have only two to choose from.) And choice **d** is not logical, so you could eliminate that one too. You are left with the correct choice, **a**.

4. a. How you used the process of elimination here depends on which words you recognized as being spelled incorrectly. If you knew that the correct spellings were *outrageous*, *domesticated*, and *understandable*, then you were home free. You probably knew that at least one of those words was wrong!

▶ Step 6: Know When to Guess

Time to complete: 20 minutes
Activity: Complete worksheet on Your Guessing Ability

Armed with the process of elimination, you are ready to take control of one of the big questions in test taking: Should I guess? The short answer is *yes*. Some exams have what's called a guessing penalty, in which a fraction of your wrong answers is subtracted from your right answers—but the real estate appraisal licensing or certification exam doesn't work like that. The number of questions you answer correctly yields your raw score. So you have nothing to lose and everything to gain by guessing.

The more complicated answer to the question "Should I guess?" depends on you—your personality and your guessing intuition. There are two things you need to know about yourself before you go into the exam:

- Are you a risk taker?
- Are you a good guesser?

You will have to decide about your risk-taking quotient on your own. To find out if you are a good guesser, complete the Your Guessing Ability worksheet because most real estate appraisal exams have no guessing penalty. Even if you are a play-it-safe person with lousy intuition, you're still safe in guessing. The best thing would be if you could overcome your anxieties and go ahead and mark an answer. But you may want to have a sense of how good your intuition is before you go into the exam.

Your Guessing Ability

The following are ten really hard questions. You are not supposed to know the answers. Rather, this is an assessment of your ability to guess when you don't have a clue. Read each question carefully, just as if you did expect to answer it. If you have any knowledge at all of the subject of the question, use that knowledge to help you eliminate wrong answer choices.

1. September 7 is Independence Day in
   a. India.
   b. Costa Rica.
   c. Brazil.
   d. Australia.

2. Which of the following is the formula for determining the momentum of an object?
   a. $p = mv$
   b. $F = ma$
   c. $P = IV$
   d. $E = mc^2$

3. Because of the expansion of the universe, the stars and other celestial bodies are all moving away from each other. This phenomenon is known as
   a. Newton's first law.
   b. the big bang.
   c. gravitational collapse.
   d. Hubble flow.

4. American author Gertrude Stein was born in
   a. 1713
   b. 1830
   c. 1874
   d. 1901

5. Which of the following is NOT one of the Five Classics attributed to Confucius?
   a. *I Ching*
   b. *Book of Holiness*
   c. *Spring and Autumn Annals*
   d. *Book of History*

6. The religious and philosophical doctrine that holds that the universe is constantly in a struggle between good and evil is known as
   a. Pelagianism.
   b. Manichaeanism.
   c. neo-Hegelianism.
   d. Epicureanism.

7. The third chief justice of the U.S. Supreme Court was
   a. John Blair.
   b. William Cushing.
   c. James Wilson.
   d. John Jay.

8. Which of the following is the poisonous portion of a daffodil?
   a. the bulb
   b. the leaves
   c. the stem
   d. the flowers

9. The winner of the Masters golf tournament in 1953 was

    a. Sam Snead.

    b. Cary Middlecoff.

    c. Arnold Palmer.

    d. Ben Hogan.

10. The state with the highest per capita personal income in 1980 was

    a. Alaska.

    b. Connecticut.

    c. New York.

    d. Texas.

Answers

Check your answers against the correct answers below.

1. c.

2. a.

3. d.

4. c.

5. b.

6. b.

7. b.

8. a.

9. d.

10. a.

▶ How Did You Do?

You may have simply gotten lucky and actually known the answers to one or two questions. In addition, your guessing was more successful if you were able to use the process of elimination on any of the questions. Maybe you didn't know who the third chief justice was (question 7), but you knew that John Jay was the first. In that case, you would have eliminated choice **d** and therefore improved your odds of guessing correctly from one in four to one in three.

According to probability, you should get $2\frac{1}{2}$ answers correct, so getting either two or three right would be average. If you got four or more right, you may be a really terrific guesser. If you got one or none right, you may not be a great guesser.

Keep in mind, though, that this is only a small sample. You should continue to keep track of your guessing ability as you work through the sample questions in this book. Circle the numbers of questions you guess on as you make your guesses; or, if you don't have time while you take the practice exams, go back afterward and try to remember which questions you guessed on. Remember, on an exam with four answer choices, your chances of getting a correct answer is one in four. So keep a separate guessing score for each exam. How many questions did you guess on? How many did you get right? If the number you got right is at least one-fourth of the number of questions you guessed on, you are at least an average guesser, maybe better—and you can go ahead and guess on the real exam. If the number you got right is significantly lower than one-fourth of the number you guessed on, you would be safe in guessing anyway, but maybe you would feel more comfortable if you guessed only selectively, when you can eliminate a wrong answer or at least have a good feeling about one of the answer choices.

▶ Step 7: Reach Your Peak Performance Zone

Time to complete: Ten minutes to read; weeks to complete!
Activity: Complete the Physical Preparation Checklist

To get ready for a challenge like a big exam, you have to take control of your physical, as well as your mental, state. Exercise, proper diet, and rest will ensure that your body works with, rather than against, your mind on test day, as well as during your preparation.

Exercise

If you don't already have a regular exercise program going, the time during which you are preparing for an exam is actually an excellent time to start one. And if you are already keeping fit—or trying to get that way—don't let the pressure of preparing for an exam fool you into quitting now. Exercise helps reduce stress by pumping wonderful good-feeling hormones called endorphins into your system. It also increases the oxygen supply throughout your body, including your brain, so you will be at peak performance on test day.

A half hour of vigorous activity—enough to raise a sweat—every day should be your aim. If you are really pressed for time, every other day is okay. Choose an activity you like, and get out there and do it. Jogging with a friend always makes the time go faster, or take a radio.

But don't overdo it; you don't want to exhaust yourself. Moderation is the key.

Diet

First, cut out the junk. Go easy on caffeine and nicotine, and eliminate alcohol and any other drugs from your system at least two weeks before the exam. Promise yourself a special treat the night after the exam, if need be.

What your body needs for peak performance is simply a balanced diet. Eat plenty of fruits and vegetables, along with lean protein and complex carbohydrates. Foods high in lecithin (an amino acid), such as fish and beans, are especially good "brain foods."

The night before the exam, you might "carbo-load" the way athletes do before a contest. Eat a big plate of spaghetti, rice and beans, or your favorite carbohydrate.

Rest

You probably know how much sleep you need every night to be at your best, even if you don't always get it. Make sure you do get that much sleep, though, for at least a week before the exam. Moderation is important here, too. Extra sleep will just make you groggy.

If you are not a morning person and your exam will be given in the morning, you should reset your internal clock so that your body doesn't think you are taking an exam at 3:00 A.M. You have to start this process well before the exam. The way it works is to get up half an hour earlier one morning, and then go to bed half an hour earlier that night. Don't try it the other way around; you will just toss and turn if you go to bed early without having gotten up early. The next morning, get up another half an hour earlier, and so on. How long you will have to do this depends on how late you are used to getting up. Use the Physical Preparation Checklist on page 29 to make sure you are in tip-top form.

▶ Step 8: Get Your Act Together

Time to complete: Ten minutes to read; time to complete will vary
Activity: Complete Final Preparations worksheet

You are in control of your mind and body; you are in charge of test anxiety, your preparation, and your test-taking strategies. Now it's time to take charge of external factors, such as the testing site and the materials you need to take the exam.

Find Out Where the Exam Is and Make a Trial Run

Do you know how to get to the testing site? Do you know how long it will take to get there? If not, make a trial run, preferably on the same day of the week at the same time of day. Make note, on the Final Preparations worksheet on page 30, of the amount of time it will take you to get to the exam site. Plan on arriving 30–45 minutes early so you can get the lay of the land, use the bathroom, and calm down. Then, figure out how early you will have to get up that morning, and make sure you get up that early every day for a week before the exam.

Gather Your Materials

The night before the exam, lay out the clothes you will wear and the materials you have to bring with you to the exam. Plan on dressing in layers; you won't have any control over the temperature of the examination room. Have a sweater or jacket you can take off if it's warm. Use the checklist on the Final Preparations worksheet to help you pull together what you will need.

Don't Skip Breakfast

Even if you don't usually eat breakfast, do so the morning of the exam. A cup of coffee doesn't count. Don't eat doughnuts or other sweet foods, either. A sugar high will leave you with a sugar low in the middle of the exam. A mix of protein and carbohydrates is best: Cereal with milk, or eggs with toast, will do your body a world of good.

Physical Preparation Checklist

For the week before the exam, write down 1) what physical exercise you engaged in and for how long and 2) what you ate for each meal. Remember, you are trying for at least 30 minutes of exercise every other day (preferably every day) and a balanced diet that's light on junk food.

Exam minus 7 days

Exercise: _____ for ____ minutes
Breakfast: _____
Lunch: _____
Dinner: _____
Snacks: _____

Exam minus 6 days

Exercise: _____ for ____ minutes
Breakfast: _____
Lunch: _____
Dinner: _____
Snacks: _____

Exam minus 5 days

Exercise: _____ for ____ minutes
Breakfast: _____
Lunch: _____
Dinner: _____
Snacks: _____

Exam minus 4 days

Exercise: _____ for ____ minutes
Breakfast: _____
Lunch: _____
Dinner: _____
Snacks: _____

Exam minus 3 days

Exercise: _____ for ____ minutes
Breakfast: _____
Lunch: _____
Dinner: _____
Snacks: _____

Exam minus 2 days

Exercise: _____ for ____ minutes
Breakfast: _____
Lunch: _____
Dinner: _____
Snacks: _____

Exam minus 1 day

Exercise: _____ for ____ minutes
Breakfast: _____
Lunch: _____
Dinner: _____
Snacks: _____

Getting to the Exam Site

Location of exam: _____

Date: _____

Departure time: _____

Do I know how to get to the exam site? Yes _____ No _____
If no, make a trial run.

Time it will take to get to exam site: _____

Things to Lay Out the Night Before

Clothes I will wear   _____

Sweater/jacket   _____

Watch   _____

Photo ID   _____

No. 2 pencils   _____

Calculator   _____

_____   _____

_____   _____

▶ Step 9: Do It!

Time to complete: Ten minutes, plus test-taking time
Activity: Ace the real estate appraisal exam!

Fast-forward to exam day. You are ready. You made a study plan and followed through. You practiced your test-taking strategies while working through this book. You are in control of your physical, mental, and emotional states. You know when and where to show up and what to bring with you. In other words, you are better prepared than most of the other people taking the real estate appraisal exam with you. You are psyched.

Just one more thing: When you are done with the exam, you will have earned a reward. Plan a celebration. Call up your friends and plan a party, or have a nice dinner for two—whatever your heart desires. Give yourself something to look forward to.

And then do it. Go into the exam, full of confidence, armed with the test-taking strategies you have practiced until they're second nature. You are in control of yourself, your environment, and your performance on the exam. You are ready to succeed. So do it. Go in there and ace the exam. And look forward to your future career!

3 ▶ Residential Appraisal Practice Exam 1

CHAPTER SUMMARY

This is the first of the two practice tests in this book based on the Appraiser Qualifications Board's (AQB) National Uniform Exam Content Outlines for state-licensed real estate appraisers and state-certified residential appraisers. Take this test to see how you would do if you took the exam today and to get a handle on your strengths and weaknesses.

TAKE THIS EXAM in as relaxed a manner as you can, without worrying about timing. You can time yourself on the second exam. You should, however, make sure that you have enough time to take the entire exam in one sitting. Find a quiet place where you can work without interruptions.

The answer sheet is on the following page, and is followed by the exam. After you have finished, use the answer key and explanations to learn your strengths and your weaknesses. Then use the scoring section at the end of this chapter to see how you did overall. Good luck!

► Residential Appraisal Practice Exam 1 Answer Sheet

1.	ⓐ	ⓑ	ⓒ	ⓓ
2.	ⓐ	ⓑ	ⓒ	ⓓ
3.	ⓐ	ⓑ	ⓒ	ⓓ
4.	ⓐ	ⓑ	ⓒ	ⓓ
5.	ⓐ	ⓑ	ⓒ	ⓓ
6.	ⓐ	ⓑ	ⓒ	ⓓ
7.	ⓐ	ⓑ	ⓒ	ⓓ
8.	ⓐ	ⓑ	ⓒ	ⓓ
9.	ⓐ	ⓑ	ⓒ	ⓓ
10.	ⓐ	ⓑ	ⓒ	ⓓ
11.	ⓐ	ⓑ	ⓒ	ⓓ
12.	ⓐ	ⓑ	ⓒ	ⓓ
13.	ⓐ	ⓑ	ⓒ	ⓓ
14.	ⓐ	ⓑ	ⓒ	ⓓ
15.	ⓐ	ⓑ	ⓒ	ⓓ
16.	ⓐ	ⓑ	ⓒ	ⓓ
17.	ⓐ	ⓑ	ⓒ	ⓓ
18.	ⓐ	ⓑ	ⓒ	ⓓ
19.	ⓐ	ⓑ	ⓒ	ⓓ
20.	ⓐ	ⓑ	ⓒ	ⓓ
21.	ⓐ	ⓑ	ⓒ	ⓓ
22.	ⓐ	ⓑ	ⓒ	ⓓ
23.	ⓐ	ⓑ	ⓒ	ⓓ
24.	ⓐ	ⓑ	ⓒ	ⓓ
25.	ⓐ	ⓑ	ⓒ	ⓓ
26.	ⓐ	ⓑ	ⓒ	ⓓ
27.	ⓐ	ⓑ	ⓒ	ⓓ
28.	ⓐ	ⓑ	ⓒ	ⓓ
29.	ⓐ	ⓑ	ⓒ	ⓓ
30.	ⓐ	ⓑ	ⓒ	ⓓ
31.	ⓐ	ⓑ	ⓒ	ⓓ
32.	ⓐ	ⓑ	ⓒ	ⓓ
33.	ⓐ	ⓑ	ⓒ	ⓓ
34.	ⓐ	ⓑ	ⓒ	ⓓ
35.	ⓐ	ⓑ	ⓒ	ⓓ
36.	ⓐ	ⓑ	ⓒ	ⓓ
37.	ⓐ	ⓑ	ⓒ	ⓓ
38.	ⓐ	ⓑ	ⓒ	ⓓ
39.	ⓐ	ⓑ	ⓒ	ⓓ
40.	ⓐ	ⓑ	ⓒ	ⓓ
41.	ⓐ	ⓑ	ⓒ	ⓓ
42.	ⓐ	ⓑ	ⓒ	ⓓ
43.	ⓐ	ⓑ	ⓒ	ⓓ
44.	ⓐ	ⓑ	ⓒ	ⓓ
45.	ⓐ	ⓑ	ⓒ	ⓓ
46.	ⓐ	ⓑ	ⓒ	ⓓ
47.	ⓐ	ⓑ	ⓒ	ⓓ
48.	ⓐ	ⓑ	ⓒ	ⓓ
49.	ⓐ	ⓑ	ⓒ	ⓓ
50.	ⓐ	ⓑ	ⓒ	ⓓ
51.	ⓐ	ⓑ	ⓒ	ⓓ
52.	ⓐ	ⓑ	ⓒ	ⓓ
53.	ⓐ	ⓑ	ⓒ	ⓓ
54.	ⓐ	ⓑ	ⓒ	ⓓ
55.	ⓐ	ⓑ	ⓒ	ⓓ
56.	ⓐ	ⓑ	ⓒ	ⓓ
57.	ⓐ	ⓑ	ⓒ	ⓓ
58.	ⓐ	ⓑ	ⓒ	ⓓ
59.	ⓐ	ⓑ	ⓒ	ⓓ
60.	ⓐ	ⓑ	ⓒ	ⓓ
61.	ⓐ	ⓑ	ⓒ	ⓓ
62.	ⓐ	ⓑ	ⓒ	ⓓ
63.	ⓐ	ⓑ	ⓒ	ⓓ
64.	ⓐ	ⓑ	ⓒ	ⓓ
65.	ⓐ	ⓑ	ⓒ	ⓓ
66.	ⓐ	ⓑ	ⓒ	ⓓ
67.	ⓐ	ⓑ	ⓒ	ⓓ
68.	ⓐ	ⓑ	ⓒ	ⓓ
69.	ⓐ	ⓑ	ⓒ	ⓓ
70.	ⓐ	ⓑ	ⓒ	ⓓ
71.	ⓐ	ⓑ	ⓒ	ⓓ
72.	ⓐ	ⓑ	ⓒ	ⓓ
73.	ⓐ	ⓑ	ⓒ	ⓓ
74.	ⓐ	ⓑ	ⓒ	ⓓ
75.	ⓐ	ⓑ	ⓒ	ⓓ
76.	ⓐ	ⓑ	ⓒ	ⓓ
77.	ⓐ	ⓑ	ⓒ	ⓓ
78.	ⓐ	ⓑ	ⓒ	ⓓ
79.	ⓐ	ⓑ	ⓒ	ⓓ
80.	ⓐ	ⓑ	ⓒ	ⓓ
81.	ⓐ	ⓑ	ⓒ	ⓓ
82.	ⓐ	ⓑ	ⓒ	ⓓ
83.	ⓐ	ⓑ	ⓒ	ⓓ
84.	ⓐ	ⓑ	ⓒ	ⓓ
85.	ⓐ	ⓑ	ⓒ	ⓓ
86.	ⓐ	ⓑ	ⓒ	ⓓ
87.	ⓐ	ⓑ	ⓒ	ⓓ
88.	ⓐ	ⓑ	ⓒ	ⓓ
89.	ⓐ	ⓑ	ⓒ	ⓓ
90.	ⓐ	ⓑ	ⓒ	ⓓ
91.	ⓐ	ⓑ	ⓒ	ⓓ
92.	ⓐ	ⓑ	ⓒ	ⓓ
93.	ⓐ	ⓑ	ⓒ	ⓓ
94.	ⓐ	ⓑ	ⓒ	ⓓ
95.	ⓐ	ⓑ	ⓒ	ⓓ
96.	ⓐ	ⓑ	ⓒ	ⓓ
97.	ⓐ	ⓑ	ⓒ	ⓓ
98.	ⓐ	ⓑ	ⓒ	ⓓ
99.	ⓐ	ⓑ	ⓒ	ⓓ
100.	ⓐ	ⓑ	ⓒ	ⓓ

► Residential Appraisal Practice Exam 1

1. Which of the following principles states that the value of an income-earning property is the present value of the future financial benefits?
   a. anticipation
   b. increasing and decreasing returns
   c. opportunity cost
   d. supply and demand

2. Which of the following economic or demographic changes will cause the price of housing to decline while housing starts to increase?
   a. New construction takes place, but the number of buyers stays constant.
   b. Construction costs increase, but the number of buyers stays constant.
   c. The number of buyers increases, and the mortgage interest rate declines.
   d. Construction costs decrease, and the number of buyers also decreases.

3. Each of the following is a critical issue in defining the appraisal problem EXCEPT
   a. identifying the property and ownership rights.
   b. identifying the effective date of the appraisal.
   c. identifying the highest and best use.
   d. identifying the scope of work.

4. Which of the following statements is NOT correct?
   a. Cost to construct can be greater than the current market value.
   b. Sales price can be greater than the cost to construct.
   c. Market value and sales price are always equal.
   d. Market value can be greater than the cost to construct.

5. Which of the following is the legal description of the method that uses lines of longitude and latitude?
   a. government rectangular survey
   b. lot and block
   c. metes and bounds
   d. plat map

6. Financial feasibility of a vacant site is determined by the
   a. appraiser's expert opinion.
   b. current use of the site.
   c. property market conditions.
   d. zoning officials.

7. A mortgage or a deed of trust is a document that
   a. makes a property the security or collateral for a debt.
   b. identifies the money the seller owes the lender.
   c. notifies the buyer of a foreclosure sale.
   d. serves as evidence of the borrower's debt.

8. Standard 1 has six associated rules. Which of these Standard Rules discusses the need for a highest and best use analysis?
   a. Standard Rule 1–1
   b. Standard Rule 1–3
   c. Standard Rule 1–4
   d. Standard Rule 1–6

9. Which of the following statements is NOT true about a real estate appraisal?
   a. It is an estimate or opinion of the value of real property.
   b. It is an orderly, step-by-step process.
   c. It focuses exclusively on the physical property.
   d. It must be free of the appraiser's preferences.

10. What type of appraisal report is characterized by the use of tables of data?
   a. self-contained
   b. summary
   c. restricted use
   d. oral

11. Which of the following is the best definition of a fee simple estate?
   a. a representation of the rights of ownership that are not affected by public regulations like the zoning ordinance
   b. an estate in which the current owner cannot dispose of the property through a sale or gift, but can lease the property to a third party
   c. an estate in which the owner has the right to dispose of the property in addition to the rights of use, possession, and exclusion
   d. a representation of the rights of ownership in real estate that are possessed for only a short period of time (less than a lifetime)

12. Which of the following principles states that the price of the property can change as market factors change?
   a. anticipation
   b. increasing and decreasing returns
   c. opportunity cost
   d. supply and demand

13. If a buyer bought a $200,000 house and the lender gives that buyer an 80% loan at an interest rate of 7% per year, the monthly interest payment in the first month will be which of the following?
   a. $1,400
   b. $1,166.67
   c. $933.33
   d. $900

14. Which of the following is the legal description of the method that uses a zero milepost, monuments, and points of beginning?
   a. government rectangular survey
   b. lot and block
   c. metes and bounds
   d. plat map

15. Each of the following factors directly affects the physical possibility of a property EXCEPT
   a. development costs of the site.
   b. shape and size of the site.
   c. property market conditions.
   d. bedrock characteristics.

16. Which of the following principles states that the value of a component of the appraisal property is measured in terms of what it adds to the value of the whole property?
   a. change
   b. competition
   c. conformity
   d. contribution

17. Which of the following statements best describes the cost approach?

   a. The appraiser estimates the depreciated construction cost of the improvement and adds it to the value of the land.

   b. The appraiser formulates his or her estimate of the market value based on the analysis of the sales price and the nature of comparable properties.

   c. The appraiser generates a stream of future income payments to the owner and uses this as an estimate of value.

   d. The appraiser identifies several comparable properties and divides their sales prices by rent revenues.

18. When an appraiser estimates the reproduction cost of the subject property by establishing the cost of construction per square foot for a comparable property and then makes adjustments for differences in special features and the quality of fixtures, he or she is utilizing which of the following techniques?

   a. the quantity survey method

   b. the unit-in-place method

   c. the comparative-unit method

   d. the replacement method

19. The current market value of real property is

   a. the highest price offered by a buyer and accepted by the seller.

   b. the first price offered by a buyer and accepted by the seller.

   c. the sales price that is eventually accepted by the seller.

   d. the most probable sales price offered in the market.

20. Which statement best relates the concepts of land and site?

   a. Land and site are the same (synonyms).

   b. Land is used to describe large parcels, while site is used for small parcels.

   c. Land is used in agricultural areas, while site is used in urban and suburban areas.

   d. Land is in its natural condition, while site has been improved upon and made ready for use.

21. Which principle states that the prudent buyer will not pay more for one site than for a comparable site offering the same satisfaction and amenities?

   a. anticipation

   b. demand

   c. substitution

   d. supply

22. Which of the following is the best definition of a life estate?

   a. a representation of the rights of ownership that are not affected by public regulations like the zoning ordinance

   b. an estate in which the current owner cannot dispose of the property through a sale or gift, but can occupy the property

   c. an estate in which the owner has the right to dispose of the property in addition to the rights of use, possession, and exclusion

   d. a representation of the rights to ownership in real estate that are possessed for less than a lifetime

23. Which of the following is an example of external obsolescence?

   a. Residential structures in the neighborhood undergo physical deterioration.

   b. The subject property experiences incurable physical deterioration.

   c. The consumer attitudes toward older homes change and lead to rehabilitation of these structures.

   d. The cost to repair the foundation in the subject property exceeds the value increase that the subject property would experience if the repair were made.

24. A developer discovers that a certain neighborhood does not have adequate retail facilities for the population in the area. This is what type of determinant of value?

   a. economic

   b. governmental

   c. physical/environmental

   d. social

25. Which of the following refers to the value of a property to a specific individual who is considering its purchase?

   a. assessed value

   b. insurance value

   c. investment value

   d. market value

26. If a single-family house with a fully equipped kitchen is leased to a tenant for $1,400 per month, and the owner must make annual payments of $1,400 for repairs, $2,000 for an improvement, $300 for property insurance, $600 for property tax, and reserves for replacement are $300, the net operating income is which of the following?

   a. $15,400

   b. $14,500

   c. $14,200

   d. $12,200

27. When the owner of a property is analyzing the relationship between the price he or she paid for the property ten years ago and its current net operating income (NOI), he or she is considering the property's

   a. capitalization rate.

   b. operating expense ratio.

   c. vacancy rate.

   d. none of the above

28. *Appraiser's peers* are defined as appraisers who

   a. hold the same certification, such as a certified residential or certified general.

   b. practice in the same market area.

   c. have expertise and competency in a similar type of assignment.

   d. have the same magnitude of education and experience hours.

29. *Scope of work* is defined as

   a. a plan for the use of professional and staff time to complete a report.

   b. the process and cost of gathering relevant data.

   c. the process of identifying the start and completion dates of the report.

   d. the type and extent of research and analysis in an assignment.

30. The legal permissibility of a site as vacant is determined by the
   a. appraiser's expert opinion.
   b. current use of the site.
   c. property market conditions.
   d. zoning officials.

31. Which of the following statements represents the relationship between contract rent and market rent?
   a. Market rent and contract rent are always the same.
   b. Contract rent is the amount of money the tenant is currently paying, while market rent is the rent that is currently being negotiated for comparable space.
   c. Contract rent is always less than market rent.
   d. Contract rents are renegotiated; so by necessity, they always reflect market rent.

32. Which of the following calculations yields a present value of $734.67?
   a. $900 due at the end of two years at a discount rate of 9%
   b. $900 due at the end of three years at a discount rate of 7%
   c. $1,000 due at the end of four years at a discount rate of 6%
   d. $1,100 due at the end of four years at a discount rate of 8%

33. When the appraiser uses information about revenue and operating expenses of the subject property to form the opinion of value, he or she is using the
   a. cost approach.
   b. income approach.
   c. sales comparison approach.
   d. highest and best use approach.

34. A loan agreement in which the builder provides a portion of the interest payment during the early years of the mortgage term is known as
   a. a graduated payment mortgage agreement.
   b. an adjustable-rate mortgage agreement.
   c. a shared appreciation mortgage agreement.
   d. a buydown mortgage agreement.

35. A neighborhood has a reputation for having a low crime rate and respect for the private property of others. This is what type of determinant of value?
   a. economic
   b. governmental
   c. physical/environmental
   d. social

36. The measure of the width of a property along the street that the property abuts is called
   a. assemblage.
   b. frontage.
   c. plottage.
   d. salvage.

37. A physically deteriorated item in the structure is considered to be curable if
   a. the item can easily be repaired.
   b. the cost of the repair is not excessive.
   c. the repair cost is less than the increase in value due to the repair.
   d. the resulting value increase is less than the repair bill.

38. Which of the following statements best describes the sales comparison approach?
  a. The appraiser estimates the cost to build the improvement and adds it to the value of the land.
  b. The appraiser formulates his or her estimate of the market value based on the analysis of the sales price and the nature of comparable properties.
  c. The appraiser generates a stream of future income payments to the owner and uses this as an estimate of value.
  d. The appraiser identifies several comparable properties and divides their sales prices by rent revenues.

39. Which technique for site valuation uses a capitalization rate in the value determination?
  a. allocation
  b. extraction
  c. land residual
  d. land development

40. Which technique for site valuation is based on developing the contributory value of the value of all improvements on an improved comparable property and deducts it from the total property sale price?
  a. allocation
  b. extraction
  c. ground rent capitalization
  d. sales comparison

41. When a potential buyer and seller of a property enter into the negotiation for that property, which of the following statements is correct?
  a. The property has value in use, but not in exchange.
  b. The property has value in exchange, but not in use.
  c. The property has value in use and exchange.
  d. The value in use and in exchange cannot be determined.

42. Each of the following is a characteristic of market value EXCEPT
  a. the buyer and seller are typically motivated.
  b. the buyer and seller are well informed.
  c. the buyer and seller each acts in his or her own best interest.
  d. the buyer and seller make special financial arrangements.

43. Which of the following calculations yields a future value of $900.52?
  a. $800 at 5% for three years
  b. $800 at 4% for five years
  c. $700 at 7% for three years
  d. $700 at 6.5% for four years

44. Which of the following principles states that the economic, physical, social, and governmental forces influence real property value?
  a. change
  b. competition
  c. conformity
  d. contribution

45. The capitalization rate is used in which of the appraisal techniques?
  a. cost approach
  b. income approach
  c. sales comparison approach
  d. highest and best use approach

46. The age-life method based on effective age is used in which of the appraisal techniques?
  a. cost approach
  b. income approach
  c. sales comparison approach
  d. highest and best use approach

Use the following to answer questions 47–50.

An appraiser discovers the following information about the acreage of seven land parcels. The appraiser calculates the descriptive statistics for this data set. (Rounded to one decimal.)

	# of Acres
Parcel 1	1.4
Parcel 2	4.9
Parcel 3	5.5
Parcel 4	2.9
Parcel 5	3.2
Parcel 6	3.8
Parcel 7	2.8

47. Parcel 5 represents the
  a. average number of acres.
  b. median number of acres.
  c. range of acreage.
  d. standard deviation.

48. 3.5 acres represents the
  a. average size of the parcels.
  b. median size of the parcels.
  c. range in size of the parcels.
  d. standard deviation.

49. 4.1 acres represents the
  a. average size of the parcels.
  b. median size of the parcels.
  c. range in size of the parcels.
  d. standard deviation.

50. 1.4 acres represents the
  a. average number of acres.
  b. median number of acres.
  c. range of acreage.
  d. standard deviation.

51. Which of the following economic or demographic changes will cause the price of housing to increase while housing starts to increase?
  a. New construction takes place, but the number of buyers stay constant.
  b. Construction costs increase, but the number of buyers stay constant.
  c. The number of buyers increases, and the mortgage interest rate declines.
  d. Construction costs decrease, and the number of buyers also decreases.

52. When the appraiser estimates the reproduction cost new of the subject property by calculating the cost of constructing each of the major components of the structure and then adding these together, which of the following techniques is he or she utilizing?
  a. the quantity survey method
  b. the unit-in-place method
  c. the comparative-unit method
  d. the replacement method

53. Which of the following is the most likely reason for the local government to place a lien on a property?
   a. The owner refused to sell the property to the county government.
   b. The owner's property has been escheated.
   c. The owner violated a zoning ordinance.
   d. The owner failed to pay a sidewalk assessment charge.

54. Mr. Smith dies, and in his will, he has left real property to his son for as long as the son lives, with the property then belonging to Mr. Smith's daughter upon the son's death. Mr. Smith has created
   a. an easement.
   b. a fee simple estate.
   c. a life estate.
   d. a restrictive covenant.

55. Which of the following principles states that the real property value is created and maintained when the attributes of the property match the desires of consumers in the market?
   a. change
   b. competition
   c. conformity
   d. contribution

56. Which of the following activities is NOT part of the scope of work rule?
   a. identifying the problem to be solved
   b. determining the use of professional and staff resources and quoting the fee
   c. determining and performing the scope of work necessary to develop credible results
   d. disclosing the scope of work in the report

57. When at least two sites are combined to produce greater utility, what is the increment of value that is created?
   a. assemblage
   b. frontage
   c. plottage
   d. salvage

58. How many square feet is the following site?

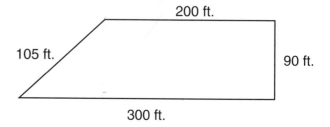

   a. 18,000 square feet
   b. 22,500 square feet
   c. 27,000 square feet
   d. 33,000 square feet

59. An appraiser can be each of the following EXCEPT
   a. an unbiased analyst.
   b. an impartial researcher.
   c. an objective reporter.
   d. a confidential advocate.

60. When the appraiser estimates the reduction in value caused by changes in consumer attitudes toward the design of the structure and its fixtures, he or she is estimating
   a. physical deterioration.
   b. functional obsolescence.
   c. external obsolescence.
   d. taxable depreciation.

61. Which of the following statements best describes the procedure for calculating the capitalization rate from data in the property market?
   a. The appraiser obtains the average net operating income and sales price for properties in the market and divides net operating income by the sales price.
   b. The appraiser obtains figures for net operating income and sales price for comparable properties and divides the sales price by net operating income.
   c. The appraiser identifies comparable properties and obtains figures for NOI and sales price and divides NOI by the sales price.
   d. The appraiser obtains the net operating income for the subject property and divides it by the sales price on comparable properties.

62. The Ethics Rule has four major parts. They are
   a. confidentiality, finances, credit, and ethics.
   b. confidentiality, conduct, management, and record keeping.
   c. conduct, accounting, management, and finances.
   d. conduct, accounting, management, and record keeping.

63. Which technique for site valuation is based on developing a ratio of land value to total property value from recently sold improved properties?
   a. allocation
   b. extraction
   c. ground rent capitalization
   d. sales comparison

64. Which of the following is NOT a private restriction on the rights of ownership?
   a. zoning
   b. liens
   c. easements
   d. deed restrictions

65. What part of the Ethics Rule states that the appraiser must prepare a workfile and keep it for five years after preparation?
   a. conduct
   b. confidentiality
   c. management
   d. record keeping

66. A loan agreement in which the contract interest rate can change as the market interest rate changes is known as
   a. a graduated payment mortgage agreement.
   b. an adjustable-rate mortgage agreement.
   c. a shared appreciation mortgage agreement.
   d. a 1-2-3 buydown mortgage agreement.

Use the following information to answer questions 67–71 about cash flow analysis.

The appraiser obtains the following income and expense data for the subject property.

Market rent per unit per month	$1,200
Units	4
Market vacancy	8%
Operating expenses	
per unit per year	$3,200
Market value of the property	$340,000

67. When the appraiser develops the cash flow statement, the figure of $52,992 is the
   a. potential gross income.
   b. net operating income.
   c. effective gross income.
   d. before-tax cash flow.

68. When the appraiser develops the cash flow statement, the figure of $40,192 is the
a. potential gross income.
b. net operating income.
c. effective gross income.
d. before-tax cash flow.

69. When the appraiser develops the cash flow statement, the figure of $12,800 is the
a. total operating expenses.
b. potential gross income.
c. net operating income.
d. effective gross income.

70. When the appraiser develops the cash flow statement, the figure of 24.15% is the
a. operating expense ratio.
b. vacancy rate.
c. discount rate.
d. overall property capitalization rate.

71. When the appraiser develops the cash flow statement, the figure of 11.8% is the
a. operating expense ratio.
b. vacancy rate.
c. discount rate.
d. overall property capitalization rate.

72. Which of the following is an example of a governmental determinant of value?
a. smaller household sizes
b. land use restrictions
c. increasing divorce rate
d. the opening of a production facility

73. A subdivision of a neighborhood has an excellent view of the ocean. This is what type of determinant of value?
a. economic
b. governmental
c. physical/environmental
d. social

74. What part of the Ethics Rule states that the appraiser cannot report predetermined opinions or conclusions?
a. conduct
b. confidentiality
c. management
d. record keeping

75. Which legal description system uses measurements of distances and angles to identify real property?
a. lot and block
b. plat map
c. government survey
d. metes and bounds

76. When an income property appraiser extracts a capitalization rate from the property market (not the mortgage market), he or she will do which of the following?
a. Divide the sales price for each comparable property by the market rent.
b. Divide the sales price of the subject property by the market rent level.
c. Divide the sales price of each comparable property by the average price of the comparable properties.
d. none of the above

77. The difference between potential gross income and effective gross income is caused by
   a. appreciation.
   b. capitalization.
   c. operating expenses.
   d. vacancy.

78. A property is sold and the buyer promises the seller in writing that he or she, the buyer, will take the legal responsibility to repay the existing loan. This is called
   a. assuming the loan.
   b. buying down the loan.
   c. loan satisfaction.
   d. amortizing the loan.

79. The Competency Rule requires that the appraiser must have the knowledge and experience to complete an assignment competently. If the knowledge and experience do not exist, then each of the following must occur EXCEPT
   a. disclosure of the lack of knowledge in the completed report.
   b. the taking of all necessary steps to complete the assignment competently.
   c. describing the lack of knowledge or experience in the report.
   d. describing the steps taken to complete the report competently.

80. When an appraiser undertakes a sales comparison approach of a single-family house, which of the following pieces of information can be ignored in arriving at the current market value?
   a. the neighborhood features of the subject property and the comparable properties
   b. the market rent for similar-sized apartments in the immediate area
   c. the time of sale for the comparable properties
   d. the financial terms under which the comparable properties are sold

81. Each of the following is a critical issue in defining the appraisal problem EXCEPT
   a. identifying the client and intended users.
   b. identifying the comparable properties.
   c. identifying the purpose of the appraisal.
   d. identifying the scope of work.

82. Each of the following statements is necessary to let an appraiser know that the scope of work is acceptable EXCEPT
   a. it meets the needs and expectations of parties who are regular, intended users.
   b. it meets what an appraiser's peers' actions would be in performing the same assignment.
   c. it does not allow assignment conditions to limit it under any circumstance.
   d. it does not allow the intended use to cause the assignment results to be biased.

83. Which of the following principles states that additional expenditures to build a property will generate more net income until a certain level of those expenditures is reached, and at that point, net income reaches its maximum?
   a. anticipation
   b. increasing and decreasing returns
   c. opportunity cost
   d. supply and demand

84. The scope of work rule requires each of the following EXCEPT
   a. identifying the problem to be solved.
   b. identifying the professional staff involved in the analysis.
   c. determining the necessary scope of work to produce credible results.
   d. disclosing the scope of work in the report.

85. If the subject property has a patio and the comparable property does not, and the market value of a patio is $1,000, what is the correct adjustment?
   a. Subtract $1,000 from the comparable property.
   b. Add $1,000 to the comparable property.
   c. Subtract $1,000 from the subject property.
   d. Add $1,000 to the subject property.

86. Each statement about the scope of work is correct EXCEPT
   a. it is developed at the outset of the assignment and remains fixed.
   b. it is necessary to solve the appraisal problem.
   c. it may be quick because a familiar assignment is being handled.
   d. it may change over the course of the assignment.

87. When an appraiser estimates the reduction in value that is caused by wear and the disintegration of structural components of the building, he or she is making an estimate of
   a. physical deterioration.
   b. functional obsolescence.
   c. external obsolescence.
   d. tax depreciation.

88. Which of the terms describes land that is not needed for the current use, can be separated from the full site, and can be sold?
   a. excess
   b. functional
   c. salvageable
   d. surplus

89. When the appraiser discusses the need to have the bedrock structure and drainage on the site evaluated, the general term for this discussion is
   a. plottage.
   b. topography.
   c. soil analysis.
   d. accessibility.

90. Which of the following residential appraisers are the appraiser's peers to Appraiser X?
   a. Appraiser A performs office and retail assignments.
   b. Appraiser B performs less sophisticated residential assignments.
   c. Appraiser C performs residential assignments using the same techniques and sophistication.
   d. Appraiser D holds the same type of state certification.

91. Which of the following is an example of an economic determinant of value?
   a. smaller household size
   b. land use restrictions
   c. an increasing divorce rate
   d. a production facility opening

92. When an appraiser uses information about actual sales of properties to form the opinion of value, he or she is using the
   a. cost approach.
   b. income approach.
   c. sales comparison approach.
   d. direct capitalization approach.

93. Which of the following is a characteristic of market value?

    a. The buyer and seller make special financial arrangements.

    b. The buyer and seller negotiate special price concessions.

    c. The property is on the market for a reasonable amount of time.

    d. The property does not have value in exchange.

94. If the comparable property has a deck worth $6,000 but the subject property does not, what is the correct adjustment?

    a. Subtract $6,000 from the comparable property.

    b. Add $6,000 to the comparable property.

    c. Subtract $6,000 from the subject property.

    d. Add $6,000 to the subject property.

95. A loan agreement in which a person other than the borrower provides funds for the down payment is known as

    a. a graduated payment mortgage agreement.

    b. an adjustable-rate mortgage agreement.

    c. a shared appreciation mortgage agreement.

    d. a 1-2-3 buydown mortgage agreement.

96. When the appraiser estimates the capitalization rate from the financial market, each of the following items is used EXCEPT

    a. loan-to-value ratio.

    b. the interest rate (or mortgage constant) on the loan.

    c. the investor's expected rate of return.

    d. loan balance percentage.

97. In the appraisal process, which of the following statements is a correct sequence of actions?

    a. land value opinion, highest and best use, approaches to value

    b. highest and best use, approaches to value, land value opinion

    c. land value opinion, data analysis, approaches to value

    d. highest and best use, land value opinion, approaches to value

98. Which of the following items is NOT necessary to perform a sales comparison technique?

    a. a subject property inspection

    b. an element of comparison research

    c. net operating income

    d. an adjustment grid for the comparable properties

99. Which of the following loans does NOT amortize?

    a. fixed-rate mortgage

    b. buydown loan

    c. adjustable-rate mortgage

    d. interest-only loan

100. A thorough site inspection requires which of the following items?

    a. a map or drawing of the perimeter of the site

    b. facts about the characteristics of the site

    c. knowing the reasons for doing the inspection

    d. all of the above

▶ Answers

1. a. Anticipation is the perception that value is created by the expectation of financial or psychological benefits (pride of ownership, shelter, etc.) to be derived in the future.

2. a. New construction is an increase in the supply of housing; if there is more housing available but the number of buyers doesn't increase, the price of housing will decline.

3. c. Identifying the highest and best use (HBU) is the part of the analysis that takes place after the problem is identified.

4. c. Market value and sales price *can* be equal, but they are not always. Sales price can be at, greater than, or less than market value, depending on a number of factors.

5. a. The government rectangular survey system is a land survey system used in Florida, Alabama, Mississippi, and all states north of the Ohio River or west of the Mississippi River, except Texas. It starts with the intersection of lines of longitude (meridians) and lines of latitude (baselines), and then divides land around these intersections into "townships" approximately six miles squared. Each township contains 36 sections of 640 acres each.

6. c. Financial feasibility is a function of market conditions. The current use might be losing money. Zoning affects the legal uses. The expert opinion is based on the HBU criteria.

7. a. Identifying the property as collateral is a key element of a mortgage or a deed of trust.

8. b. Standard Rule 1–3 discusses the need for a highest and best use analysis. See the subparts of Standard 1 in Uniform Standards of Professional Appraisal Practice (USPAP).

9. c. The appraisal focuses on physical factors but also legal, market, location, etc.

10. b. According to USPAP, the summary appraisal report is characterized by summarizing data. The best way to summarize is to place the data in a table.

11. c. Fee simple ownership includes the rights of use, possession, exclusion, and disposition.

12. d. Supply and demand is the principle that states that the price of real property is directly influenced by the demand for it, further influenced by its availability (supply); in other words, a need or a desire for property in a particular community, coupled with a scarce availability, will drive up the prices. Conversely, little interest and a high availability of real property will drive the prices down.

13. c. Do the math as follows.

$200,000 (sale price) $\times$ .80 = $160,000 (loan amount)

.07 (interest rate) $\div$ 12 (months in a year) = 0.005833

$160,000 $\times$ 0.005833 = $933.33

14. c. The metes and bounds system is defined as a system for the legal description of land that refers to the property's boundaries, which are formed by the point of beginning (POB) and all intermediate points. It uses the distances and angles of each point.

15. c. Financial feasibility is a function of the property market conditions. The other three choices affect the physical possibilities.

16. d. Contribution is the concept that the value of a particular component of the property is measured in terms of its contribution to the value of the whole property, or as the amount that its absence would detract from the value of the whole.

17. a. The cost approach is a set of procedures used to estimate the current cost to construct a reproduction of (or replacement for) the existing structure, including an entrepreneurial incentive, deducting accrued depreciation from the total cost, and adding the estimated land value.

18. c. The comparative-unit method uses a pre-established construction cost manual that shows these costs on a square foot basis.

19. d. It is the most probable sales price, not the highest (**a**). It is not the first price offered (**b**), and it is not the one that the seller eventually takes (**c**).

20. d. A site is land that is improved upon so that it is ready to be used for a specific economic purpose such as residential, commercial, or industrial development.

21. c. Substitution is the principle that states that when several similar commodities, goods, or services are available, the one with the lowest price will attract the greatest demand and widest distribution. It is also stated that a prudent buyer will not pay more for an item than he or she will pay for a similar item. Substitution is the primary principle upon which the cost and sales comparison approaches are based.

22. b. In a life estate, the holder of the estate in possession does not have the right to dispose of the land; however, he or she can occupy the property for his or her lifetime.

23. a. External obsolescence occurs off site.

24. a. Retail facilities are economic determinants of value.

25. c. Investment value is both property- and person-specific. The other three choices are only property-specific.

26. c. Potential gross income (PGI) = effective gross income (EGI) = $1,400 × 12 = $16,800

Operating expenses = $1,400 + $300 + $600 + $300 = $2,600

Improvement expenditures are not part of NOI.
NOI = $16,800 − $2,600 = $14,200

27. d. There is no valuation relationship between a sale price ten years ago and current NOI. Current NOI divided by current sales price equals the capitalization rate.

28. c. Appraiser's peers are defined as appraisers who have expertise and competency in a similar type of assignment. See the definition in the "Definitions" section of USPAP.

29. d. Scope of work is defined as the type and extent of research and analysis in an assignment. See the definition in the "Definitions" section of USPAP.

30. d. Zoning affects the legal uses.

31. b. See the definitions of contract rent and market rent in the glossary for a more in-depth explanation.

32. b. Remember, whichever choice yields $734.67 is your answer.

The math solution is as follows, using a Hewlett Packard 12c:

Keystrokes: 900 FV, 3 n, 7 i/Yr, then press PV to get −734.67 (ignore the minus sign).

33. b. The income approach is a set of procedures through which an appraiser derives a value for an income-earning property by converting its anticipated revenues and expenses into property value.

34. d. In a buydown mortgage agreement, the buyer qualifies at a below-market interest rate in the first year and the builder pays the difference in the interest payment to the lender. This typically happens for the first three years, with the buyer's interest rate increasing to the market rate.

35. d. A low crime rate and respect for property in a community are social determinants of value.

36. b. Frontage is the measured footage of a site that abuts a street (as well as a stream, railroad, or other facility).

37. c. The increase in value needs to be equal to or greater than the cost to repair.

38. b. This statement best describes the sales comparison approach.

39. c. Land residual technique is the method of estimating land value in which the net operating income attributable to the land is estimated and then capitalized to produce an estimate of the land's contribution to the total property.

40. b. Extraction technique is a method of estimating land value in which the depreciated cost of the improvements on the improved property is estimated and deducted from the total sale price to arrive at an estimated sale price for the land. It is most effective when the improvements contribute little to the total sale price of the property.

41. c. The buyer must have a value in use for the property, and both the buyer and the seller must have value in exchange.

42. d. Special financing, which typically refers to below-market interest rate financing, is not a characteristic of market value. For the financing to be characterized as market value, it must be typical for the market.

43. d. Remember, whichever choice yields $900.52 is your answer.

The math solution is as follows, using a Hewlett Packard 12c:

Keystrokes: 700 PV, 4 n, 6.5 i/Yr, then press FV to get –900.52 (ignore minus sign).

44. a. Change is caused by the economic, physical, social, and governmental forces that influence real property value.

45. b. Of the four choices, only the income approach—direct capitalization—uses a capitalization rate.

46. a. The age-life method is used to estimate the percent of total depreciation. It is a technique used in the cost approach.

Please refer to the following for the answer explanations for questions 47–50.

The numbers in the table have to be rearranged from high to low or low to high.

	# of Acres	Low to high	High to low
Parcel 1	1.4	1.4 (Parcel 1)	5.5 (Parcel 3)
Parcel 2	4.9	2.8 (Parcel 7)	4.9 (Parcel 2)
Parcel 3	5.5	2.9 (Parcel 4)	3.8 (Parcel 6)
Parcel 4	2.9	3.2 (Parcel 5)	3.2 (Parcel 5)
Parcel 5	3.2	3.8 (Parcel 6)	2.9 (Parcel 4)
Parcel 6	3.8	4.9 (Parcel 2)	2.8 (Parcel 7)
Parcel 7	2.8	5.5 (Parcel 3)	1.4 (Parcel 1)

47. b. Parcel 5, which is 3.2 acres, represents the median number of acres.

48. a. 3.5 acres represents the average size of all the parcels. The total sum acreage of the seven parcels is 24.5. Divide that sum acreage by the number of parcels, 7, to get the average parcel size, 3.5 acres.

49. c. 4.1 acres represents the range of the parcels. To find the range, subtract the smallest parcel size from the largest.
5.5 − 1.4 = 4.1.

50. d. 1.4 acres represents the standard deviation. A calculator with statistical capabilities is needed to find this answer.

51. c. Both the number of buyers increasing and the mortgage interest rate declining will cause demand to increase, and the prices will rise.

52. b. The statement is an explanation of the unit-in-place method, which is also known as the subcontractors' method.

53. d. The government can place a tax lien on a property if a special assessment, such as a sidewalk assessment charge, is not paid.

54. c. A life estate is an ownership form in which rights of use, possession, and exclusion are held by one party for his or her lifetime (the estate in possession). The right of disposition is held by another person (estate in expectancy). Upon the death of the owner of the state in possession, the physical property and the rights pass on to the person holding the estate in expectancy.

55. c. Conformity is the principle that states that real property value is created and sustained when the characteristics of a property conform to the demands of its market.

56. b. Determination of the use of professional and staff resources and the quote of the fee are not part of the scope of work requirement; the other three options are part of the scope of work requirement.

57. c. Plottage is the increment of value that is created when at least two sites are combined to produce greater utility. You may have been tempted to pick choice **a**, but you would have been wrong: Assemblage is the process that creates plottage value; it is the combining into one ownership or the use of at least two parcels that are normally—but not necessarily—contiguous.

58. b. The easiest way to do this is to simply split the figure into a rectangle and a triangle.

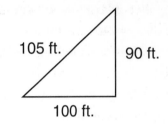

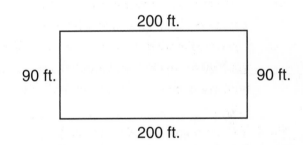

The rectangle portion is 200 × 90 = 18,000 square feet.

The triangle portion is 90 feet high with a 100-foot base. The formula for the area of a triangle is $\frac{1}{2}bh$ (*b* for base, *h* for height). Plug in the numbers:

$\frac{1}{2}(100) \times 90 = 50 \times 90 = 4{,}500$ square feet

Add the total square feet of the two portions together:

18,000 + 4,500 = 22,500

59. d. An appraiser cannot act as an advocate under any circumstance or for any party. See the discussion in the "Conduct" section of the "Ethics Rule" in USPAP.

60. **b.** The reduction in value caused by changes in consumer attitudes toward the design of the structure and its fixtures is known as functional obsolescence.

61. **c.** This is the verbal statement of the valuation formula $V = NOI \div Ro$.

62. **b.** Confidentiality, conduct, management, and record keeping are the four sections of the Ethics Rule. See the discussion in the "Ethics Rule" in USPAP.

63. **a.** Allocation technique is the process of separating total property value between the component parts of a property. A ratio of land value to total property value is applied to the subject property or the comparable sale being analyzed.

64. **a.** Zoning is a public limit on ownership—it limits the right of use.

65. **d.** The record-keeping section of the Ethics Rule states that the appraiser must prepare a workfile and keep it for five years after its preparation. See the discussion in the "Ethics Rule" of the "Record Keeping" section in USPAP.

66. **b.** In an adjustable-rate mortgage (ARM) agreement, the contract interest rate can change as the index rate (a proxy for the market interest rate) changes.

67. **c.** PGI = 1,200 × 4 × 12 = 57,600
PGI less Vacancy = EGI
57,600 − (57,600 × 8%) = 57,600 − 4,608 = 52,992

68. **b.** NOI = EGI less total operating expenses = 52,992 − 4(3,200) = 40,192

69. **a.** Total operating expenses = 4 units × 3,200 = 12,800.

70. **a.** The operating expense ratio is $\frac{12,800}{52,992} = 24.15\%$.

71. **d.** The overall cap rate is NOI/Property Value $= \frac{40,192}{340,000} = 11.8\%$

72. **b.** Land use restriction in the zoning ordinance is the governmental determinant.

73. **c.** An ocean view is a physical/environmental determinant of value.

74. **a.** The conduct part of the Ethics Rule states that the appraiser cannot report predetermined opinions or conclusions. See the discussion in the "Ethics Rule" in the "Conduct" section in USPAP.

75. **d.** A metes and bounds system is defined as a system for the legal description of land that refers to the property's boundaries, which are formed by the POB and all intermediate points. It uses the distances and angles of each point.

76. **d.** None of the options is correct. The correct formula is $Ro = NOI \div V$.

77. **d.** PGI minus vacancy loss equals the EGI.

78. **a.** A loan assumption occurs when a new buyer takes the legal and financial responsibility to pay off the mortgage for the original buyer and borrower.

79. **a.** The Competency Rule does not require that the appraiser disclose the lack of knowledge in the completed report. It does require that the lack of knowledge is revealed "before accepting the assignment," not in the completed report. See the discussion in the "Competency Rule" section in USPAP.

80. **b.** The market rent for comparable-sized apartments in the immediate area can be ignored: Apartments are not good comparables for single-family units.

81. **b.** Identifying the comparable properties is the part of the analysis that takes place *after* the problem is identified.

82. c. The scope of work does not allow assignment conditions to limit it under any circumstance. The other three options are required by the scope of services. See the discussion in the "Scope of Work Rule" and the "Scope of Work Acceptability" section in USPAP.

83. b. Increasing and decreasing returns is the concept that successive increments of one or more agents of production (labor or capital) added to fixed amounts of another agent (land) will enhance income—in dollars, benefits, or amenities—until a maximum return is reached. Then, income will decrease until the increment to value becomes increasingly less than the value of the added agent or agents.

84. b. The scope of work does not require the identity of the professional staff involved in the analysis. The other three choices are required by the scope of services. See the discussion in the "Scope of Work Rule" in USPAP.

85. b. The comparable property must be adjusted to the subject property; here, the appraiser would add the market value of the patio ($1,000) to the price of the comparable property.

86. a. The scope of work is developed at the outset of the assignment, but it does not remain fixed. The other three choices are required by the scope of services. See the discussion in the "Scope of Work Rule" in USPAP.

87. a. The reduction in value that is caused by wear and the disintegration of structural components of the building is known as physical deterioration.

88. a. Excess land is the part of a site not needed to serve or support the existing improvement in regard to a vacant site or a site considered as vacant (the land not needed to accommodate the site's primary highest and best use). Such land may be separated from the larger site and have its own highest and best use, or it may allow for future expansion of the existing or anticipated improvement. Surplus land (choice **d**) is the portion of a site not necessary to support the highest and best use of the existing improvement but, because of physical limitations, building placement, or neighborhood norms, cannot be sold off separately.

89. c. Soil analysis is the study of the attributes of the soil on the land. Drainage ability and bedrock are two important aspects of soil analysis. It is not topography (choice **b**), which focuses on the surface of the parcel (slope, at grade level, etc.).

90. c. Appraiser C, who performs residential assignments using the same techniques and sophistication as Appraiser X, is an appraiser peer. The other three appraisers are not peers to Appraiser X. See the definition of appraiser's peers in the "Definitions" section of USPAP.

91. d. Of the choices, the opening of a production facility is the economic determinant. Smaller household sizes (**a**) and an increasing divorce rate (**c**) are social determinants of value; land use restrictions (**b**) are a governmental determinant of value.

92. c. The sales comparison approach is a set of procedures in which a value indication is derived by comparing the property being appraised to similar properties that have been sold recently, then applying appropriate units of comparison and making adjustments to the sales prices of the comparables based on the elements of comparison.

93. c. For the property to be characterized as having market value, it must have reasonable exposure. The incorrect choices focus on special financing and price, and no value in exchange.

94. a. The comparable property must be adjusted to the subject property; here, the appraiser would subtract the market value of the deck ($6,000) from the price of the comparable property.

95. c. In a shared appreciation mortgage agreement, a third party other than the buyer or the lender provides money for the down payment and negotiates a portion of the appreciation over a fixed period of time as the return on the investment.

96. d. The loan balance percentage is not involved in the calculation of the capitalization rate using financial data. The rate of growth in value as given by appreciation or the change in NOI is part of the solution.

97. d. HBU analysis takes place before land is valued and before the three approaches to value are used.

98. c. Net operating income (NOI) is used in the income method.

99. d. Interest-only loans do not amortize; these loans only have an interest payment, so the loan balance stays constant. Each of the other three loan options has its payments split between an interest payment and loan repayment.

100. d. All three of the choices are a required part of a site inspection.

▶ Scoring

Evaluate how you did on this practice exam by first finding the number of questions you answered correctly. Only the number of correct answers is important—questions that you skipped or got wrong don't count against your score. On your official exam, you will most likely only receive a score of pass or fail. However, you should check with your state to find out what the official scoring criteria is for the particular exam you will be taking. Generally, to achieve a passing score for the exam, you must answer at least 75% of the questions correctly. On this practice exam, a passing score would be 75 correct.

Use your scores in conjunction with the Learning-Express Test Preparation System in Chapter 2 of this book to help you devise a study plan using the real estate appraisal refresher course in Chapter 5, the real estate math review in Chapter 6, and the real estate glossary in Chapter 7. You should plan to spend more time on the sections that correspond to the questions you found hardest and less time on the lessons that correspond to areas in which you did well.

For now, what is much more important than your overall score is how you performed on each of the areas tested by the exam. You need to diagnose your strengths and weaknesses so that you can concentrate your efforts as you prepare. The different question types are mixed in the practice exam, so in order to diagnose where your strengths and weaknesses lie, you will need to compare your answer sheet with the following table, which shows which of the categories each questions falls into.

Once you have spent some time reviewing, take the second residential appraisal practice exam in Chapter 8 to see how much you have improved.

Residential Appraisal Practice Exam 1 for Review

Topic	Question Numbers	
Influences on Real Estate	24, 35, 72, 73, 91	1
Legal Considerations in Appraisal	11, 22, 53, 64, 75	2
Types of Value	4, 25, 41, 42, 93	1
Economic Principles	1, 12, 16, 44, 55, 83	3
Real Estate Markets and Analysis	2, 7, 13, 34, 51, 66, 78, 95, 99	2
Valuation Process	3, 33, 45, 46, 81, 92, 97	4
Property Description	5, 14, 20, 36, 57, 58, 88, 89, 100	4
Highest and Best Use Analysis	6, 15, 30, 67, 68, 69, 70, 71	3
Appraisal Math and Statistics	10, 32, 43, 47, 48, 49, 50	3
Sales Comparison Approach	9, 19, 38, 80, 85, 94, 98	3
Site Value	21, 39, 40, 63	1
Cost Approach	17, 18, 23, 37, 52, 60, 87	0
Income Approach	26, 27, 31, 61, 76, 77, 96	3
Valuation of Partial Interests	54	
Appraisal Standards and Ethics	8, 28, 29, 56, 59, 62, 65, 74, 79, 82, 84, 86, 90	2

4 ▶ Certified General Appraisal Practice Exam 1

CHAPTER SUMMARY

This is the first of the two practice tests in this book based on the Appraiser Qualifications Board's (AQB) National Uniform Exam Content Outlines for certified general appraisers. Take this test to see how you would do if you took the exam today and to get a handle on your strengths and weaknesses.

TKE THIS EXAM in as relaxed a manner as you can, without worrying about timing. You can time yourself on the second exam. You should, however, make sure that you have enough time to take the entire exam in one sitting. Find a quiet place where you can work without interruptions.

The answer sheet is on the following page, and is followed by the exam. After you have finished, use the answer key and explanations to learn your strengths and your weaknesses. Then use the scoring section at the end of this chapter to see how you did overall. Good luck!

▶ Certified General Appraisal Practice Exam 1 Answer Sheet

#						#						#				
1.	ⓐ	ⓑ	ⓒ	ⓓ		46.	ⓐ	ⓑ	ⓒ	ⓓ		91.	ⓐ	ⓑ	ⓒ	ⓓ
2.	ⓐ	ⓑ	ⓒ	ⓓ		47.	ⓐ	ⓑ	ⓒ	ⓓ		92.	ⓐ	ⓑ	ⓒ	ⓓ
3.	ⓐ	ⓑ	ⓒ	ⓓ		48.	ⓐ	ⓑ	ⓒ	ⓓ		93.	ⓐ	ⓑ	ⓒ	ⓓ
4.	ⓐ	ⓑ	ⓒ	ⓓ		49.	ⓐ	ⓑ	ⓒ	ⓓ		94.	ⓐ	ⓑ	ⓒ	ⓓ
5.	ⓐ	ⓑ	ⓒ	ⓓ		50.	ⓐ	ⓑ	ⓒ	ⓓ		95.	ⓐ	ⓑ	ⓒ	ⓓ
6.	ⓐ	ⓑ	ⓒ	ⓓ		51.	ⓐ	ⓑ	ⓒ	ⓓ		96.	ⓐ	ⓑ	ⓒ	ⓓ
7.	ⓐ	ⓑ	ⓒ	ⓓ		52.	ⓐ	ⓑ	ⓒ	ⓓ		97.	ⓐ	ⓑ	ⓒ	ⓓ
8.	ⓐ	ⓑ	ⓒ	ⓓ		53.	ⓐ	ⓑ	ⓒ	ⓓ		98.	ⓐ	ⓑ	ⓒ	ⓓ
9.	ⓐ	ⓑ	ⓒ	ⓓ		54.	ⓐ	ⓑ	ⓒ	ⓓ		99.	ⓐ	ⓑ	ⓒ	ⓓ
10.	ⓐ	ⓑ	ⓒ	ⓓ		55.	ⓐ	ⓑ	ⓒ	ⓓ		100.	ⓐ	ⓑ	ⓒ	ⓓ
11.	ⓐ	ⓑ	ⓒ	ⓓ		56.	ⓐ	ⓑ	ⓒ	ⓓ		101.	ⓐ	ⓑ	ⓒ	ⓓ
12.	ⓐ	ⓑ	ⓒ	ⓓ		57.	ⓐ	ⓑ	ⓒ	ⓓ		102.	ⓐ	ⓑ	ⓒ	ⓓ
13.	ⓐ	ⓑ	ⓒ	ⓓ		58.	ⓐ	ⓑ	ⓒ	ⓓ		103.	ⓐ	ⓑ	ⓒ	ⓓ
14.	ⓐ	ⓑ	ⓒ	ⓓ		59.	ⓐ	ⓑ	ⓒ	ⓓ		104.	ⓐ	ⓑ	ⓒ	ⓓ
15.	ⓐ	ⓑ	ⓒ	ⓓ		60.	ⓐ	ⓑ	ⓒ	ⓓ		105.	ⓐ	ⓑ	ⓒ	ⓓ
16.	ⓐ	ⓑ	ⓒ	ⓓ		61.	ⓐ	ⓑ	ⓒ	ⓓ		106.	ⓐ	ⓑ	ⓒ	ⓓ
17.	ⓐ	ⓑ	ⓒ	ⓓ		62.	ⓐ	ⓑ	ⓒ	ⓓ		107.	ⓐ	ⓑ	ⓒ	ⓓ
18.	ⓐ	ⓑ	ⓒ	ⓓ		63.	ⓐ	ⓑ	ⓒ	ⓓ		108.	ⓐ	ⓑ	ⓒ	ⓓ
19.	ⓐ	ⓑ	ⓒ	ⓓ		64.	ⓐ	ⓑ	ⓒ	ⓓ		109.	ⓐ	ⓑ	ⓒ	ⓓ
20.	ⓐ	ⓑ	ⓒ	ⓓ		65.	ⓐ	ⓑ	ⓒ	ⓓ		110.	ⓐ	ⓑ	ⓒ	ⓓ
21.	ⓐ	ⓑ	ⓒ	ⓓ		66.	ⓐ	ⓑ	ⓒ	ⓓ		111.	ⓐ	ⓑ	ⓒ	ⓓ
22.	ⓐ	ⓑ	ⓒ	ⓓ		67.	ⓐ	ⓑ	ⓒ	ⓓ		112.	ⓐ	ⓑ	ⓒ	ⓓ
23.	ⓐ	ⓑ	ⓒ	ⓓ		68.	ⓐ	ⓑ	ⓒ	ⓓ		113.	ⓐ	ⓑ	ⓒ	ⓓ
24.	ⓐ	ⓑ	ⓒ	ⓓ		69.	ⓐ	ⓑ	ⓒ	ⓓ		114.	ⓐ	ⓑ	ⓒ	ⓓ
25.	ⓐ	ⓑ	ⓒ	ⓓ		70.	ⓐ	ⓑ	ⓒ	ⓓ		115.	ⓐ	ⓑ	ⓒ	ⓓ
26.	ⓐ	ⓑ	ⓒ	ⓓ		71.	ⓐ	ⓑ	ⓒ	ⓓ		116.	ⓐ	ⓑ	ⓒ	ⓓ
27.	ⓐ	ⓑ	ⓒ	ⓓ		72.	ⓐ	ⓑ	ⓒ	ⓓ		117.	ⓐ	ⓑ	ⓒ	ⓓ
28.	ⓐ	ⓑ	ⓒ	ⓓ		73.	ⓐ	ⓑ	ⓒ	ⓓ		118.	ⓐ	ⓑ	ⓒ	ⓓ
29.	ⓐ	ⓑ	ⓒ	ⓓ		74.	ⓐ	ⓑ	ⓒ	ⓓ		119.	ⓐ	ⓑ	ⓒ	ⓓ
30.	ⓐ	ⓑ	ⓒ	ⓓ		75.	ⓐ	ⓑ	ⓒ	ⓓ		120.	ⓐ	ⓑ	ⓒ	ⓓ
31.	ⓐ	ⓑ	ⓒ	ⓓ		76.	ⓐ	ⓑ	ⓒ	ⓓ		121.	ⓐ	ⓑ	ⓒ	ⓓ
32.	ⓐ	ⓑ	ⓒ	ⓓ		77.	ⓐ	ⓑ	ⓒ	ⓓ		122.	ⓐ	ⓑ	ⓒ	ⓓ
33.	ⓐ	ⓑ	ⓒ	ⓓ		78.	ⓐ	ⓑ	ⓒ	ⓓ		123.	ⓐ	ⓑ	ⓒ	ⓓ
34.	ⓐ	ⓑ	ⓒ	ⓓ		79.	ⓐ	ⓑ	ⓒ	ⓓ		124.	ⓐ	ⓑ	ⓒ	ⓓ
35.	ⓐ	ⓑ	ⓒ	ⓓ		80.	ⓐ	ⓑ	ⓒ	ⓓ		125.	ⓐ	ⓑ	ⓒ	ⓓ
36.	ⓐ	ⓑ	ⓒ	ⓓ		81.	ⓐ	ⓑ	ⓒ	ⓓ						
37.	ⓐ	ⓑ	ⓒ	ⓓ		82.	ⓐ	ⓑ	ⓒ	ⓓ						
38.	ⓐ	ⓑ	ⓒ	ⓓ		83.	ⓐ	ⓑ	ⓒ	ⓓ						
39.	ⓐ	ⓑ	ⓒ	ⓓ		84.	ⓐ	ⓑ	ⓒ	ⓓ						
40.	ⓐ	ⓑ	ⓒ	ⓓ		85.	ⓐ	ⓑ	ⓒ	ⓓ						
41.	ⓐ	ⓑ	ⓒ	ⓓ		86.	ⓐ	ⓑ	ⓒ	ⓓ						
42.	ⓐ	ⓑ	ⓒ	ⓓ		87.	ⓐ	ⓑ	ⓒ	ⓓ						
43.	ⓐ	ⓑ	ⓒ	ⓓ		88.	ⓐ	ⓑ	ⓒ	ⓓ						
44.	ⓐ	ⓑ	ⓒ	ⓓ		89.	ⓐ	ⓑ	ⓒ	ⓓ						
45.	ⓐ	ⓑ	ⓒ	ⓓ		90.	ⓐ	ⓑ	ⓒ	ⓓ						

► Certified General Appraisal Practice Exam 1

1. An appraiser accepts an assignment to appraise a quadraplex. Unable to find reliable sales of comparable quadraplexes, the appraiser uses duplexes—multiplying rents, sale prices, and sizes by two to match the characteristics of his or her subject. The appraiser's behavior is best described as
   a. an appropriate application of the seldom-used appraisal principle of doubling.
   b. a violation of Uniform Standards of Professional Appraisal Practice (USPAP).
   c. mathematic approximation.
   d. statistical estimation.

2. What is the most critical element in the appraiser's decision to apply an income capitalization technique?
   a. client demands
   b. the motivation of buyers in the subject market
   c. The subject is tenant-occupied.
   d. The contract rent exceeds market rent.

3. An appraiser may reveal the details concerning the development of an appraisal and the value conclusion to
   a. the homeowner.
   b. the lender.
   c. the party who hired the appraiser.
   d. no one.

4. What kind of depreciation may be found in a structure that is part of a subject judged to be highest and best use of the property as improved?
   a. incurable short-lived and incurable long-lived
   b. incurable short-lived only
   c. incurable long-lived only
   d. curable

5. Concerning the criteria for highest and best use, which of the following is correct?
   a. It is legally permitted and marginally profitable.
   b. It is appropriately financed and maximally productive.
   c. It is physically possible and legally permitted.
   d. It is marginally productive and financially feasible.

6. A waterfront residential property is traded in a rental market impacted by seasonal changes in demand. Which is true concerning the application of income capitalization as an appraisal technique?
   a. Income capitalization should not be used in a seasonal market.
   b. Monthly rent should be converted into value using a gross rent multiplier.
   c. Annual rent should be converted into value using a gross rent multiplier.
   d. Seasonal rents are converted into value using a net rent multiplier.

7. Building plans and specifications indicate the measurement of one wall in a rectangular building to be 90'9". The intersecting wall is 32'6". Replacement cost of the improvement is estimated at $140 per square foot. What is the total replacement cost of this building?
   a. $412,912
   b. $414,867
   c. $416,220
   d. $418,980

8. An appraiser is examining plans and specifications for proposed construction. The effective date is established as of the anticipated time of completion. This is a
   a. current effective date.
   b. retrospective effective date.
   c. prospective effective date.
   d. violation of USPAP.

9. As of the effective appraisal date, the appraiser has determined that the 50-year-old subject improvement has experienced typical maintenance. The appraiser would estimate the effective age at
   a. zero.
   b. less than actual age.
   c. same as actual age.
   d. greater than actual age.

10. After the factors of production of labor, capital, and entrepreneurial ability have received their share of net operating income, the income left over is paid to the land. This is described by the appraisal principle of
   a. surplus productivity.
   b. conformity.
   c. substitution.
   d. competition.

11. Upon inspection, an appraiser notes a malfunctioning septic system. Which of the following indicated this condition?
   a. low water pressure
   b. standing water in the backyard
   c. healthy vegetation growth
   d. leaking water meter

12. What is an example of a construction component that would likely exhibit long-lived physical depreciation?
   a. load-bearing walls
   b. water heater
   c. floor covering
   d. air conditioning compressor

13. The buyer makes a $50,000 down payment, financing the balance of the purchase price with a $500,000 loan. The lender charged four points in a discount that the seller agreed to pay. What is the cash equivalent price of this sale?
   a. $570,000
   b. $550,000
   c. $530,000
   d. $520,000

14. What is the depreciated value of a building that has an anticipated total economic life of 100 years and an effective age of 20 years if the replacement cost is $500,000?
   a. $100,000
   b. $200,000
   c. $300,000
   d. $400,000

15. A two-bedroom, one-bath subject property has been estimated to have a market value of $200,000 as is. The market prefers three-bedroom, two-bath homes that typically sell for $230,000. It would now cost $18,500 to construct the third bedroom and $16,200 to add a bath. If this work had been included in the original construction, the third bedroom would have cost $12,000 and the second bath would have cost $8,000. If the work were performed now, the subject would conform to the expectations of the market. What depreciation is being demonstrated?

a. curable functional
b. incurable functional
c. curable physical
d. incurable physical

16. A father sold a duplex to his daughter as her first real estate investment. You would like to use this sale as a comparable, but you are concerned about the familial relationship between buyer and seller. You are considering an adjustment for

a. property rights.
b. financing.
c. conditions of sale.
d. market conditions.

17. An appraiser uses reconciliation for what purpose?

a. to increase the value estimate to achieve the client's objective
b. to weigh the results to obtain a single estimate of value
c. to satisfy the client's expectations as to the amount of the value
d. to adjust approaches to value that are inappropriate for the type of property being appraised

18. An appraiser is using comparables that vary in size. A decision is made to convert the sale prices into price per square foot. What is the benefit of using this unit of comparison?

a. Adjustments for size differences may be unnecessary.
b. Adjustments for location may be unnecessary.
c. Reconciliation of value becomes unnecessary.
d. Measurement of gross adjustment percentages becomes redundant.

19. What appraisal approach is based on the premise that a person will pay the same amount for properties of similar quality and amenities?

a. income approach
b. sales comparison
c. cost approach
d. regression

20. A property is purchased for $75,000 today. The property is anticipated to increase in value 6% each year. How much is the property projected to be worth at the end of five years (rounded to the nearest $1,000)?

a. $97,000
b. $98,000
c. $99,000
d. $100,000

21. Comparable property A is a wooded and sloped lot that recently sold for $500,000. Comparable property B is a wooded and level lot that recently sold for $530,000. The subject is wooded and level. The comparables are identical to the subject in all other respects. What type of adjustment should be made?

a. $30,000 positive adjustment to A
b. $30,000 negative adjustment to B
c. $30,000 negative adjustment to A
d. $30,000 positive adjustment to B

22. Comparables and subject must share which of the following?

a. market area
b. neighborhood
c. district
d. community-wide appeal

23. A 70-year-old home is traded in an active market in which there are plenty of sales of similar properties. There are no rental homes in the market. What appraisal approach will likely provide the most reliable indicator of market value for this subject?

a. cost
b. sales comparison
c. regression
d. income

24. Most appraisal assignments are undertaken to measure the most probable sale price of improved property. This is the basis of what type of value?

a. value in use
b. investment value
c. market value
d. going-concern value

25. An appraiser is unable to locate a sufficient number of comparable land sales, although sales of improved land are plentiful. What land valuation technique is appropriate?

a. allocation
b. sales comparison
c. building residual
d. mortgage equity

26. An example of a business or personal expense of the property owner and NOT a real property operating expense is

a. management.
b. debt service.
c. collection loss.
d. vacancies.

27. Land value may be measured by deducting the contributory improvement value from the total sale price of a property. This describes which of the following?

a. allocation
b. extraction
c. land residual
d. ground rent capitalization

28. Which of the following would cause an increase in the discount rate?

a. increase in the quantity of income
b. decrease in the quantity of income
c. irregular income stream
d. increase of risk in the investment

29. Total income generated from all operations of the real property after an allowance for vacancy and collection loss is

a. potential gross income.
b. effective gross income.
c. net operating income.
d. cash dividend.

30. If the overall capitalization rate exceeds the mortgage constant, leverage is
   a. positive.
   b. negative.
   c. zero.
   d. There is insufficient information provided to answer this question.

31. Extraction is most reliably used as a land valuation technique when
   a. improvements were virtually identical at the time of sale.
   b. improvements contribute an insignificant amount of value.
   c. improvements are all in the same physical condition.
   d. the land is vacant.

32. The portion of an office building that is capable of generating rent is represented by which of the following?
   a. gross income ratio
   b. net income ratio
   c. efficiency ratio
   d. useable ratio

33. The criteria for highest and best use that will normally eliminate the most alternatives from consideration and will therefore be considered first is
   a. financially feasible.
   b. maximally productive.
   c. legally permitted.
   d. marginally profitable.

34. The idea that a comparable property with superior amenities should sell for a higher price is explained by the appraisal principle of
   a. highest and best use.
   b. competition.
   c. conformity.
   d. externalities.

35. The minimum report format required for oral appraisal reports is
   a. letter.
   b. form.
   c. restricted use.
   d. summary.

36. What type of value would be measured for a water treatment plant where the appraiser is considering the number of gallons of water capable of being processed each hour?
   a. investment value
   b. market value
   c. value in use
   d. going-concern value

37. The combination of two or more properties under a single ownership to increase value is
   a. assemblage.
   b. plottage.
   c. surplus land.
   d. excess land.

38. What is the annual market absorption rate if 50 of the available 500 units sell every six months?
   a. 10%
   b. 15%
   c. 20%
   d. 30%

39. Which of the following factors strongly influences the appraiser's selection of discount rates?
   a. the relationship between market and contract rents
   b. the credit rating of the tenant
   c. the quality of the income stream
   d. all of the above

40. The content and type of an appraisal report should never be influenced by
   a. the appraiser's fee.
   b. subject property characteristics.
   c. client requirements.
   d. the intended use of the appraisal.

41. Land is vacant and available to be developed to its highest and best use. Zoning and utility are considered appropriate in the market area. This tract of land should be valued as
   a. vacant, to be developed to its highest and best use.
   b. improved, with the most feasible use.
   c. improved, with the most probable use.
   d. improved, with the maximally productive use.

42. An appropriately sized improvement is constructed on a site. Construction of this improvement achieves highest and best use of the land as though vacant. What principle applies?
   a. balance
   b. over-improvement
   c. under-improvement
   d. super-adequacy

43. An appraiser has an assignment to value an apartment complex. Historical sales of this property must be researched for how many years?
   a. one year
   b. two years
   c. three years
   d. four years

44. Any current agreement of sale, option, or listing of the subject property
   a. must be considered and analyzed.
   b. must be ignored, as it would bias the appraisal result.
   c. must not be considered until the property has a closed sale.
   d. must be considered and analyzed only if relative to the function of the assignment.

45. A measurement of variance is found in the
   a. range.
   b. mean.
   c. median.
   d. mode.

46. What appraisal principle suggests that even though historical data is analyzed, buyers make decisions based on expectations of future benefits?
   a. conformity
   b. anticipation
   c. expectations
   d. consistent use

47. Construction of a new interchange for the local community has been rumored for several months. The interchange will be located nearby the subject. When will the interchange influence values in the subject's neighborhood?
a. completion of the project
b. beginning of construction
c. funding of the project is complete
d. market reacts

48. A 40-year-old single-family home with 5,000 square feet of gross living area recently sold for $600,000. Land value at the time of sale was $120,000. Replacement cost of similar homes is $200 per square foot of gross living area. What is the depreciation in the home at the time of sale?
a. 48%
b. 49%
c. 50%
d. 52%

49. A roof must be replaced in three years. Contributions are made into an interest-bearing account that yields 4% interest. The contributions are made at the end of each year. How much must be contributed annually to meet the goal of roof replacement if the roof will cost $40,000 to replace (rounded to the nearest $100)?
a. $12,300
b. $12,800
c. $13,200
d. $13,400

50. Which limits the applicability of income capitalization as an appraisal technique?
a. lack of a rental market
b. income varies in an irregular pattern
c. improvements are more than 70 years old
d. lack of sales activity

51. A market that is oversupplied with available product is a
a. buyer's market.
b. seller's market.
c. tight market.
d. broad market.

52. A neighborhood that is experiencing an influx of new purchasers who are demolishing or renovating existing improvements is in what phase of the neighborhood life cycle?
a. growth
b. stability
c. decline
d. revitalization

53. Zoning, building codes, and deed restrictions are all examples of what type of value influence?
a. social
b. governmental
c. economic
d. environmental

54. Return of investment capital is represented by which of the following?
a. discount rate
b. yield rate
c. interest rate
d. recapture rate

55. All of the following are components of the market value definition EXCEPT
a. typically informed buyers and sellers.
b. reasonable exposure to the market.
c. highly motivated buyers and sellers.
d. consummation of sale as of a particular date.

56. Smith and Jones, who are both state-certified general appraisers, collaborated on the appraisal of a retail shopping center. Smith conducted all of the research and analysis of market rents used in support of income capitalization techniques, while Jones completed the remainder of the appraisal. Because the client was only familiar with Jones, Jones was the only appraiser who signed the certification. Which of the following is correct?

   a. Because Jones and Smith both contributed in such a significant manner, both must sign the certification and the details regarding the extent of both their contributions must be described.

   b. If Jones is the only appraiser signing the certification, Smith should not have participated in the appraisal.

   c. As long as either Jones or Smith signs the certification, there is no violation of USPAP.

   d. If Smith does not sign the certification, the extent of Smith's contribution must be noted in the report and Smith must be named as having contributed in a significant way in the certification.

57. When supply exceeds demand at the current price, the most likely result is

   a. a price decline.

   b. inflationary pressure.

   c. market equilibrium.

   d. a price increase.

58. What condition is indicated in a market with a 60% vacancy ratio?

   a. buyer's market

   b. seller's market

   c. equilibrium

   d. transition

59. In which of the following appraisal techniques is the income attributed to improvements deducted from net operating income?

   a. land residual

   b. building residual

   c. allocation

   d. extraction

60. What is the operating expense ratio for a property with the following characteristics?

Sale Price	$150,000
Potential Gross Income	$10,000
Operating Expenses	$3,150
Debt Service	$6,200
Effective Gross Income	$9,000
Net Operating Income	$5,850

   a. .315

   b. .35

   c. .42

   d. .538

61. Two properties are anticipated to be ready for high-rise office building construction in about five years. One site has a commercial interim use that produces $40,000 more net operating income per year than the other property, which has a parking lot as its interim use. The present value of the future cost to demolish the commercial building is $50,000 and the parking lot will entail no significant demolition cost. Based on a discount rate of 10.5%, what is the difference in value of these two interim uses? (Answer is rounded to the nearest thousand.)

   a. $150,000

   b. $125,000

   c. $100,000

   d. $50,000

62. Which of the following pairs of terms are synonymous?
   a. contract rent/economic rent
   b. contract rent/scheduled rent
   c. contract rent/market rent
   d. economic rent/scheduled rent

63. Effective rent would be reduced by what concession by a landlord?
   a. installing dental chairs
   b. carpeting the floors
   c. painting the walls
   d. all of the above

64. Four residential units have been constructed on a tract of land now rezoned to allow only two residential units. During a market value appraisal of the existing four units, how should income from the over-improvments be treated?
   a. It should be allocated between land and improvements.
   b. It should be attributed to the land only.
   c. It should be attributed to the improvements only.
   d. It should be ignored.

65. An appraiser lacks vacant land sales in his or her market. However, sales of improved properties are plentiful. Because the improvements built on the sale properties are of minimal value, the appraiser would choose which as the most reliable land valuation technique?
   a. sales comparison
   b. extraction
   c. allocation
   d. land residual

66. A residential community has experienced significant growth in recent years. Similar communities have experienced success in rezoning residential properties along the most heavily traveled streets. The appraiser's subject is located along the street where the zoning has been changed from residential to commercial usage. If appraised for market value as a residential property, land value would be $10,000 and the value of improvements would be $40,000. If appraised for market value as a commercial property, land value would be $60,000 and the value of the improvements would be $10,000. How should this property be appraised for market value?
   a. residential land and commercial improvement
   b. commercial land and residential improvement
   c. commercial land and commercial improvement
   d. residential land and residential improvement

67. What type of depreciation is possible if a property is judged to be at its highest and best use as improved?
   a. physical curable
   b. functional curable
   c. functional incurable
   d. Depreciation is not possible.

68. Which of the following is NOT a step in defining the appraisal problem?
   a. identifying the interest to be appraised
   b. legal description
   c. collection of specific data
   d. identifying the client

69. Following the acceptance of an appraisal assignment of a water treatment plant, the appraiser finds that data collection is much more difficult than originally anticipated. After working on the assignment for more than three weeks, the appraiser decides that he or she is in over his or her head and informs the client that he or she will be unable to complete the appraisal by the following Friday, the agreed delivery date. When should the appraiser have reached this conclusion?

a. within 72 hours of acceptance
b. within 24 hours of acceptance
c. subsequent to acceptance
d. prior to acceptance

70. A property owner has two contiguous lots that measure 55' × 125'. Market evidence indicates that the ideal lot size is 100' × 130'. Conducting a market value appraisal, the appraiser decides to value this property as one lot. This is known as

a. assemblage.
b. excess land.
c. surplus land.
d. overage.

71. Scarcity, transferability, utility, and demand are all requirements for what type of value?

a. market value
b. insurable value
c. investment value
d. value in use

72. Three sales of comparable properties have been identified in a neighborhood. Comparable A sold one year ago for $566,000; Comparable B sold last week for $556,000; and Comparable C sold two years ago for $590,000. With no other significant differences, what adjustment should be made to Comparable C to bring it to the current market?

a. −6.11%
b. −5.76%
c. +5.76%
d. +6.11%

73. The location of the subject is 5% inferior to that of the comparable. Market conditions indicate an increase in sales prices of 0.5% per month for the past six months since the comparable sold. Market conditions adjustments are calculated linearly. What would be the net adjustment to the comparable?

a. −2.15%
b. −2%
c. +2%
d. +2.15%

74. An appraiser is analyzing sales comparable to the subject. One comparable has a lower rent than the subject and the other comparables. If this sale has a higher gross income multiplier than any of the other comparables, what condition may be indicated?

a. The buyers anticipated reducing rent.
b. The buyers anticipated increasing rent.
c. an oversupplied market
d. a buyer's market

75. Which of the following appraisal products requires a new appraisal of the subject?
   a. update
   b. recertification
   c. extension
   d. assignment

76. The work-service zone of a home does NOT include which of the following?
   a. the kitchen
   b. the pantry
   c. the bedroom
   d. the laundry room

77. The most efficient configuration for a parking garage allows for parking at
   a. 30°.
   b. 45°.
   c. 70°.
   d. 90°.

78. What type of insulation may have a dangerous chemical as a component?
   a. asbestos
   b. fiber
   c. foam
   d. blanket

79. The population in the local community is declining due to closing of the region's major industry. The declining size of the population is an example of what kind of value influence?
   a. social
   b. economic
   c. governmental
   d. environmental

80. What is the anticipated value of a home that currently sells for $810,000 in five years if the market is improving by 3% each year (rounded to the nearest $1,000)?
   a. $942,000
   b. $939,000
   c. $936,000
   d. $934,000

81. What is the most reliable way to determine the appropriate adjustment for changes in market conditions?
   a. Compare similar properties that have recently sold in different neighborhoods.
   b. Compare successive sale prices of similar properties that have recently sold at least twice.
   c. Consult the consumer price index for changes in the market during the time in question.
   d. Subtract the annual cost of the actual debt service from the annual cost of the market debt service and capitalize the difference.

82. The value of all of the tangible and intangible assets of an established and operating business with an indefinite life is
   a. investment value.
   b. business value.
   c. market value.
   d. going-concern value.

83. What appraisal report is prepared only for the appraiser's client?
   a. letter
   b. restricted use
   c. summary
   d. self-contained

84. A duplex recently sold for $435,000. The site is valued at $125,000. The remaining economic life of the improvement at the time of the sale was 25 years and the site value is anticipated to remain unchanged. If the net operating income for this property is $57,000, what is the discount rate?
a. 9.25%
b. 9.75%
c. 10.25%
d. 10.5%

85. A property has net operating income of $15,000 and operating expenses of $10,000. Based on a capitalization rate of 10%, what is the property value?
a. $50,000
b. $100,000
c. $125,000
d. $150,000

86. Personal property owned by a tenant and attached to leased property in such a way as to assist the tenant in the conduct of business is a
a. fixture.
b. trade fixture.
c. real estate.
d. chattel fixture.

87. If there are no recognizable potential purchasers for a property, appraisers will find it difficult to measure
a. market value.
b. replacement cost.
c. potential gross income.
d. depreciation.

88. The current use of the subject is a golf course. The location of the course places it in the path of multifamily development. An appraiser determines that if sold, the sale price would reflect the potential for apartment development. The current use is
a. a multiple use.
b. an interim use.
c. a consistent use.
d. an inconsistent use.

89. Which of the following adjustments to a comparable sale price would be made first when using percentage adjustments?
a. market conditions
b. physical condition
c. view
d. access

90. Land not needed to accommodate the site's highest and best use, which will not accommodate future expansion, is known as
a. excess land.
b. surplus land.
c. super-adequacy.
d. under-improvement.

91. When several similar properties are available in the market, the property with the lowest price will attract the greatest level of demand. What appraisal principle supports this premise?
a. competition
b. conformity
c. market
d. substitution

92. The subject property produces $42,000 in annual net operating income for the first year of the investment. Net operating income is anticipated to increase 3% for each subsequent year during the five-year projection period. Net operating income for the sixth year is projected to be 3% greater than the fifth year. The appropriate discount rate is 9%, and the value of the reversion is calculated by capitalizing the projected income of year six using a terminal capitalization rate of 12%. What is the indicated value of the subject (rounded to the nearest $1,000)?
   a. $271,000
   b. $379,000
   c. $436,000
   d. $498,000

93. The right to use property owned by another may be granted by
   a. encroachment.
   b. easement.
   c. trespass.
   d. appurtenant.

94. The process of enforcing the right of government to take privately held property for public use is known as
   a. eminent domain.
   b. condemnation.
   c. police power.
   d. zoning.

95. A property owner contracts for installation of an addition to an existing home. The addition costs $50,000 to construct. After the addition is built, the home is found to be worth only $10,000 more than it was worth prior to the addition. What appraisal principle best applies?
   a. conformity
   b. consistent use
   c. contribution
   d. competition

96. A use that was lawfully established and maintained, but no longer conforms to the use regulations of current zoning, is a(n)
   a. legal non-conforming use.
   b. illegal non-conforming use.
   c. legal conforming use.
   d. illegal conforming use.

97. What is the maximum number of years that an appraiser must maintain workfiles?
   a. seven years
   b. five years
   c. four years
   d. No maximum has been established.

98. A single-family residence was sold for $550,000. A down payment of $50,000 was made, and the seller financed the balance with a purchase money mortgage of $500,000 for a 15-year term with monthly payments at 5% interest. Payments are discounted on a monthly basis. The outstanding balance is discounted on an annual basis. If the market interest rate is 6% and the market typically suggests this loan is in existence for five years, what is the cash equivalent sale price (rounded to the nearest hundred dollars)?
a. $533,000
b. $527,500
c. $515,500
d. $502,600

99. The gradual recession of a body of water from the usual high-water mark is
a. accretion.
b. riparian.
c. reliction.
d. alluvion.

100. What is the required contribution from a developer to offer a buydown interest rate of 4% for the first year on financing in the amount of $80,000, when market rates are 8% on 30-year monthly amortizing loans?
a. $2,357
b. $2,135
c. $1,982
d. $1,934

101. The monetary worth of a property to buyers and sellers at a given time is the
a. price.
b. cost.
c. value.
d. all of the above

102. The subject is a quadraplex with one efficiency, two one-bedroom units, and one two-bedroom unit. All comparables are quadraplexes with four one-bedroom units. What is the least appropriate unit of comparison?
a. gross rent multiplier (GRM)
b. value per room
c. value per unit
d. value per square foot

103. Which of the following is true?
a. One link equals .66 of a foot.
b. One chain has 100 links.
c. One chain has 66 feet.
d. all of the above

104. All elements suggest good functional design EXCEPT
a. location of windows and doors.
b. location of electrical outlets.
c. condition of plumbing.
d. good interior layout.

105. Timberland that is being utilized as land available for a hunting lease would be considered a(n)
a. interim use.
b. multiple use.
c. consistent use.
d. speculative use.

106. The Federal Reserve Board has increased the reserve requirement for local banks. What impact does this action have on the availability of mortgage money?
a. increases
b. decreases
c. stabilizes
d. no change

107. The minimum report format required by USPAP for oral appraisal reports is
a. limited.
b. self-contained.
c. summary.
d. restricted use.

108. A state-certified appraiser has offered rebates to his or her clients for each appraisal assignment offered to him or her. This payment is made to encourage the client to send the assignments to him or her. The payment of this rebate
a. violates the requirements of USPAP.
b. must be disclosed in each appraisal report.
c. must be approved by the property owner.
d. violates state and federal law.

109. A poorly designed home with an effective age of 80 years located near an airport exhibits
a. physical depreciation and external obsolescence.
b. functional obsolescence and external obsolescence.
c. functional obsolescence and physical depreciation.
d. physical depreciation, functional obsolescence, and external obsolescence.

110. For a fee simple value indication of a property to exceed its leased fee value,
a. the contract rent must exceed market rent.
b. the deficit rent must exceed market rent.
c. the market rent must exceed contract rent.
d. the deficit rent must exceed contract rent.

111. A pool was recently installed as the subject improvement at a cost of $30,000. The subject was appraised prior to the pool installation for $220,000 and following the pool installation, the subject was appraised for $229,000. The pool construction represents
a. a highest and best use.
b. a super-adequacy.
c. external obsolescence.
d. economic obsolescence.

112. What legal appraisal reports are NOT recognized in federally related transactions?
a. self-contained
b. summary
c. restricted
d. oral

113. Walls, windows, and doors are part of the home's
a. super-structure.
b. infrastructure.
c. interstructure.
d. sub-structure.

114. Zoning changes reduced the permitted intensity of property use. The result will be
a. non-conforming under-improvements.
b. non-conforming over-improvements.
c. conforming under-improvements.
d. conforming over-improvements.

115. Which portion of a home is NOT measured as part of the gross living area?
a. a master closet
b. an attached garage
c. a master bath
d. interior walls

116. Contract rent of the subject may be analyzed and converted into the value of what type of estate?
a. fee simple
b. leased fee
c. leasehold
d. equity

117. The most reliable date for an appraiser to use as the basis for a market conditions adjustment is the
a. sales contract date.
b. loan origination date.
c. effective appraisal date.
d. title closing date.

118. A neighborhood has several streets that end with an enlarged turnaround area. The residential lots at the turnaround area are
a. corner lots.
b. interior lots.
c. flag lots.
d. cul-de-sac lots.

119. Corner lots in a subdivision are selling for $125,000. Interior lots are selling for $118,000. The difference in sale prices due to the quality of location is known as
a. developer's profit.
b. agglomeration.
c. corner influence.
d. plottage.

120. Given the same square footage for construction, what configuration is the most cost-effective to build?
a. square
b. rectangular
c. octagonal
d. hexagonal

121. Sections, townships, and ranges are found in the legal description of which of the following techniques?
a. metes and bounds
b. surveyor's method
c. lot and block
d. rectangular survey

122. A measurement taken from N90E results in a line drawn from a point from which direction?
a. northerly
b. northeasterly
c. easterly
d. southerly

123. A neighborhood's improvements are exhibiting deferred maintenance and changes in use from owner occupancy to tenant occupancy. This neighborhood is in what phase of the neighborhood life cycle?
a. growth
b. stability
c. decline
d. revitalization

124. An appraiser is valuing a residence in an area that has been recently zoned commercial. The appraiser finds three comparable properties, all with residential zoning. If the appraiser makes no adjustment on the sales for the subject's commercial zoning, the appraiser
   a. ignored the principle of balance.
   b. ignored the principle of highest and best use.
   c. ignored the principle of consistent use.
   d. should not be using the sales comparison approach.

125. What is the minimum report format allowed by the requirements of USPAP?
   a. limited
   b. summary
   c. letter
   d. restricted use

► Answers

1. **b.** It is a violation of USPAP to fabricate data to make it suitable as a comparable sale.

2. **b.** The motivation of buyers would determine if an income capitalization technique could be applied because the buyers determine how a property will be used. Buyers would have to be buying property as an investment in order for income capitalization to be applicable.

3. **c.** It is a violation of USPAP to reveal any details of an appraisal to anyone other than the client without the client's consent. The client is the party who engaged the appraiser.

4. **a.** In order for a property to be at its highest and best use, the property must have no depreciation or have incurable short- and long-lived components. If any part of the property has curable depreciation, the property is not at its highest and best use.

5. **c.** The four criteria for highest and best use are physically possible, legally permissible, financially feasible, and maximally productive.

6. **c.** In a rental market with seasonal changes in demand, rents can vary greatly month to month; therefore, annual rent should be used. Seasonal changes do not impact the applicability of income capitalization.

7. **a.** The mathematic solution is as follows: You must first convert the inches to tenths of a foot.

    $\frac{9"}{12"} = .75$, so $90'9" = 90.75'$

    $\frac{6"}{12"} = .50$, so $32'6" = 32.50'$

    $90.75' \times 32.50' = 2,949.375'$

    $2,949.375' \times \$140$ per square foot $= \$412,912$

8. **c.** An effective date established as a future date is a *prospective effective date*.

9. **c.** In order for effective age to be less than actual age, maintenance would have to be better than average. The subject would have to have experienced less-than-typical maintenance to have a effective age greater than actual age.

10. **a.** Surplus productivity is associated with land rent. Land is the last factor of production to receive its benefits, because land is not built, and as a result, supply of land is limited.

11. **b.** Standing water in the backyard is indicative of a malfunctioning septic system. Low water pressure (choice **a**) relates to the water entering a home. Healthy vegetation growth (choice **c**) is a sign of a functional septic system. A leaking water meter (choice **d**) does not relate to the septic system.

12. **a.** Water heater, floor covering, and air conditioning compressor are short-lived items that are replaced periodically throughout the life of the building. Load-bearing walls cannot be replaced without replacing the entire building.

13. **c.** The math solution is as follows:
    $\$550,000$ (sale price) $- \$50,000$ (down payment) $= \$500,000$ (loan amount)
    $\$500,000 \times .04 = \$20,000$
    $\$550,000 - \$20,000 = \$530,000$ (cash equivalent)

14. **d.** The math solution is as follows:
    $\frac{20}{100} = .20$
    $.20 \times \$500,000 = \$100,000$ (amount of depreciation)
    $\$500,000 - \$100,000 = \$400,000.$

15. b. In this example, the answer is incurable functional because the costs to add the components now exceed the potential value gained. Physical depreciation would not be a choice because it is a deficiency, not a problem related to wear and tear.

16. c. A sale between family members will likely influence sale price. Conditions of sale adjustment are required when buyers and sellers are not typically motivated.

17. b. Reconciliation is a process of weighted averaging that resolves differences between alternative value indications.

18. a. Price per square foot is a size characteristic. By converting sales prices to a price per square foot, all the sales become the same size for the purpose of analysis.

19. b. The income approach is based on the income potential of a property. The cost approach is based on the cost of construction. Regression is not an approach to value.

20. d. The math solution is as follows using a Hewlett Packard 12c.
Keystrokes: $75,000 present value (PV), 6 i, 5 n
Solve for future value (FV) = $100,366, which should be rounded down to $100,000.

21. a. Comparable A is different from the subject and therefore needs the adjustment. Because the property is inferior, it requires a positive adjustment. A simple rule of thumb: When it's bad, you add; when it's nice, you slice.

22. a. Comparables must be competitive with the subject, and properties are only truly competitive when they share the same market area.

23. b. A sales comparison will likely provide the most reliable indicator of market value for this subject. The cost approach (choice **a**) would not be a reliable indicator of value due to the age of the property. Regression (choice **c**) is not an approach to value. Because there are no rental properties in the subject's market, the income approach (choice **d**) would not be applicable, as no rent comparables are available.

24. c. Market value assumes the subject of the appraisal will sell to the most likely purchaser. Investment value (choice **b**) is what the property is worth to a specific investor. Value in use (choice **a**) does not assume a sale. Going-concern value (choice **d**) is what an ongoing enterprise is worth.

25. a. Allocation uses a land ratio multiplied by an improved property sale price to establish land value for a comparable sale. Sales comparison (choice **b**) requires land sales; building residual and mortgage equity (choices **c** and **d**) are not land valuation techniques.

26. b. Subtracting debt service from gross income reduces the net operating income, which implies that the property is worth less if it is financed. The property would be worth the same amount regardless of financing.

27. b. Land value may be measured by deducting the contributory improvement value from the total sale price of a property by extraction. Allocation (choice **a**) uses a land ratio multiplied by an improved property sale price. Land residual and ground rent capitalization (choices **c** and **d**) are income capitalization techniques.

28. d. Discount rates are composed of the cost of money and risk; therefore, an increase in risk increases the discount rate.

29. b. The potential gross income (choice **a**) is the total income generated from all income operations at 100% occupancy. Deducting vacancy and collection loss results in effective gross income.

30. a. When the capitalization rate is greater than the mortgage constant, then the equity rate would exceed the capitalization rate, which makes leverage positive. The goal of leverage is to make the yield to the equity position higher.

31. b. Extraction requires the appraiser to subtract the depreciated value of the improvement from the comparable sale price. If the improvement has insignificant value, the comparable is nearly a vacant land sale and inaccuracies in measuring cost depreciation in the improvements are minimized.

32. c. The efficiency ratio is the result of the portion of building rentable divided by total building area. The net income ratio (choice **b**) is an incorrect choice because it is a result of the net operating income divided by effective gross income. Gross income ratio and useable ratio (choices **a** and **d**) do not exist.

33. c. By testing for legally permitted uses first, the appraiser is able to verify that such items as zoning and building codes will allow the considered use. Anything not allowed would no longer be considered as a potential highest and best use.

34. b. Because comparable properties are traded in the same market, they are competitive with each other. Better properties should sell for higher prices.

35. d. Summary is the minimum report format required for oral appraisal reports. See USPAP Standard Rule 2–4.

36. c. An appraiser who values a property not likely to be sold often measures the utility of the property without considering a potential sale. Utility of a property is measured in value-in-use appraisals.

37. a. The combination of two or more properties under a single ownership to increase value is called *assemblage*. Plottage (choice **b**) is the increment of value earned when two or more properties are combined under a single ownership. Surplus land (choice **c**) exists when a parcel is larger than that required by the market. Excess land (choice **d**) requires division into smaller parcels to achieve highest and best use.

38. c. To answer this question, you must first convert 50 units every six months to an annual amount by multiplying by two.
$50 \times 2 = 100$ units sold per year
Divide the number of units sold per year into the number of available units (500) to find the annual absorption rate.
$\frac{100 \text{ sold}}{500 \text{ available}} = .20$, or 20%

39. d. Risk is one of the components of the discount rate; all of the choices influence the risk of the investment.

40. a. Appraiser's fees can be based only on the difficulty and time it takes to complete an assignment.

41. a. Because the property is not improved, the land should be valued as vacant, to be developed to its highest and best use. If the property were improved, land would be valued as vacant because the improvements cannot influence land value.

42. a. The principle of balance indicates that maximum values are achieved when the correct improvement is constructed on a site.

43. **c.** USPAP states that a three-year sale history must be researched for the subject of all appraisals.

44. **a.** It is a requirement of USPAP to review any sales contract, option, or listing of the subject property. Knowledge of the information in these contracts indicated how the market has and is treating the property.

45. **a.** The range is the difference between the highest and lowest values in a sample. Mean, median, and mode are all measurements of central tendency.

46. **b.** The principle of anticipation is the perception that value is created by the expectations of benefits to be derived in the future. The current value of a property is usually not based on its historical prices or costs. Historical data is analyzed only to project benefits for the future.

47. **d.** The buyers and sellers often react to the proposed construction of improvements well before plans are finalized.

48. **d.** The math solution is as follows.
$600,000 − $120,000 = $480,000 (value of improvement)
$200 × 5,000 = $1,000,000 (replacement cost)
$1,000,000 − $480,000 = $520,000 (total amount of depreciation)
$\frac{\$520,000}{\$1,000,000} = .52$ (52%)

49. **b.** The math solution is as follows using a Hewlett Packard 12c.
Keystrokes: 3 n, 4 i, $40,000 FV
Solve for payment (PMT) = $12,813, which is rounded to $12,800.

50. **a.** The income approach is used to convert income into value. Therefore, with no rental market, there would be no income to convert *t* value.

51. **a.** When a market is oversupplied, prices decrease and the buyers have more control.

52. **d.** Revitalization is a period of renewal, redevelopment, modernization, and increasing demand.

53. **b.** Governmental considerations relate to the laws, codes, and regulations in a market area.

54. **d.** Return of investment is required through the income stream whenever the property is anticipated to depreciate. Recapture is the provision in a capitalization rate for recovery of a loss in value from the income stream.

55. **c.** Market value requires buyers and sellers with typical motivation. Highly motivated buyers and sellers influence prices paid and, as a result, the market value.

56. **d.** Anyone who contributes to an appraisal must state the extent of the contribution in the certification, even if he or she is not signing the report.

57. **a.** Excess supply will cause a decrease in price, as sellers seek to maintain a competitive advantage because of the lack of buyers. Sellers will reduce the price to ensure that their properties will sell.

58. **a.** A 60% vacancy ratio indicates an oversupply of units, which favors buyers. Sellers reduce asking prices for their properties.

59. **a.** Improvement income subtracted from net operating income equals land income, which is the *land residual* technique.

60. **b.** To find the operating expense ratio, the formula and solution is as follows:
$\frac{\text{Operating Expenses}}{\text{Effective Gross Income}} = \text{Operating Expense Ratio}$
$\frac{\$3,150}{\$9,000} = .35$

61. **c.** The math solution is as follows, using the Hewlett Packard 12c:
Keystrokes: 5 n, 10.5 i, $40,000 PMT

Solve for present value (PV) = $149,714

$149,714 – $50,000 = $99,714

62. b. Both contract and scheduled rent represent the rent appearing in the lease.

63. a. Installation of dental chairs is considered a concession because it is tenant-specific. All tenants need carpet and painted walls.

64. c. Improvements cannot impact land value. If income from the over-improvement is attributed to the land, it would affect the land value. Land is valued as vacant.

65. b. Extraction is a method of estimating land value in which the depreciated cost of the improvements is estimated and deducted from the total sale price to arrive at an estimated value for the land.

66. c. The property must be valued as commercial land and commercial improvement based on the principle of consistent use. The principle of consistent use states that land cannot be valued based on one use while the improvements are valued based on another use.

67. c. A property that is highest and best use as improved cannot be made more valuable as of the effective appraisal date. Any depreciation existing in the improvement would have to be incurable when property is at its highest and best use.

68. c. The appraisal problem must be defined to determine what specific data is applicable.

69. d. It is a violation of the competency rule in USPAP to accept an assignment without properly identifying the problem and having the knowledge and experience to complete the assignment competently.

70. a. The property owner must assemble the two lots to achieve the highest and best use of the property.

71. a. Market value is the only type of value that requires all four factors of value. Insurable value does not require any of those components; it is a replacement cost estimate. Investment value is a value to a particular investor client. Value in use measures only the utility of a property.

72. b. The math solution is as follows:

$590,000 – $556,000 = $34,000

$\frac{\$34,000}{\$590,000} = .0576 \ (5.76\%)$

73. a. The market conditions adjustment must be made prior to the location adjustment. Assume a sale price of $1.

0.5% × 6 months = 3%

$1 + .03 = 1.03

1.03 × .05% = .0515

.0515 – .03 = .0215

The adjustment is negative because the adjusted sale price is less than the beginning sale price.

74. b. The gross income multiplier is a result of the sale price divided by the gross income. In order for the income to be lower, the sale price must be higher. The only plausible explanation is that the buyers anticipated increasing rent.

75. a. An update requires a new effective date. A recertification verifies a condition existing in the prior appraisal without changing the effective date. Assignment is no longer allowed under the requirement of USPAP.

76. c. The bedroom is included in the private-sleeping zone.

77. d. Parking at a right angle takes up less space.

78. c. Formaldehyde was used as a chemical component in foam insulation until 1983. Formaldehyde emits a gas that irritates the respiratory system.

79. a. Value influences that relate to the characteristics of the population are social value influences.

80. b. The math solution is as follows, using a Hewlett Packard 12c:
Keystrokes: 5 n, 3 i, $810,000 PV
Solve for future value (FV) = $939,012.

81. b. By comparing successive sale prices, differences in market conditions may be identified by examining differences in sale prices.

82. d. This is the definition of going-concern value.

83. b. The restricted-use report must contain a prominent use restriction that limits the use of the report to the client and warns that any other user is unauthorized.

84. c. The math solution is as follows:
$435,000 − $125,000 = $310,000
$\frac{1}{25} = .04$
$310,000 × .04 = $12,400
$57,000 − $12,400 = $44,600
$\frac{\$44,600}{\$435,000} = .1025$

85. d. The math solution is as follows
$\frac{\$15,000}{.10} = \$150,000$

86. b. Trade fixtures remain the property of the tenants because they are essential in conducting the business of the tenant.

87. a. Market value requires an appraiser to anticipate a sale of the subject. With no potential purchasers, there will be no sale and no measurable market value.

88. b. An interim use is a temporary use that does not fully explain the motivation of buyers in the marketplace. In this case, the purchase price would reflect the long-term highest and best use potential of the property to be developed into apartments.

89. a. Adjustments affecting the overall value of the comparable sale should be made prior to any adjustment for individual property features.

90. b. Because of physical limitations or building placement, the land cannot be sold as a separate parcel. This surplus land may or may not positively contribute to value.

91. d. As market participants make comparisons among similar properties, they substitute one property for another as they make their buying decisions.

92. c. The math solution is as follows, using a Hewlett Packard 12c:
Year 1: $42,000
Year 2: $42,000 × 1.03 (3% per year) = $43,260
Year 3: $43,260 × 1.03 = $44,557
Year 4: $44,557 × 1.03 = $45,894
Year 5: $45,894 × 1.03 = $47,271
Year 6: $47,271 × 1.03 = $48,689
Using the cash flow keys: 9 I, $42,000 g CFj, $43,260 g CFj, $44,557 g CFj, $45,894 g CFj, $47,271 g CFj,
f NPV = $172,584
$\frac{\$48,689}{12\%} = \$405,741$
5 n, 9 i, $405,741 FV,
Solve for PV = $263,703
$172,584 + $263,703 = $436,287

93. b. This is the definition of an easement.

94. b. This is the definition of condemnation. Condemnation is the process; eminent domain is the right.

95. c. Improvements are valued based on their contribution to total property value, regardless of construction cost. In this example, the addition is worth $10,000 based on the appraisal principle of contribution.

96. a. It is a legal use because it was lawfully established. It no longer conforms to current zoning, creating a non-conforming use.

97. d. Minimum time periods are established, but no maximum.

98. a. The math solution is as follows using a Hewlett Packard 12c:

Mortgage Payments: 15 g n, 5 g i, $500,000 PV

Solve for PMT = $3,953

Market Value of Payments: 5 g n, 6 g i, $3,953 PMT

Solve for PV = $204,471

Loan Balance: 10 g n, 5 g i, $3,953 PMT

Solve for PV = $372,694

Market Value of Loan Balance: 5 n, 6 i, $372,694 FV

Solve for PV = $278,498

Cash Equivalent Sale Price: $204,471 + $278,498 + $50,000 = $532,969

99. c. The gradual recession of a body of water from the usual high-water mark is the definition of reliction.

100. a. The math solution is as follows, using a Hewlett Packard 12c:

Find the debt service for the advertised rate and the market rate.

Keystrokes: 30 g n, 8 g i, $80,000 PV

Solve for PMT = $587.01

30 g n, 4 g i, $80,000 PV

Solve for PMT = $381.93

$587.01 − $381.93 = $205.08 (savings per month)

Amount of the buydown: 1 g n, 8 g i, $205.08 PMT

Solve for PV = $2,357

101. c. Cost is the expenditure of resources to create a product. Price is the amount paid.

102. c. The value per unit would be the least appropriate due to the varying rooms per unit.

103. d. All of the above are true concerning a chain measurement.

104. c. The condition of the plumbing is not a functional issue, but a physical issue.

105. a. A combination of compatible land uses to achieve highest and best use is a multiple use.

106. b. The supply of mortgage funds reduces if more money is required to be held by the bank.

107. a. The limited format is the minimum report format required by USPAP for oral appraisal reports. See USPAP Standard Rule 2–4.

108. b. USPAP states that anything of value paid to clients for the purpose of procurement of an appraisal must be disclosed in the appraisal report.

109. d. The home exhibits physical depreciation because of the age, functional obsolescence because it is poorly designed, and external obsolescence because of the location near an airport.

110. c. Market rent converts to fee simple value and contract rent converts to leased fee value. If market rent is higher than contract rent, the fee simple value would be higher than the leased fee value.

111. b. A super-adequacy is a type of functional obsolescence caused by something in the subject property (pool) that does not contribute to a value amount equal to its cost.

112. d. Oral reports are not recognized in federally related transactions because oral representations are difficult to prove.

113. a. Super-structure is the improvements above ground. Sub-structure (choice **d**) is the improvements underground; infrastructure (choice **b**) is the utilities; interstructure (choice **c**) is a fabricated answer choice.

114. b. The result is non-conforming because it does not meet the current zoning regulations, and is considered an over-improvement because the zoning changes reduced the permitted intensity. Therefore, the improvement is larger than what the current zoning would allow to be built.

115. b. An attached garage is not part of gross living area because it is not a finished residential space.

116. b. Contract rent converts into a leased fee value, market rent converts into fee simple estate, and deficit rent converts into leasehold estate. Equity is not a type of estate.

117. a. Using the date of closing, an appraiser ignores all the changes in the market that have taken place between the contract date and closing date.

118. d. The residential lots at the turnaround area are known as cul-de-sac lots. Corner lots (choice **a**), interior lots (choice **b**), and flag lots (choice **c**) do not have a turnaround area.

119. c. Corner lots may be larger, offer additional design flexibility for improvements, and sell for a higher or lower price.

120. a. Square construction results in the least amount of wall area to be built.

121. d. Metes and bounds and surveyor's method are the same and are measurements and boundaries. Lot and block is used only in subdivisions. The rectangular survey, also known as *government survey*, is the only method that uses sections, townships, and ranges.

122. c. N90E is true east.

123. c. The decline phase is a period of diminishing demand. When there is a transition from owner occupancy to tenant occupancy, there is a decline in maintenance resulting in depreciation, which is a character of the decline phase.

124. c. The principle of consistent use states that land improvements must be valued based on the same highest and best use. Therefore, all of the comparables used must be adjusted for zoning in order to share the same highest and best use as the subject.

125. b. Limited and letter are not a type of format. Summary report is more detailed than restricted and, therefore, would not be the minimum report format.

▶ Scoring

Evaluate how you did on this practice exam by first finding the number of questions you answered correctly. Only the number of correct answers is important—questions that you skipped or got wrong don't count against your score. On your official exam, you will most likely only receive a score of pass or fail. However, you should check with your state to find out what the official scoring criteria is for the particular exam you will be taking. Generally, to achieve a passing score for the exam, you must answer at least 75% of the questions correctly. On this practice exam, a passing score would be 113 correct.

Use your scores in conjunction with the Learning-Express Test Preparation System in Chapter 2 of this book to help you devise a study plan using the real estate appraisal refresher course in Chapter 5, the real estate math review in Chapter 6, and the real estate glossary in Chapter 7. You should plan to spend more time on the sections that correspond to the questions you found hardest and less time on the lessons that correspond to areas in which you did well.

For now, what is much more important than your overall score is how you performed on each of the areas tested by the exam. You need to diagnose your strengths and weaknesses so that you can concentrate your efforts as you prepare. The different question types are mixed in the practice exam, so in order to diagnose where your strengths and weaknesses lie, you will need to compare your answer sheet with the following table, which shows which of the categories each questions falls into.

Once you have spent some time reviewing, take the second certified general appraisal practice exam in Chapter 8 to see how much you have improved.

Certified General Appraisal Practice Exam 1 for Review

Topic	Question Numbers
Influences on Real Estate Value	53, 79, 106
Legal Considerations in Appraisal	93, 94, 114, 121, 122
Types of Value	24, 36, 55, 71, 82, 87, 101
Economic Principles	10, 34, 42, 46, 66, 91, 95, 124
Real Estate Markets and Analysis	22, 30, 38, 47, 51, 57, 58, 74, 119, 120, 123
Valuation Process	17, 23, 32, 39, 50, 52, 62, 63, 68
Property Description	11, 12, 76, 77, 78, 99, 103, 104, 113, 115, 118
Highest and Best Use Analysis	4, 5, 33, 37, 64, 67, 70, 88, 96, 105
Appraisal Math and Statistics	20, 45, 49, 60, 61, 80, 84, 100
Sales Comparison Approach	13, 16, 18, 19, 21, 72, 73, 81, 86, 89, 98, 102, 117
Site Value	25, 27, 31, 41, 59, 65, 90
Cost Approach	7, 9, 14, 15, 48, 109, 111
Income Approach	2, 6, 26, 28, 29, 54, 85, 92
Valuation of Partial Interests	110, 116
Appraisal Standards and Ethics	1, 3, 8, 35, 40, 43, 44, 56, 69, 75, 83, 97, 107, 108, 112, 125

5 ▶ Real Estate Appraisal Refresher Course

CHAPTER SUMMARY

If you want to review basic real estate appraisal concepts for your exam, this is the chapter you need. Using this chapter, you can review just what you need to know for the test.

HOW YOU USE this chapter is up to you. You may want to proceed through the entire course in order, or perhaps, after taking the first practice exam, you know that you need to brush up on just one or two areas. In that case, you can concentrate only on those areas.

Following are the major sections of the real estate appraisal refresher course and the page on which you can begin your review of each one. Please note that some sections reviewed here apply to concepts tested only on specific exams for different levels of licensure and certification. An (L) denotes a concept that will be tested only on state-licensed real estate appraiser exams, an (R) denotes a concept that is found on state-certified residential appraiser exams, and a (G) signals a concept tested on certified general appraiser exams.

▶ Influences on Real Estate Value

The only constant about property values is that they change. They may increase or decrease based on complex stock market fluctuations, current events, or even the weather. Values may also depend on point of view: The value of just one piece of real estate may vastly differ depending on an individual's interest in it. What does the homeowner estimate his or her property is worth? What does the seller believe the buyer should pay for it? What do the sales agents of the two parties advise? Each brings to the table a measure of wishful thinking. Their points of view of a property's value probably also differ considerably from those of the lender, such as a bank; the insurance provider; and anyone else, such as accountants, involved in sale negotiations.

Appraisers, however, need to be objective, shouldn't have agendas, are usually not personally involved, and are guided mainly by property characteristics. These characteristics are fairly inflexible and unemotional. To help accurately determine the value of a property, appraisers must be able to ask and answer the following questions about the major influences on real estate value:

- How do **physical and environmental** influences such as the weather (e.g., hurricanes and flooding); the topography (e.g., mudslides); and high pollution, fires, and drought affect value?
- How do **economic** influences affect value? In other words, how prosperous is the region in which the property is located? The answer to this question is determined by such factors as the percentage of employment and how many local businesses have recently opened or closed.
- How do **governmental and legal** influences affect value? The services provided by the municipality in which a property is located are important to know. Building codes and taxation levels severely affect the value of a property—adversely or positively. So do the uses to which taxes are put, such as education, police and fire departments, sanitation, and recreation. Appraisers must also be aware of planning and zoning regulations, two issues that are often major obstacles in property negotiation.
- How do **social** influences affect value? In other words, who lives in the area? The number of people living in an area and the uses of nearby land and buildings also affect the value of a property.

▶ Legal Considerations in Appraisal

Appraisers must be familiar with a wide range of laws, rules, and regulations that affect property in the area they are appraising.

Real Estate versus Real Property

Real estate is the land and everything that is permanently attached to it. Real property is the legal rights attached to real estate that are inherited with it. This means a buyer may automatically receive an easement or access to a water line or to a road across a neighboring property. Or it might be a parking space outside the property. Local laws or codes sometimes declare particular objects on real estate to be real property.

Real Property versus Personal Property

In legal language, property is "valuable rights held to the exclusion of others." Property may be **real property** or **personal property**. Personal property is any movable object, such as a TV or jewelry. Almost everything else is considered real property, which is called **real estate** in some parts of the United States, and refers only to the rights that go with the ownership of land. Today, in many states, real property refers to owning the land itself. Real property usually includes the following:

- **Land.** In its most simple definition, land includes the earth below a property and the air above it. Gases and liquids found below the land fall into a separate, complex legal area. The airspace of a property has become so valuable in many places that it, too, has its own set of rules.

- **Permanently affixed objects.** These are objects that would be physically difficult to remove from the land, such as houses, trees, barns, gazebos, and bridges. Doors and windows, which are permanently attached to buildings, are also part of real estate. Some objects, though, are affixed but might not be permanent, such as small statues or birdbaths. Although they are personal property, they are considered **fixtures** and may fall into a legal gray area. To resolve disputes over whether objects are personal property or fixtures, courts have devised these five tests.

  Test 1: How did the person who owned the object intend to use it?

  Example: After selling her house, did the seller intend to remove and take along the washer-dryer that she had originally installed?

  Test 2: What is the degree of annexation (how permanently is the object attached)?

  Example: Built-in bookcases are fixtures. A freestanding case is personal property.

  Test 3: How important is the object to the property?

  Example: A handmade mirror that was made to fit over a fireplace is unique to it. A conventional mirror in an office would not be.

  Test 4: Was there ever an agreement concerning the object?

  Example: Drapes and carpeting may have been part of the original lease.

  Test 5: What is the relationship between the people involved in the dispute?

  Example: The courts may base their decision on who is involved in the dispute: A tenant may have a stronger case than an investor, for instance.

- **Machinery** and **equipment** are known as **trade fixtures** and are considered personal property that belong to the owner of a rented space.

Limitations on Real Property Ownership

Just about every kind of real estate has restrictions placed on it that affect its use and ownership. Restrictions remain part of the property even after it has been sold unless the buyer or seller addresses and legally removes them.

Private Restrictions

For private property, restrictions may include the following.

- **Deed restrictions** are set down in deed clauses to specify how land or property may be used. At one time, deed restrictions were often used to restrict land or property use by race, religion, or creed, a practice that is now illegal. Today, a deed restriction might say that the property could never be used for hunting, for example, or that a house must be surrounded by a specified amount of land.
- **Leases** are significant agreements between property owners and property users that describe the conditions under which the properties can be leased, for how long, and at what cost (the rent).
- **Mortgages** are recorded documents that create a lien on property as security for payment of a debt. If the mortgage payment is not made in a timely manner based on an agreed-upon schedule, the mortgage holder can sell the property. This means that the property has been foreclosed.

- **Easements** allow the owner of one property to use property belonging to another for a specific purpose. Easements are frequently invoked so that a hard-to-reach property can be more easily accessed, that a utility company can install lines across two properties, or that public water drainage is undisturbed by the owner of the property it crosses.
- **Liens** are claims against property owners. Such claims may be a way of collecting unpaid taxes or bills.
- **Encroachments** may be property, part of a property, or an obstruction that overlaps or intrudes a neighboring property. In some pre–World War II residential buildings, for example, electrical lines for one apartment may run through the apartment next door, making individual electricity use difficult to assign.

Public Restrictions

Most property is restricted by governmental rules, regulations, and ordinances that, unlike private restrictions, are meant to benefit all citizens of a municipality. **Police power** is the government's right to regulate property to protect public safety, health, morals, and general **welfare**. This includes imposing laws, statutes, and ordinances, including:

- **Zoning** ordinances, which designate an area's purpose: residential, commercial, or industrial. Municipalities use zoning regulations to monitor details from stores' hours of operation, noise levels, height and size of buildings, fixtures such as balconies and decks, and the color of building materials. As Americans have become increasingly aware of the heritage of their buildings, regulations that zone for landmarking have become more common.
- **Building** and **fire codes**, which set down structural requirements that construction must meet before it can pass inspection. Areas that must be up to code include electrical wiring, foundations, plumbing, and roofing.
- **Environmental regulations**. Many areas require environmental impact reports before construction is allowed to begin. These reports study how a new building will impact traffic, pedestrian patterns, air and water pollution, and utility needs. Environmental regulations also protect endangered species, coastal areas, and historic preservation.

Municipalities also have the right to impose **taxation**. Among these taxes are local taxes based on the property's value, known as **property taxes**, which must be paid in addition to federal and state income taxes. Taxes, as we know, are inescapable and greatly affect the real estate market.

Municipalities may assess property owners to help pay for public improvements, even if the owners pay taxes for them as well. These **special assessments** may occur one time or be spread over a specified period. They may help pay for widening a sidewalk, for example, or for improving security in an area.

A state or local government can acquire real estate under the following two circumstances.

- **Eminent domain.** Frequently controversial and fraught with emotion, eminent domain allows a government or a public utility to acquire private property for "necessary" public use. The owner must be compensated with **fair market value**, which is often determined by the courts. In some cases, property owners—often people who have lived on the property for many years—do not want to sell. The government can then seize the property by condemning it, but must still pay. The owner is forced to leave, whether or not compensation has been agreed on.

- **Escheat.** If a property owner dies without leaving a will and has no legal heirs, the property reverts to the government. In other words, the assets of a person who dies without a will **escheat** to the state.

Legal Rights and Interests

In a **fee simple estate**, an owner has absolute ownership of a property with no established conditions on how it must be transferred. In a **life estate**, an individual has the use of a property during his or her lifetime. On his or her death, it goes to a person called the **remainderman**, who may be a child or surviving spouse.

The real estate on which a tenant holds the lease is known as a **leasehold interest**. In some cases, such as a long lease with the tenant paying less than market rates, the lease may be extremely valuable to the tenant. The owner's interest in a property that is under lease is known as a **leased fee interest**.

An **easement** is the right one party has on the property of another. An **encroachment** is an obstruction from one property that overlaps a second property owned by a different party.

Forms of Property Ownership

Gone are the days when appraisers dealt with only a few conventional forms of property. The field has become far more complex, with a variety of ownership concepts and distinctive residences.

In an **individual ownership**, the owner has a simple title interest that includes both the building and the land under it.

All but two forms of **tenancy** have to do with **freeholds**. The most common forms of tenancy are as follows:

- **Tenancy in severalty** is ownership by one person.
- **Tenancy in common** is ownership by two or more people, each of whom owns an **undivided interest**. Each interest does not have to be an equal amount. By owning a fraction of the real estate, each person is responsible for a share of the expenses and is entitled to a share of the profits. The shareholders may leave their shares to an heir or give them away.
- In a **joint tenancy**, the conditions are similar to a tenancy in common, but the shares owned by shareholders who die are divided proportionately among the survivors of the group.
- **Tenancy by the entirety** is joint ownership allowed only to married couples.
- California, Texas, Arizona, Idaho, Louisiana, Nevada, New Mexico, Washington, and Wisconsin have **community property** laws. Half of all property that a couple acquires during their marriage is considered to be owned equally by both partners.

Two kinds of tenancies refer to **non-freehold estates**.

1. **Tenancy at will** means that a tenant has a lease, but it specifies no time period, so the tenant or the landlord can end the lease at will. In some cases, courts have ruled that tenants and landlords must give ample warning if the lease is to be terminated.
2. **Tenancy at sufferance** means that a tenant refuses to leave a property even when a lease has ended.

There are also a number of **special ownership forms**. The most popular forms of special ownership include **condominiums**, **cooperatives**, and **time-sharing**.

Condominiums have become increasingly common since the 1960s; in many cases, the property was purpose built. Basically, in a "condo," each member of the condominium community has exclusive ownership of the airspace (height and width) occupied by his or her unit. However, the land on which the building stands—common areas, such as lobbies and outside areas, such as parking lots—are jointly owned.

Appraisals of condominiums most often rely on the **sales comparison approach**. Appraisers need to take a condominium's unique aspects into account. They must ask themselves these questions as they do comparables.

- How well have condominiums sold in this area? The concept is more popular in some areas than in others, which may affect the value.
- As we all know, location rules in real estate. In this case, where is the unit located? How close is it to public transportation or major roads? Does it have a view? Is it private? How big are the rooms and how generously spaced are foyers or hallways? What is the condition of the unit? What amenities and common areas (such as swimming pools and gardens) does the building offer?
- How well is the homeowners association doing? Is it adequately financed? How do the assessments compare with those of similar condominiums?
- What part, if any, does the developer still play in the management/ownership of the building?

Cooperatives have played a unique role in the real estate field. Some have existed since the 1950s and even before, which means that much of the building stock is prewar (pre–World War II). In a **stock cooperative**, each owner in a multiunit building holds a percentage ownership in the cooperative association. The association, usually overseen by a board of directors, owns the property and allows individual shareholders to reside in the building permanently and to use the common areas.

When doing an appraisal of a cooperative, an appraiser deals with the same important questions as he or she did when appraising a condominium. But, because cooperatives are sometimes financed differently, additional questions come into play. For example, are mortgages allowed? What loan arrangements does the cooperative have? What does the sale price of the unit reflect?

In **time-sharing**, a buyer acquires rights to use or occupy a property, often a vacation home in a subdivision or resort, for a designated period of time, usually several weeks at the same time each year. In making an appraisal of this unique approach to partial rights, an appraiser has to keep in mind the location of the property and how it is priced. A property near a ski slope, for example, gains in value the more accessible it is to the slope, and probably sells at a premium during winter holidays. Discounts, however, may be offered in the warmer months.

Legal Descriptions

Accurately and exactly describing land is essential if a land transaction is to be legal and binding. The description does not have to include jargon or big words; it must be understandable and easy to follow.

Metes and bounds descriptions show the surveyor where the corners of a tract are located. With this information, the sides of the tract are also apparent. This description must show:

- an identified point of beginning
- distance and direction for each side

The **government rectangular survey** system is a land survey system used in Florida, Alabama, Mississippi, and all states north of the Ohio River or west of the Mississippi River, except Texas. It starts with the intersection of lines of longitude (meridians) and lines of latitude (baselines), and then divides land around these intersections into **"townships"** approximately six miles squared. Each township contains 36 sections of 640 acres each.

Lot and block are two common legal terms that describe how land is subdivided and shown on recorded maps.

Transfer of Title

There are two **basic types of deeds**—**warranty** (also known as **general warranty**)and **quitclaim**. Either is sufficient to show that a grantor is interested in a property.

The **warranty** promises that the grantor:

- has title to the property and the power to convey it
- has the title, which will stand up against claims
- except as specified, offers the property free of encumbrances
- will do whatever is needed to make sure the title is free and clear
- will guarantee the rights of the grantee

The **quitclaim**, on the other hand, makes no promises; it offers no warranties and no guarantees. A quitclaim deed is most often used to clear up a problem with the deed.

Recordation (recording) takes place when a document, such as a mortgage, trust deed, lease, or lien, is filed with the appropriate public agency by the parties involved in the transaction.

► Types of Value

Most types of value fall into two legal categories: **value in use** and **value in exchange**. The first is subjective, the second objective.

Value in use refers to the value an object has to a particular user. An apartment with a home office, for example, may hold more value to a person who works mainly at home than to someone who works mainly in an office building. A house within walking distance of shops and a railroad station may be worth more to a person who doesn't like to drive than to someone who would rather live in a more isolated area.

Value in exchange is the value an object holds for people in general when the object, or in this case, property, is bought and sold in the open market.

Market value is the most probable price that a property should bring in a competitive and open market under all conditions requisite to a fair sale, the buyer and seller each acting prudently, knowledgeably, and assuming the price is not affected by undue stimulus.

In determining or estimating value, an appraiser has to consider many variants, such as:

- **Price**, which is the amount a would-be buyer is willing to pay for a property.
- **Cost**, which is how much it will cost an owner to buy or improve.
- **Investment value**, which is how much a particular investor will pay for the right to collect the earnings generated by the property.
- **Assessed value**, which is the amount the County Appraisal District (CAD) assesses a property's value and on which it bases its property taxes.
- **Insurable value**, which is the maximum amount that an insurer will pay for an insured loss.
- **Going-concern value**, which is the worth of a business based on its operations. The property of the business may be worth more than the operations are worth.

▶ Economic Principles

The factors involved in production are land, labor, capital, and entrepreneurship. In some cases, economists believe that there are only three factors of production because profit is considered what the owner earns in return for taking risks and contributing management and entrepreneurship. Following are the economic principles that are part of real estate valuation. Knowing them will help a real estate appraiser make informed decisions.

- **Anticipation** is the basis of the income approach to appraisal. The value of a property today is the present value of the total of anticipated benefits.
- **Balance** is the principle that refers to the optimal mix of factors of production that result in the greatest land value when combined with land.
- **Change** in real estate, as in all parts of life, is constant. Changing patterns in the political, social, physical, and economic environment affect the way real estate is used and how it is valued. Appraisers must understand that neighborhoods, cities, and states are constantly in transition. They may experience change in four stages: development, stability, decline, and rebirth. Although these stages are fairly predictable, the rate and degree of change never are; what happened in the past is not necessarily an indication of what will happen in the future.
- **Competition** is an important principle to consider when estimating the value of a property that is selling for more than the cost of its replacement. Profits result from competition and competition results from profits. Competition can cause profits to fall. When demand for real estate is high, profits exceed the income needed to pay for the factor of production. This can lead to an oversupply of property and a resulting collapse of prices.
- **Conformity** is important in some markets and not in others. In a suburban neighborhood, for example, properties may achieve their highest value when they are similar in size, style, quality, and type to the buildings in their immediate vicinity. A starkly modern home, for instance, may lose its value amid street after street of center-hall colonials. On the other hand, innovative architectural details and luxury amenities, such as high-end kitchen appliances in apartment buildings with unique designer-created public spaces, may be essential in adding to the value of properties in urban areas.

- **Contribution** is the amount a property's value or the net income it produces is affected by the addition or lack of improvements. A seller might, for example, remodel the kitchen in her home. This may add considerable value to the property for buyers who want a home in move-in condition. But, it may add no value for buyers who want to install their own kitchen. For a builder, the principle of contribution may hinge on what it would cost to add an amenity, such as a rooftop swimming pool to a residential building, and what would enhance the overall value.

- **Increasing and decreasing returns** refers to a general rule about the value of adding improvements to real estate. A builder can add details to a property that will proportionately increase his or her profits until a theoretical point is reached at which no amount of improvements will increase profits. If the remodeling of a kitchen and bath can increase the sale price of an existing property, the cost of construction is justified. But if adding a bathroom will cost more than the buyer is willing to pay, there is no economic justification.

- **Opportunity cost** refers to the money lost by choosing one alternative over another. A person may choose to use a business bonus to buy a time-share rather than to deposit the bonus money in an interest-bearing bank account. The opportunity cost is the bank interest that the person will not receive.

- **Substitution** refers to the cost of replacing a property with one that is exactly the same. A buyer would not purchase a house for more money than is being asked for an identical house next door.

- **Supply and demand** in real estate, as in life in general, work together to affect prices. The lower the supply and higher the demand, the more value properties have. Prices will go up if the number of properties goes down, while the number of interested buyers remains the same.

- **Surplus productivity** remains after the costs of labor, capital, and entrepreneurship are deducted.

▶ Real Estate Markets and Analysis

Characteristics of Real Estate Markets

An appraiser needs to know price levels, price movements, and levels of activity in order to study what is happening to the market surrounding the property that is being considered.

Availability of Information

Finding reliable and consistent data is essential for an appraiser hoping to make a successful appraisal. Finding a source of information about rental and operating expenses isn't difficult; several national and local organizations specialize in disseminating such information. But, because the real estate market is fragmented, it's important to focus on data that is appropriate to the area being studied.

For office buildings: The Building Owners and Managers Association International (BOMA) uses information from its members across the country on office building rental rates and operating expenses.

Building Owners and Managers Association International

1201 New York Avenue NW, Suite 300

Washington, D.C. 20005

202-408-2662

www.boma.org

For shopping centers: Every two years, the Urban Land Institute (ULI) releases the latest edition of *Dollars and Cents of Shopping Centers.* Another group, the National Retail Merchants Association, issues the *Department Store Lease Study.*

Urban Land Institute

1025 Thomas Jefferson Street NW, Suite 500 West

Washington, D.C. 20007

202-624-7000

www.uli.org

For rental apartments, condominiums, and cooperatives: The Institute of Real Estate Management (IREM) periodically issues income/expense analyses of various types of buildings.

Institute of Real Estate Management

430 North Michigan Avenue

Chicago, IL 60611

800-837-6706

www.irem.org

For motels and hotels: Smith Travel Research provides information about national and local trends.

Smith Travel Research

735 East Main Street

Hendersonville, TN 37075

615-824-8664

www.smithtravelresearch.com

Local groups may also supply information.

- In most metropolitan areas, brokers who belong to local Boards of REALTORS® that sponsor multiple-listing services (MLS) provide information about the terms of sale once a transaction is completed. This information may be available to members only or through other real estate organizations.
- Local tax assessing offices keep files on every property in their area, including property characteristics, estimates of value, and the data on which they were based. The offices also keep updates of properties that are sold or for which building permits have been issued.
- Local credit bureaus and tax map companies occasionally have information about parcels of land.
- University research centers are often supported by state broker and salesperson license fees and may collect data on transactions across the state. Such information is useful in establishing trends for different types of property in various cities and areas.
- Private sources may include real estate investors, who are sometimes willing to share information about their properties, and property owners, who may have detailed information about specific holdings. Because personal records are often untidily kept and vary widely in the quality of their data, they may be a source of last resort.

Appraisers must carefully watch the direction demand for a property is taking. Changes in **supply versus demand** directly affect the market. To get the highest rents or top prices for property means that demand must be high. Then the prospects for resale will be good. Demand for real estate is affected by:

- **Economic growth.** New jobs and more residents with rising incomes are good signs for an area and indicate that rents, property prices, and retail sales will go up as well.
- High-quality property that has the basic features of other property in an area, as well as valued amenities, raises demand.
- **Location.** Even a property that is not desirable will gain in value if it is in the right location.
- **Competitive pricing** can make demand go up and help move properties that are not in great condition. Property should be priced appropriately so it will appeal to the population for which it is intended.
- **The cost of alternatives** often determines demand. When house prices are high, apartments become more desirable. But, when interest rates are low, demand for houses rises.

The term *immobility of real estate* refers to the idea that unlike other goods and services that are bought and sold in a marketplace, real estate is immoveable. Real estate for sale can be improved on and advertised, but because property from an area that has a high supply cannot be brought to an area that has a high demand, **location** is always the most important factor in determining value.

Real estate is not one single market, even within a small area, but **segmented markets** that operate independently of one another. The need for banks in a residential part of New York City, for example, may differ from that of a business area a few streets away.

Regulations that restrict property use, such as zoning, building permits, and safety codes, tend to make buyers and sellers more cautious.

Absorption Analysis

A **feasibility analysis** is a study of the cost-benefit relationship of a proposed real estate development. An essential component of many feasibility analyses is an **absorption analysis**. To complete this analysis, an appraiser must take all of the following into account.

- **Demographic data** includes information about the age, gender, and income of an area's residents, which are important elements of real estate market research.
- **Competition**, which becomes a factor when a property's value is higher than its replacement value. Net values fall when competition enters the market.
- **Absorption**, which is the time it may take to sell, lease, trade, or place in use a property at market price or rent.
- **Forecasts** are projections of future space needs and availability.
- **Existing space inventory**, which refers to vacant square feet of retail or office space.
- **Current and projected space surplus**, which refers to the amount of vacant office and retail space that is currently available.
- **New space**, which projects the availability of office and retail space in new construction.

Role of Money and Capital Markets

Real estate competes with other potential investments. The components of the real estate investment are the cash flow and appreciation. For a commercial property, the investor may compare the return on his or her investment with other instruments in the market. Treasury bills (T-bills) are typically referred to as a "safe investment" because they are guaranteed by the U.S. government. The investor's projected return on the real estate investment should surely be higher than T-bills, due to the risks associated with real estate. Other potential investments include certificates of deposit (CDs), U.S. bonds, municipal tax exempt bonds, corporate bonds, real estate investment trusts (REITs), and common stocks.

The funding of a real estate investment depends on the type of real estate involved. There are a number of **sources of capital** available for single-family housing, including mortgages from banks, mortgage companies, the Federal Housing Administration (FHA) and Veterans Administration (VA), and private investors. Some home purchases are made with seller financing provided. Many of the single-family home loans financed by banks and mortgage companies are resold to the Federal National Mortgage Association (Fannie Mae) or Federal Home Loan Mortgage Corporation (Freddie Mac). Commercial properties are typically characterized as either investment grade or non-investment grade. These are also referred to as **institutional grade** or **non-institutional grade**. Investment grade or institutional grade properties are typically the cream-of-the-crop, and as the title suggests, they are typically purchased by life insurance companies and pension funds. Non-investment grade properties may be financed by banks, funding companies, or private investors.

Real Estate Financing

There are number of mortgage terms and concepts essential to every appraiser's vocabulary.

- The **mortgagor** is the person who pledges personal property as security for a loan.
- The **mortgagee** is the person who holds a lien on property pledged as security for a debt.
- **Principal** is the amount of money raised by a mortgage.
- **Interest** is the amount of money paid for the use of money raised by a mortgage.

It is important for an appraiser to be familiar with the many different types of mortgage payment plans. **Fixed rate, level payment** means that the mortgage loan has an interest and payment rate that remains consistent through the term of the loan. An **adjustable-rate** mortgage loan has an interest rate that varies during the term of the loan. **Buydown** refers to the payment of discount points at the start of a loan in order to get a lower interest rate. This may apply to the first few years of the loan or the full term.

Other mortgage payment plans include **balloon mortgages** that offer relatively low rates for several years, after which the amount outstanding must be paid or the mortgage refinanced. An **assumable mortgage** is transferred from the seller to the buyer. Once the seller assumes the mortgage, the buyer is no longer responsible for it.

Mortgages fall into two very broad categories: conventional and insured. A **conventional mortgage** is a private-sector loan that is not insured by the FHA. Conventional loans may require larger down payments than insured loans. An **insured loan** is usually insured by the FHA or guaranteed by VA.

▶ Valuation Process

Definition of the Problem

Real estate experts define an appraisal as "the act or process of estimating value." The appraiser is often the only objective person involved in a sale of real estate and is an invaluable member of the team. The appraiser's assignment must be clearly stated so that there is no doubt about the kind of appraisal needed.

A valuation includes eight important steps that define the scope of an appraisal. A valuation identifies:

1. **The client and other intended users.** An appraiser's clients may be buyers and sellers, banks, institutions, and public agencies. Each has a unique purpose and a variety of requirements.

2. **The intended use** of the appraiser's opinions and conclusions. Appraisals may be done for partial interests in real estate, such as leased fee, leasehold, or life estates. More often, appraisers work on undivided interests in commonly held property, such as condominiums and cooperatives.

3. **The purpose of the appraisal**, including the type and definition of the value to be developed. The purpose of an appraisal is to estimate market value—the most probable value a property will bring. Appraisals are also used to assess other kinds of value, including insurable value, going-concern value, assessed value, or a property's rental value. Whatever the purpose and use of the appraisal, the type of value must be precisely and formally defined.

4. **The effective date** of the appraiser's opinions and conclusions. Real estate values are in constant flux, so it is important for the appraiser and client to agree on the effective date of the appraiser's opinions and conclusions. The appraiser's conclusion is then valid only for a particular moment in time. Appraisals are sometimes needed for figuring out divorce settlements, taxes, or other legal reasons, and must therefore estimate value for a past or future date. The appraisal is then retrospective (a past date) or prospective (a future date). Whichever it is, the appraisal must clearly state the date so no misunderstandings result.

5. **The property and property rights to be appraised.**

6. **The scope of work** necessary to complete the assignment.

7. **Any extraordinary assumptions necessary in the assignment.**

8. **Any hypothetical conditions** necessary in the assignment. **Limiting conditions** must be determined just before an appraisal is made. Suppose the appraisal is being made subject to the addition of an indoor swimming pool in an apartment building. Work on the pool is underway. The appraiser must be told the exact dimensions and other details of the pool so they can be considered during the appraisal process.

Collection and Analysis of Data

The valuation process includes a narrative that discusses the data the appraiser has collected, including national, regional, and local trends, and a description of the neighborhood in which the property is located.

The appraiser must analyze factors such as **national and regional trends** that affect market value, such as the population, employment, income, price levels, and market conditions in force at the time of the appraisal. An analysis of local trends would include growth rate, supply and demand, length of time properties have spent on the market, and how land use has changed. **Social factors** can also be taken into account. These would include living standards, ages of occupants, and family makeup.

Studying the **economic base** of an area is an essential part of any appraisal. Are the income levels of neighborhood occupants high enough to support local housing? In residential neighborhoods, this is a question the appraiser must study. The answer most likely depends on employment levels, opportunities, and the percentage of household income dedicated to housing costs. Appraisals of commercial neighborhoods must look at store sales, volume per square foot, and the area of the building floor.

The *Dictionary of Real Estate Appraisal* defines a **neighborhood** as "a group of complementary land uses; a congruous grouping of inhabitants, buildings, or business enterprises." But the definition of neighborhood has historically been open to much interpretation—and misinterpretation. It is important for an appraiser to objectively yet sensitively understand the personality and the concept of the neighborhood being examined.

Issues affecting neighborhoods include:

- **Employment.** The stability of a neighborhood greatly depends on the employment opportunities available to inhabitants, as well as the jobs that they currently hold.
- **Income.** In residential neighborhoods, the quality of an area is related to the percent of income the people living there spend on housing. The measure in commercial neighborhoods is stores' sales volume per square foot size of building floor area.
- **Trends.** The cycles that neighborhoods experience over the years affect the value of property. Gentrification, for example, may result in a total change in the housing stock and in the people who can afford to live there.
- **Access.** The value of property relates directly to its access. In a suburban neighborhood, the accessibility and proximity of highway exits and/or railroad stations are important. In urban areas, the availability of public transportation is essential when judging property value.
- **Locational convenience.** Climate, topography, visual amenities (such as trees and waterways), and geological conditions affect the appeal of neighborhoods. Closeness to earthquake zones, flood zones, or to the possibilities of firestorms and mudslides may negatively affect value.

Site and improvements is an illustrated section of the appraisal report that deals with the size and shape of the property, problems that may impede development, and improvements that may add to the value. Here, maps and photographs are essential. Among the questions that must be addressed:

- Does the parcel have a strange or awkward shape?
- How easy is the access? Is there frontage on a road?
- What is the availability of utilities such as sewers and water, gas and electric, and amenities such as cable television?
- What uses are allowed under current zoning or will be allowed if zoning changes?
- What improvements have been made and how do they affect the property?

Analysis of Highest and Best Use

Analysis of highest and best use refers to the legally permitted use of a land parcel that is either vacant or improved, that will result in the greatest return in income or amenities. See page 106 for a more in-depth explanation of this concept.

Application and Limitations of Each Approach to Value

The **sales comparison approach** involves four steps. The appraiser must:

1. Look into information about recent sales, listings, and the attributes of similar properties being offered.
2. Research the market data to make sure it is reliable and accurate.
3. Do a comparative analysis on appropriate units, such as price per square foot.
4. Adjust the value of the property for sale based on the comparisons made with similar properties.

The **cost approach** takes into account the age, condition, and improvements of a property. Cost manuals, which appraisers can purchase, can help in making the cost estimate once the appraiser has gathered the relevant information.

The **income capitalization approach** estimates the value of property by dividing the estimated annual net operating income by a capitalization rate.

Reconciliation and Final Value Estimate

Doing a **reconciliation** is the appraiser's last step before submitting a report. As the word suggests, this process brings together all the conflicting information the appraiser has gathered while doing comparisons, then uses it to estimate a market value for the property being studied.

The Appraisal Report

The appraiser typically prepares a written report to let the client know the estimated value of the property in question, but he or she may also deliver an oral report with required backup in the workfile. The report can be prepared in a variety of ways, depending on what the client needs to know.

A **narrative appraisal** report discusses at length the information gathered for the appraisal and the reasons for the value estimate that the appraiser recommends.

A **form** report is usually used for single-family residential appraisals. Agencies, banks, and other lenders require a Uniform Residential Appraisal Report (URAR), which can be computer generated. This report must detail interior and exterior inspections and cover qualities such as the outward appearance of the property; its privacy; the level of light, ventilation, and fire protection; and its sanitation facilities.

The USPAP also allows reports written in several other formats. A **self-contained** report is a narrative report, but also includes the methods that the appraiser used to reach the estimate. Another narrative report—the **summary** report—is less detailed than the self-contained report. A **restricted** report is the least detailed narrative report and is meant only for clients. Clients must give their permission for the summary or restricted reports to be used.

▶ Property Description

The client or anyone who reads the appraisal must understand the design of a property, what is available on the site, and improvements made to it.

Site Description

Every appraisal must include the cost, restrictions, service, and reliability of utilities. **Utilities** include telephone, cable, natural gas or propane, as well as the essentials—electricity service, water supply, and trash collection. The absence or presence of septic tanks, sewer systems, and storm runoff systems must also be taken into account. Public records are an excellent source for information about utilities. For example, records kept about server lines are an indication that a septic tank will be permitted.

In municipalities without a general water supply, property owners depend on private wells. If a well needs to be drilled on the appraised property, the locations of existing wells provide clues to the placement of any new wells. Providing utilities in areas beyond municipal boundaries can be costly and will, of course, impact the land value. So it is worth the appraiser's time to thoroughly investigate the utilities situation.

The ease with which a property can be accessed plays a crucial role in determining its value. In most cases, rents and prices paid for urban dwellings are considerably lower when they are not conveniently near major public or private transportation, or when more than one mode of transportation, such as a bus to a train, is necessary to get to workplaces, shopping, or entertainment. In suburban areas, the length of the commute, the frequency of service, the fares, the location of train stations, and the availability of parking affect rents and house prices. Commercial properties benefit from being near main roads, easy-to-reach exits, or well-traveled arteries.

Topography is one of the physical features that affect construction cost. The topography of a property involves its access, slope and drainage, and view. **Size** of a property informs not only its value, but also its usefulness. Size can be measured in square feet, acres, or hectares (about 2.5 acres).

Improvement Description

The appraiser can submit photographs to illustrate the **size**, **condition**, and **utility** of a property.

Basic Construction and Design

Among an appraiser's varied and essential skills is knowledge of the main principles of construction. The choice of construction **techniques and materials** depends on climate, availability, cost, and durability; local building styles and municipal codes must also be taken into account.

Classes of basic construction are designated as A, B, C, and D. The designation is important to understand because most cost manuals list cost factors under headings of the class of construction.

Class	Frames	Foundations
A	fireproofed structural steel	reinforced concrete or masonry
Examples: high rises, hotels		Qualities: strong, costly
B	reinforced concrete	reinforced concrete or masonry
Examples: low-rise office buildings		Qualities: fire resistant, costly
C	masonry	wood or exposed steel
Examples: low-density commercial, residential buildings in colder climates		
D	wood or light steel	concrete or concrete block
Examples: residential buildings in the West and South		

Another important element of basic construction and design is the **finish**, both exterior and interior. How extensive and luxurious a house's finishes are depends mainly on cost. Expensive stone counters and high-end wood flooring are most often found in custom homes. For house exteriors, the style will dictate the extras. Spanish-style houses, for example, are defined in part by roof tile and textured stucco. Half-timbering defines Tudor-style homes, and a small stone tower lets buyers know they are looking at a French-Norman style.

There are **mechanical** considerations as well. Rather than the more costly copper pipes that used to be ubiquitous in buildings, builders often turn to plastics and polymers for rough plumbing and electrical components. For energy-efficient heating and air conditioning systems, the trend is toward solar heating and "green" design features. In areas with extreme temperatures, insulation is an important element.

Functional utility refers to how livable and suitable a property is. In the appraisal report, the appraiser can describe how visually appealing a residential property is, how well its rooms flow, their spaciousness and light, and the level of comfort provided by the mechanical equipment.

The standards for commercial properties are slightly different, although they also focus on visual appeal and design features. In this case, functional utility involves the most up-to-date elements that appeal to tenants—of either residential or commercial properties—that will result in the highest income.

▶ Highest and Best Use Analysis

Four Tests

Four tests, or criteria, are typically applied to define highest and best use.

1. **Physically possible** refers to the practicality of a property's location, access, size, shape, and typography among its features.
2. **Legally permitted** tests whether a site is allowed under current zoning regulations and under anticipated zoning as well.
3. **Financially feasible** or **economically feasible** tests whether a property is workable in terms of cost and economic demand. The criteria is not met if a development involves high cost and a disproportionate amount of time that end up being higher than the income the development will produce.

4. **Maximally productive** means that the way a property is planned now or in the future will provide its most viable and economic use. The surrounding area and the buildings it supports serve as a guide to the appraiser providing his or her judgment on highest and best use.

Vacant Site or As If Vacant

Vacant site or **as if vacant** is a type of use based on the valuation theory. The value of land is considered to be based on its uses and profitability in the future, rather than the way it is currently being used.

As Improved

As improved acknowledges that, although the present use of a property may not be its highest and best, existing improvements add to its value.

Interim Use

Interim use results when an appraiser suggests alternative uses of an improved property that are different from the highest and best use of the property if it were vacant.

▶ Sales Comparison Approach

Research and Selection of Comparables

Appraisers choose information about comparables, or comps, based on recent sales of real estate in the same area that is comparable to the property being sold. **Data sources** include realtor websites and publications, public records, brokers, and other appraisers. The appraiser selects values that are as much like the subject as possible and then adds or subtracts plus or minus features if necessary. The greater the number of comps, the more accurate the result of the value estimate will be. Comps can be double-checked and **verified** by speaking to a person who took part in the deal.

The **unit of comparison approach** includes finding an important variable that can objectively be used to compare different sales. One good measure to use for comparing prices is to compare the price per room. First, divide the sales price of each property by the number of rooms. Then look for other prices of the comps as the subject may differ. If, for example, the price per room in the comps, which are similar apartments in the same building, are the same, but one apartment has sold for far more, the more costly place might be on a higher floor or be on a corner.

Income may be utilized as a unit of comparison in the sales comparison approach. The **potential gross income (PGI)** is the amount that rental properties would produce if all the units were filled and producing income all year. The **potential gross income multiplier (PGIM)** is the PGI divided by the selling price of the property. The **effective gross income (EGI)** is calculated by subtracting vacancy and collection losses from the PGI. The **effective gross income multiplier (EGIM)** is the EGI divided by the selling price of the property. **Overall rate** is the percentage relationship between the **net operating income (NOI)** and the sales price. NOI is EGI minus **operating expenses (OE)**. These include insurance, utilities, maintenance and repairs, payroll and payroll taxes, real estate property taxes, management fees, grounds keeping, and reserves for replacement expenditures.

Many properties are compared based on their **size**, such as **price per square foot** (calculated by adding up the "in place" costs of the building shell components and dividing this figure by the number of square feet in the building), **price per unit**, **price per acre** (one acre is equal to 43,560 square feet), **price per front foot, price per**

lot, or **price per buildable square foot**. The economic principle of economies of scale tells us that larger units typically cost less per unit than smaller ones.

Certified general appraisers are expected to have knowledge about units of comparison in specialized properties, such as **motel and apartment units and theater seats**. For multiscreen theaters, for example, the number of screens may be used as a unit of comparison.

Elements of Comparison

The following elements of comparison must be allowed for when the sales comparison approach is used.

Property Rights Conveyed

These include:

- **Easements**, which are the rights or interests held by one party in the property of another person.
- **Leased fee**, which is the owner's interest in a leased property. **Leasehold** is the tenant's interest in a leased property.
- **Mineral rights.** These rights are of consequence in some areas of the country; some comparables there may be sold with possibly valuable subsurface rights. Appraisers must take these into account and make the necessary adjustments between the comps and the subject property.
- Other property rights conveyed include **air rights, cooperatives**, and **time-shares**.

Financing Terms and Cash Equivalency

This element of comparison includes:

- **Loan payment.** Even when the buyer uses a mortgage or other loan, the payment is usually in cash. When special financing is involved, the price is affected. When financing is provided by the seller and there are fees for the loan, the price is adjusted. The kind of financing affects the price but not the value of the property.
- **Loan balance**, which is the amount of the loan, or mortgage, that remains outstanding.

Conditions of Sale

- An **arm's-length sale** is a "fair sale," which occurs in a competitive market where both the seller and buyer act independently of each other and have no relationship. A **non–arm's-length sale** involves people who are related, such as parents, siblings, cousins, or in-laws. The price at which the property is sold may not reflect market rates.
- **Personalty** refers to items, such as bookshelves, that are physically attached to commercial sites and are considered part of the property and belong to the owner.

Market Conditions at Time of Contract and Closing

Price levels shift depending on the state of local and national economies. When the market goes up, the current sale price of a comparable will likely go up as well and be higher than it was in previous months. The appraiser must make adjustments for such price changes due to **market conditions** and must note the date of each comparable.

Location

As often noted, the three most important words in real estate are "location, location, location." An appraiser must make an adjustment if the **location** of a comparable differs significantly from the subject's. In this case, the adjustment may be rather subjective. It is more objective in the case of commercial properties where foot traffic, for example, is verifiable.

Physical Characteristics

Age, condition, quality, construction, maintenance, access, visibility, and utility are among a property's **physical characteristics** that may lead to an adjustment.

Adjustment Process

Adjustments are usually necessary when comparing comparable properties to the subject property. Adjustments can be made in percentages or in actual dollar amounts. The appraiser can adjust the total sales price or apply adjustments to units of comparison.

Sequence of adjustments should be in this order:

1. real property rights
2. financing terms
3. location and physical characteristics

If the characteristics are independent, then each must be applied to the actual price of the comparable. This is known as a **dollar adjustment**. Cumulative **percentage adjustments** should be used if characteristics are interrelated or interdependent. **Paired sales analysis** is a useful technique when only one feature in a comparable property is found. The appraiser can then apply the value of that unique feature to the comparable.

Application of Sales Comparison Approach

Using this approach, the appraiser estimates the value of a property by comparing the actual sales of comparable properties.

▶ Site Value

A site is ready to be built on when it is cleared, graded, and utilities have been connected. **Site value** is estimated as part of the cost approach. Following are ways to estimate site value.

Sales Comparison

Sales comparison is the most commonly used way to value land and is similar to, but less complicated than, the valuing of improved properties.

Land Residual

Land residual involves the calculation of real or potential income that remains after deducting the income that is attributed to the buildings. This method is most practical when no comparable land sales are available and newer properties are being appraised.

Allocation

Allocation is an alternative method used in cases where no comparables of vacant sites are available—in built-up areas, for example, where no empty lots remain. It estimates the value of land as a fraction of the total value. The downside of allocation is that it cannot be depended on to be accurate.

Extraction

Extraction is a method of estimating land value in which the depreciated cost of improvements are subtracted from a property's total value. This method is best used when the improvements have little value.

Ground Rent Capitalization

Ground rent capitalization refers to unique circumstances most often found in Hawaii, Baltimore, and New York City, in which a building's owners or shareholders lease the land from another party, such as a church that owns it. The land's value is then estimated by capitalization—dividing the annual rent by an appropriate rate.

Subdivision Analysis

Subdivision analysis estimates the maximum amount a subdivider will pay for a tract of land. This method of valuation, also called the **development method**, looks at residential, industrial, and recreational land that is to be used for subdivided development. This analysis is most often used in feasibility studies and when comparative sales are limited. Important elements of this analysis are:

1. **Development cost: direct and indirect.** Design, engineering, government fees, promotion sales, and closing charges must be added up and factored in to reach an estimated lot price.
2. **Contractor's overhead and profit.** These include work, effort overhead costs, and return on capital. They may be a percentage of the capital invested in the undeveloped land or a percentage of gross sales.
3. **Forecast absorption and gross sales.** The appraiser must identify competing developments in the market and research their performance. A thorough market analysis should reveal the amount of competing inventory, sales prices, absorption, and time on the market. The appraiser's analysis of competing developments can provide estimates for the subject's product in these areas.
4. **Entrepreneurial profit.** The developer receives a return on his or her investment, which is, in part, payment for risk, entrepreneurial skills, and overhead costs.
5. **Discounted value conclusion.** The value may go down if the project takes more than a year to sell, during which the developer's capital has been tied up.

Plottage and Assemblage

Plottage and assemblage refers to the combining of two or more parcels of land, which are called an assemblage. The combination is worth more than the total of individual parcels. Plottage is the increase of added value.

▶ Cost Approach

Appraisers use the cost approach to:

- **estimate the value** of new and economically sound properties.
- **appraise** institutional or special use properties.
- **double-check** the value of improved property, whose value was estimated using other approaches.

Steps in Cost Approach

The cost approach involves five steps.

1. Estimate the value of land as if vacant and ready for use.
2. Estimate the cost of reproducing or replacing the existing improvements as of the date of value.
3. Estimate all elements for loss in value (accrued depreciation).
4. Subtract the loss in value from the cost of the new improvements.
5. Add the depreciated cost of the improvements to the estimated site value to come up with the property value.

Reproduction is the cost of building a replica. **Replacement** is building a property that may look like the original, but meets all current codes, standards, and design.

The **comparative-unit method** involves grouping all the components of a building together on a unit basis to arrive at the total cost per square or cubic foot. Materials, installation, and builder's overhead and profit are included in costs. The **unit-in-place method** measures the installed unit cost of each component, such as wall, floors, roof, ceiling, and heating. The lump sum of equipment and fixtures is added. The **quantity survey method** includes the cost of every individual piece used in construction, such as nails and bricks. A lump sum of insurance, overhead, and profit is then added. The **cost service index** updates the original cost of historic or unique buildings to be in line with current costs. Several companies publish current cost indexes that can help appraisers arrive at dependable figures.

Appraisers define **depreciation** as a dollar or percentage amount that is deducted from the estimated costs of improvement on the date of value, as if new. Depreciation, from an appraiser's point of view, is the best estimate of the actual market loss in value as compared to a new building.

Physical deterioration occurs in all structures no matter how high the quality of their materials and construction methods. Because buildings may age differently depending on location, loss in value is sometimes appraised on a component by component basis. **Curable deterioration** refers to conditions that would be cost effective to fix. The market value might be enhanced by installing a new elevator, painting hallways, or replacing windows, for example. The cost of making these changes might be less than the value added by doing so. **Incurable deterioration** means there are costly physical conditions that would cost more to take care of than they are worth for adding value. A new roof on a building might come under this category. **Short-lived deterioration** refers to repairs that could be put off, but would probably have to be taken care of in a few years. An aging, but still usable, boiler could be considered in this category. **Long-lived deterioration** refers to components that, when replaced in the future, may cost more than the value they add to the building. Replacing plumbing or electrical wiring in an aging structure might be among such components.

Functional obsolescence is a type of depreciation that is inherent in the design or construction of a property. **Curable obsolescence** means that the cost of dealing with it will cost less than the benefits it will add. A second bathroom can be added at reasonable cost, for example. **Incurable obsolescence** is a flaw that would cost more to fix than it is worth. An elaborate but deteriorating driveway on an over-designed house in a low-income street is an example.

External or **economic obsolescence** results from outside problems that are beyond an owner's control. It may be may be curable or incurable and might include chemical hazards or changes in zoning. If a highway is built close to a house, for example, the cost of a noise barrier may be higher than the value it brings.

Several **methods of estimating depreciation**, which appraisers usually combine, are used to measure actual loss in value.

- **Age-life method** is based on the assumption that the longevity of all buildings can be predicted. Also called **economic life**, it is the amount of time a structure with improvements is worth more than the value of its lot, were it vacant. Just because buildings are the same age does not mean their **effective life** is the same. An up-to-date, 50-year-old building may have a longer economic life and be worth more than a 25-year-old structure that has outdated features and has not been well maintained. The older building's effective age may be 25.
- **Breakdown method and sequence of deductions.** In this method, loss in value is separated into physical, functional, and outside causes.
- **Market extraction or depreciation** involves subtracting the depreciated cost of improvements from the total value of the property.

Application of the Cost Approach

The **application of the cost approach** gives the appraiser an estimate of the reproduction or replacement cost of a building minus depreciation.

▶ Income Approach

Using the **income approach**, the appraiser can calculate an estimate of a property's value by considering its current worth of the income it will produce during its remaining life. To estimate the worth of rental property, its annual income can be capitalized into value.

Estimation of Income and Expenses

Income property valuation is based on an estimate of income generated by a property and its operating expenses.

Potential gross income (PGI) is the total income a property generates before expenses are deducted. **Effective gross income** (EGI) is the income left after **vacancy rates** and allowances for **collection loss** (bad debts) are subtracted from potential gross, and income and miscellaneous income are added. The result should be a realistic prediction of the highest income the building could produce when efficiently managed in the current market.

Operating expenses include all property-related expenses added up to produce the gross income. These include:

- **Fixed expenses.** These expenses tend to remain the same over the years. They include insurance premiums and certain taxes.
- **Variable expenses.** These expenses change as a building's rate of occupancy changes. They include utilities, management fees, payroll and payroll taxes, security, landscaping, advertising, and agency fees.
- **Reserve for replacements.** This is a fund set aside for replacing boilers, appliances, and other short-lived items. This reserve may be a hidden loss of income and must be provided for in the appraiser's report.

Net operating income (NOI) is estimated by subtracting operating expenses and the replacement reserve from effective gross income.

Operating Statement Ratios

Operating statement ratios help the appraiser analyze income properties by mathematically showing the relationship between expenses and income. They are reached by dividing the total operating expenses by either the PGI or by the EGI. The operating expense ratios for apartment buildings are usually between 30% and 50%; office buildings' ratios often hover between 40% and 60%. **Net income ratio** is the NOI ratio divided by the effective gross income of a property. **Breakeven ratio** is the total of operating expenses plus collection service divided by potential gross income—or the occupancy rate needed to have zero cash flow.

Gross Rent Multiplier

The **gross rent multiplier** (GRM) is the sales price divided by the rental rate. In situations involving investors, the basis of the price is a multiple of the level of rent.

Direct Capitalization

Direct capitalization is a way of estimating value by dividing net operating income by an overall capitalization rate. For the estimate to be accurate, the information provided to formulate the calculation needs to be exact. Direct capitalization uses one rate to convert the income being examined to an estimate of value. The estimate may be credited to the total property, the building, the land, or the equity. This does not involve any yield assumptions.

The **overall capitalization rate** is found by dividing net operating income by the property's purchase price. The **gross income multiplier** is the total income from property divided by the sales price before any expenses are deducted, and **net income ratio** is the NOI ratio divided by the effective gross income of a property.

Band of investment (mortgage equity) techniques use a weighted average of debt and equity rates.

Residual techniques are techniques, not often used today, for capitalizing income. These techniques include:

- **Land (building value given)**, which is a residual technique used when improvements are either new or proposed and their value can be estimated, but the land value is not known.
- **Building (land value given)**, which is a residual technique that works in an opposite way from the land residual technique. It is used when the value of land is known but the improvement value is not known. Income credited to the improvements is capitalized and added to the land value. The result is the value estimate.
- **Equity (mortgage value given)**, which is a method that can be used when the mortgage amount and terms are known. The cash flow credited to the equity investment is capitalized and added to the loan amount.

▶ Valuation of Partial Interests

Partial interests result when a person holds some, but not all, the interest in real estate.

Interests Created by a Lease
- **Leased fee** is the owner's interest in a leased property.
- **Leasehold** is the tenant's interest in a leased property.
- **Sub-leasehold** is the interest in a leased property of the tenant's tenant.
- **Renewable options** in a lease gives the tenant the right to renew the lease at the rent and terms it describes.
- **Tenant improvements** may affect the value of a property after that tenant's lease expires. The following tenant might be willing to pay extra to keep the improvements or ask to have them removed, which may be costly.
- **Concessions**, such as no rent paid for six months, may be granted to attract renters during a slow market time. The appraiser must assess the value of concessions and understand the market in which they are granted.

Lease Provisions
- **Overage rent** is the amount paid over the base rent under a percentage lease.
- **Expense stops** in leases require the owner to pay operating expenses up to an agreed-upon amount, above which they become the tenant's responsibility.
- **Net leases.** In an absolute net lease, the tenant pays for taxes, insurance, and operating expenses, including repairs.
- **Minimum rent** is figured as part of a percentage lease, almost exclusively used by retail tenants. It is a percentage of rent based on gross sales that go over a certain amount. The rent is based on the retailer's anticipated sales per square foot.
- **Percentage rent** is provided at times when a landlord wants to make a property appealing to and economically feasible for a retail client. The rent is based on a percentage of the client's sales.

- **Consumer price index (CPI) adjustments.** During times of high inflation or deflation, multiple-year leases may lead to hardship for the landlord or the tenant, so a cost-of-living (COL) clause is written into the lease. The COL is usually based on the CPI, an index published by the Bureau of Labor Statistics, which is part of the U.S. Department of Labor.
- **Excess rent**, which is the difference between contract and market rents, implies that the tenant is paying a higher rent than the market calls for. In preparing an income report about a property with several different leases, the appraiser must compose a schedule that tells when each lease ends.

Other Partial Interests

A **life estate** is a type of partial interest in which a person is permitted to live on a property during his or her lifetime. When the person dies, the property reverts to the owner. The person who has lifetime use and the owner share the market value of the property.

Condominium owners have individual ownership of their units. Common areas, such as paths, roof gardens, recreational facilities, and hallways, are owned by all the unit owners for their use.

Easements refer to the rights a person has to use property that is owned by someone else. A cable company, for example, may use an easement to bury cable across privately owned land. Easements can enhance or detract from a property's value, depending on what has been done.

Time-shares are properties that are used for an agreed-upon time each year by owners who pay to use them and their amenities. The total paid by the owners of time-shares is often more than the units would cost if individually owned.

Cooperatives are owned by corporations in which shareholders own shares, occupy units, and make monthly maintenance payments. The common areas are maintained by the corporation. The corporation holds the mortgage and shareholders deduct the interest on it as a tax benefit.

A **leased fee estate** is the landlord's interest in leased property. The leased fee's value lies in the money that the landlord can earn from the lease. **A leasehold estate** may be especially valuable when the rent on a lease is below market rate and the lease is long term.

▶ Appraisal of Standards and Ethics

Uniform Standards of Professional Appraisal Practice (USPAP)

The Preamble to the most current edition of the USPAP states:

The purpose of the *Uniform Standards of Professional Appraisal Practice* (USPAP) is to promote and maintain a high level of public trust in appraisal practice by establishing requirements for appraisers. It is essential that appraisers develop and communicate their analyses, opinions, and conclusions to intended users of their services in a manner that is meaningful and not misleading.

The USPAP, which was first adopted on April 27, 1987, is currently maintained and regularly updated by the **Appraisal Foundation's Appraisal Standards Board (ASB)**. Every appraiser who is state licensed or certified must adhere to the standards outlined in the USPAP. In other words, the standards set by this important document are the minimum benchmarks to which every appraiser must adhere. Thus, it is vital that any person who wishes to pursue a career as an appraiser must be very familiar with every term, definition, and concept contained within the latest edition of USPAP.

The USPAP review found on the following pages is intended to be a simplified overview of the most important points contained within the 2006 edition of the USPAP, and is in no way intended to be a quick fix to learning and understanding the Uniform Standards before an upcoming exam. Any serious candidate for licensure or certification should visit the Appraisal Foundation's website (www.appraisalfoundation.org), where he or she can access the most recent USPAP in its entirety, as well as purchase hard copies and electronic copies of this vital document.

Structure of USPAP (Five Sections)

USPAP contains five sections, all of which are all equally important; within those five sections, there are also comments, which also are all equally important. Following is a brief overview of those sections and their key concepts.

Section 1. Definitions

As of 2006, there are 38 definitions. These important terms, which follow, are of a distinct meaning for appraisers. For more information, be sure to visit the USPAP section of the Appraisal Foundation's website.

advocacy	hypothetical condition
appraisal	intangible property (intangible assets)
appraisal consulting	intended use
appraisal practice	intended user
appraisal review	jurisdictional exception
appraiser	market value
appraiser's peers	mass appraisal
assignment	mass appraisal model
assignment results	personal property
assumption	price
bias	real estate
business enterprise	real property
business equity	report
client	scope of work
confidential information	signature
cost	supplemental standards
credible	valuation services
extraordinary assumption	value
feasibility analysis	workfile

Section 2. Preamble

The purpose of the USPAP is to help ensure the public's trust in the appraisal profession by establishing a minimum set of standards to which all appraisers must adhere. These uniform standards were created not only for the providers of the appraisal services, but also for the users of the appraisal services.

USPAP applies when **compliance may be required** under the law, regulation, or agreement with the client. **It can also apply when there is no obligation of compliance**; this is a voluntary obligation by the appraiser.

The services covered under USPAP are:

- **appraisal** (Standards 1, 2, and 6–10)
- **appraisal review** (Standard 3)
- **real property appraisal consulting** (Standards 4 and 5)
- **other services** that may be performed by an appraiser, such as **teaching, writing articles about appraising, performing cost estimates, measuring a house**, and **collecting data**. Although there are no Standards in USPAP that address these topics, the appraiser is still bound to comply with both the Ethics Rule and Competency Rule of USPAP.

USPAP covers the following property types:

- **Real property**, which is real property such as real estate, and the rights associated with it.
- **Personal property**, which could be household items, machinery equipment, artwork, etc.—all tangible items that are not real property and their rights.
- **Intangible property**, which are nonphysical assets and their rights, such as goodwill, contracts, patents, and copyrights.

Section 3. Rules

A. Ethics Rule

The Ethics Rule has four parts: conduct, management, confidentiality, and record keeping. Following is a breakdown of each part's key points.

1. **Conduct**

   The first part of the Ethics Rule deals with the manner in which an appraiser must conduct him or herself. Above all else, **an appraiser must perform his or her duties in an ethical, impartial, and noncriminal manner, as dictated by USPAP, and never discriminate**. This part applies to the accepting and performing of assignments, and the communication of an assignment's results. An appraiser must never discriminate.

2. **Management**

   The second part of the Ethics Rule **prohibits the appraiser from being paid any undisclosed fees, commissions, or anything else of value** in order to obtain an assignment. It also stipulates that an appraiser **may not advertise in an improper manner or accept unethical compensation arrangements**.

3. **Confidentiality**

The third part of the Ethics Rule stipulates **that it is every appraiser's duty to protect the confidential nature of the relationship between himself or herself and the client**, and may only disclose confidential information regarding a client or an assignment to the client or those approved by the client those authorized by law; or to an authorized professional peer review.

4. **Record Keeping**

The fourth part of the Ethics Rule applies to Standards 1 through 10. It requires that for every appraisal, appraisal review, or consulting assignment, an appraiser must prepare a detailed workfile and retain it for a minimum of five years after the date it was completed and signed, or two years after the final decision of a court case where the appraiser provided testimony.

B. Competency Rule

This rule states that **before accepting any assignment, the appraiser needs to identify the competency requirements that must be met, and should only accept work that he or she possesses the experience to perform**. The competency issue may involve the property type (residential, commercial, industrial, etc), the market area (city, rural, mountain, etc.) where the property is located, or a type of analysis (linear regression, discounted cash flow, etc.) needed in the assignment. If the appraiser does not feel that he or she is competent to complete the assignment, he or she must disclose this information to the client and take the steps necessary to becoming competent, or simply not accept the assignment.

C. Scope of Work Rule

The USPAP defines **scope of work** as "the type and extent of research and analyses in an assignment." **To properly identify the appraisal problem to be solved, an appraiser must collect and analyze information about a number of assignment elements**, such as who is the client and who are the assignment's intended users, the effective date for appraiser's opinion of value, the definition of value needed for the assignment, etc.

The scope of work is acceptable when it is performed at the level to which typical intended users expect for the particular type of an assignment, and what other competent appraisers' actions would be if they were to perform the assignment.

Every appraisal report prepared must properly disclose enough information for the intended users to fully comprehend the scope of work performed by the appraiser. Scope of work can be documented throughout the report or in a specific section.

D. Jurisdictional Exception Rule

This rule **recognizes that laws or regulations may supersede USPAP**. If a part or parts of USPAP (not USPAP as a whole) is against a particular area's law or public policy, only that part or parts of USPAP is voided. The rest of USPAP will still apply.

The appraiser needs to identify the part or parts of USPAP voided by law and identify the legal authority justifying the action. The appraiser is then required to reference the legal authority in the report. An example of a jurisdictional exception would be a situation where a county assessor might ignore existing leases and use market rents to determine assessed values.

E. Supplemental Standards Rule

Supplemental standards are additional requirements that add to the development and reporting requirements of USPAP. These additional requirements can be issued by entities that create public policy, by government agencies like FHA or VA, or by enterprises sponsored by the government, like Fannie Mae and Freddie Mac. These additional requirements or standards may be published in regulations, policies, and other documents.

Section 4. Standards

There are ten Standards. Within each Standard, there are subsections known as Standard Rules.

STANDARD 1: Real Property Appraisal, Development

- **Standard Rule 1–1:** This standard rule **discusses the appraiser's need to be competent**; an appraiser must be able to develop a credible appraisal and not commit any errors of omission or commission that would adversely affect an appraisal.

- **Standard Rule 1–2:** This standard rule **discusses the need to identify all applicable real property assignment elements.** From these assignment elements the appraiser will determine the scope of work necessary to produce credible assignment results.

- **Standard Rule 1–3:** This standard rule **discusses the appraiser's need to identify land use regulations, economic supply and demand factors, market area trends, and other similar items to develop a market value opinion.** The appraiser may also need to develop an opinion of the highest and best use of the property.

- **Standard Rule 1–4:** This standard rule **discusses the collection, verification, and analysis of the information necessary to produce a credible appraisal**, as well as the three approaches to value (cost, sales comparison, and income). An appraiser must use those approaches to value to produce credible assignment results. Not all approaches to value will always be used (vacant land does not need a cost approach).

- **Standard Rule 1–5:** This standard rule discusses the appraiser's need to **analyze for the subject property as of the effective date (date for the value estimate) any agreement of sale, options and any listings.**

- **Standard Rule 1–6:** This standard rule discusses **reconciliation of the quality and quantity of data available** within the approaches to value used, and the reconciliation **of the final value opinion from the different approaches to value used** in the assignment.

STANDARD 2: Real Property Appraisal, Reporting

- **Standard Rule 2–1:** This standard rule **discusses the appraiser's need to report the assignment results accurately and in a straightforward, ethical manner** so that the intended users can fully comprehend the report.

- **Standard Rule 2–2:** This standard rule **discusses the three reporting options used** in a real property appraisal. These options address the level of content and detail to be discussed in a real property appraisal report. Starting with the most detail to the least detail, as follows. A **self-contained report** uses the highest level of content detail; a **summary report** uses the next level of content detail; a **restricted-use report** uses the minimum level of content detail required and can any only have the client as an intended user. In a restricted-use report, the appraiser needs to disclose that this report is only to be used by the client; there are no other intended users and that the workfile will be needed to understand the report.

- **Standard Rule 2–3**: This standard rule **discusses what is present in a signed certification** by the appraiser. All assignments performed under Standards 1–10 require signed certifications, which state that the appraiser performed in an ethical manner with no bias and no contingent fee arrangements. In addition, the names of any individuals who provided significant real property appraisal assistance but did not sign the certification must be stated in the certification.
- **Standard Rule 2–4**: This standard rule **discusses oral reports**. Oral reports must address important items in a manner that is similar to a summary report. The appraiser will need to sign and date a certification from an oral report and put it into the workfile for this assignment.

STANDARD 3: Appraisal Review, Development and Reporting

An appraisal review is **a critique of an assignment and may be all or part of a report of a workfile**. Standard 3 covers both the development and reporting requirements and applies to all types of property (real, personal, and business assets). Intended uses of reviews are for quality control, audits, confirmation, or qualification.

- **Standards Rule 3–1** and **Standards Rule 3–2**: These **two rules share similar criteria**, but the **first rule applies to the development of an appraisal review**, and the **second rule applies to the reporting** in it.
- **Standards Rule 3–3**: The reviewer will **need to date and sign an appraisal review certification statement** similar to that already discussed in standards rule 2–3. **Appraisal review is not the co-signing of the original report**. A reviewer should not sign the original report under review unless the reviewer intends to accept full responsibility of the original report.

STANDARDS 4 and 5: Real Property Appraisal Consulting, Development and Reporting

These two standards **discuss the development and reporting involved in appraisal consulting assignments.**

USPAP Definition of Appraisal Consulting: "Developing an analysis, recommendation, or an opinion to solve a problem, where an opinion of value is a component of the analysis leading to the assignment results."

An appraisal consulting assignment applies only to real property and has an opinion of value as one of the components of the assignment. It does not have an appraisal or an appraisal review as its primary purpose. As always, the appraiser needs to be competent and perform in an ethical manner. The opinion of value used in the appraisal consulting assignment may be developed by the appraiser doing the consulting assignment or from a different appraiser. If the appraisal comes from a different appraiser, the consulting assignment appraiser should either perform the appraisal review or the appraisal; otherwise, an extraordinary assumption about the appraisal will need to be used before it can be incorporated into the appraisal consulting assignment. This second option is less desirable because whenever one uses extraordinary assumptions there is less certainty about the credibility of the assignment results.

The appraiser will **need to date and sign an appraisal consulting report statement** similar to that already discussed in Standards Rule 2–3.

STANDARD 6: Mass Appraisal, Development and Reporting

Standard 6 **discusses both development and reporting issues for mass appraisals**. It is similar to Standard 3 (Appraisal Review) in this manner. **Mass appraisals are used to value very large samples of real and personal property**. For mass appraisals, all of the USPAP rules apply, as do the Preamble and definitions.

As an example, tax assessors use mass appraisal for tax assessments (*ad valorem* taxation). *Ad valorem* taxation may involve the jurisdictional exception rule, as these are public agencies. In addition, holders of many properties or loans may decide to value their portfolios using mass appraisals.

Assignment identification and reporting requirements are similar to what has been previously discussed in the other Standards; however, Standard 6 also addresses issues of model specification and data requirements, model calibration methods, the mathematical form of the model, appraisal performance tests, and other issues beyond the scope of this text.

STANDARDS 7 and 8: Personal Property Appraisal, Development and Reporting

The USPAP defines personal property as "identifiable tangible objects that are considered by the general public as being 'personal'—for example, furnishings, artwork, antiques, gems and jewelry, collectibles, machinery and equipment; all tangible property that is not classified as real estate."

Standards 7 and 8 mirror Standards 1 and 2 in many ways. The major differences are as follows.

- The appraiser must determine the appropriate level of trade for the property. For example, the same property may have a different value at a wholesale level of trade versus a retail level of trade versus an auction level.
- The appraiser will need to analyze the prior sales history of the personal property that have occurred within a reasonable and applicable period. Thus, it is not a "one size fits all" as was the case for real property (three years prior). If the prior sale date occurred and it is not considered reasonable and applicable, then it does not need to be analyzed.

The appraiser will **need to date and sign a personal property report statement** similar to that already discussed in Standard Rule 2–3.

STANDARDS 9 and 10: Business Appraisal, Development and Reporting

Business appraisals are for intangible property, which are nonphysical assets.

USPAP defines a business entity as "an entity pursuing an economic activity."

Standards 9 and 10 also similar to Standards 1 and 2 in many ways. The major differences are as follows.

- Assignment identification and reporting requirements for business appraisal include items such as ownership percentage interests and elements of control and marketability.
- The appraiser needs to determine if the interest being appraised has the ability to cause liquidation of all or part of the business enterprise. If this is the case, then appraisals of the personal property and real property assets may need to be performed. For example, there may be an old, outdated manufacturing business in a downtown area. The underlying real estate may have a greater value than the continued operation of this business.

- The appraiser may have to analyze prior sales of capital stock or ownership interest of the intangible asset being appraised. No specific time period is given for the analysis of the prior sales history of the intangible asset.

Section 5. Statements on Appraisal Standards (1–10)

Statements on Appraisal Standards clarify, explain, elaborate, or interpret a Rule or Standard Rule. There are ten statements listed in USPAP, of which four have been retired as of 2006. Statements are an integral part of USPAP and can only be incorporated into USPAP by the Appraisal Standards Board after exposure and comments from the public. These are very long discussions found after Standard 10.

Real Estate Math Review

CHAPTER SUMMARY

Currently, math and statistics questions account for almost 10% of real estate appraisal exams, so you should take these topics seriously. But even if math is not your favorite subject, this chapter will help you do your best. It not only covers arithmetic, algebra, geometry, and word problems, but also has practice problems for each of the real estate math topics, not just those required for appraisers.

ERE ARE SOME of the concepts that will be tested on your exam:

Statistical concepts used in appraisal:

- Mean
- Median
- Mode
- Range
- Standard deviation

Compound interest concepts (tested only on state-certified residential and certified general appraiser exams):

- Future value of $1
- Present value of $1

- Future value of an annuity of $1 per period
- Present value of an annuity of $1 per period
- Sinking fund factor
- Installment to amortize $1 (loan constant)

This chapter starts with the simplest real estate and real estate appraisal concepts and works its way up to the most difficult material. Before you begin to review your skills, take a look at some helpful strategies for doing your best.

► Strategies for Math Questions

Answer Every Question

You should answer every single question, even if you don't know the answer. There is usually no penalty for a wrong answer, and, if there are four answer choices, you have a 25% chance of guessing correctly. If one or two answers are obviously wrong, the odds may be even higher on selecting the correct one.

Bring a Calculator

Your state *may* allow you to bring calculator to your exam. **You must check with your exam center to find out exactly what type of calculator is permitted**. In general, permissible calculators are battery operated, do not print, are not programmable, and do not have a keypad with letters. As a precaution, you should bring an extra battery with you to your exam. Try not to rely entirely on the calculator. Although using one can prevent simple adding and subtracting errors, it may take longer for you to use the calculator than to figure it out yourself.

Use Scratch Paper

Resist the temptation to "save time" by doing all your work on your calculator. The main pitfall with calculators is the temptation to work the problem all the way through to the end on the calculator. At this point, if none of the answers provided is correct, there is no way to know where the mistake lies. Use scratch paper to avoid this problem.

Check Your Work

Checking your work is always good practice, and it's usually quite simple. Even if you come up with an answer that is one of the answer choices, you should check your work. Test writers often include answer choices that are the results of common errors, which is what you may have.

▶ Real Estate Math Review

Here's a quick review of some basic arithmetic, algebra, geometry, and word problem skills you will need for your exam and career.

Arithmetic Review

Symbols of Multiplication

When two or more numbers are being multiplied, they are called **factors**. The answer that results is called the **product**.

> *Example:*
> $5 \times 6 = 30$ 5 and 6 are **factors**, and 30 is the **product**.

There are several ways to represent multiplication in this mathematical statement.

- A dot between factors indicates multiplication:

  $5 \cdot 6 = 30$

- Parentheses around any part of the one or more factors indicates multiplication:

  $(5)6 = 30$ $5(6) = 30$ $(5)(6) = 30$

- Multiplication is also indicated when a number is placed next to a variable:

  $5a = 30$ In this equation, 5 is being multiplied by a.

Divisibility

Like multiplication, division can be represented in a few different ways:

$8 \div 3$ $3\overline{)8}$ $\frac{8}{3}$

In each of these expressions, 3 is the **divisor** and 8 is the **dividend**.

If the number after the one you need to round to is five or more, make the preceding number one higher. If it is less than five, drop it and leave the preceding number the same. (Information about rounding is usually provided in the exam instructions or in the exam bulletin.)

Example:
0.0135 = 0.014 or 0.01

Decimals

The most important thing to remember about decimals is that the first place value to the right begins with tenths. The place values are as follows:

1	2	6	8	•	3	4	5	7
THOUSANDS	HUNDREDS	TENS	ONES	DECIMAL POINT	TENTHS	HUNDREDTHS	THOUSANDTHS	TEN THOUSANDTHS

In expanded form, this number can also be expressed as:

$1{,}268.3457 = (1 \times 1{,}000) + (2 \times 100) + (6 \times 10) + (8 \times 1) + (3 \times .01) + (4 \times .01) + (5 \times .001) + (7 \times .0001)$

Fractions

To do well when working with fractions, you'll need to understand some basic concepts. Here are some math rules for fractions using variables:

$$\frac{a}{b} \times \frac{c}{d} = \frac{a \times c}{b \times d}$$

$$\frac{a}{b} + \frac{c}{b} = \frac{a + c}{b}$$

$$\frac{a}{b} \div \frac{c}{d} = \frac{a}{b} \times \frac{d}{c} = \frac{a \times d}{b \times c}$$

$$\frac{a}{b} + \frac{c}{d} = \frac{ad + bc}{bd}$$

Multiplication of Fractions

Multiplying fractions is one of the easiest operations to perform. To multiply fractions, simply multiply the numerators and the denominators, writing each in the respective place over or under the fraction bar.

Example:
$$\frac{4}{5} \times \frac{6}{7} = \frac{24}{35}$$

Dividing Fractions

Dividing fractions is the same thing as multiplying fractions by their **reciprocals**. To find the reciprocal of any number, switch its numerator and denominator. For example, the reciprocals of the following numbers are:

$$\frac{1}{3} \leftarrow \frac{3}{1} = 3$$

$$x \leftarrow \frac{1}{x}$$

$$\frac{4}{5} \leftarrow \frac{5}{4}$$

$$5 \leftarrow \frac{1}{5}$$

When dividing fractions, simply multiply the **dividend** (what is being divided) by the **divisor's** (what is doing the dividing) reciprocal to get the answer.

Example:
$$\frac{12}{21} \div \frac{3}{4} = \frac{12}{21} \times \frac{4}{3} = \frac{48}{63} = \frac{16}{21}$$

Adding and Subtracting Fractions

To add or subtract fractions with like denominators, just add or subtract the numerators and leave the denominator as it is. For example,

$$\frac{1}{7} + \frac{5}{7} = \frac{6}{7} \quad \text{and} \quad \frac{5}{8} - \frac{2}{8} = \frac{3}{8}$$

To add or subtract fractions with unlike denominators, you must find the **least common denominator**, or LCD.

For example, if given the denominators 8 and 12, 24 would be the LCD because $8 \times 3 = 24$ and $12 \times 2 = 24$. In other words, the LCD is the smallest number divisible by each of the denominators.

Once you know the LCD, convert each fraction to its new form by multiplying both the numerator and denominator by the necessary number to get the LCD, and then add or subtract the new numerators.

Example:
$$\frac{1}{3} + \frac{2}{5} = \frac{5(1)}{5(3)} + \frac{3(2)}{3(5)} = \frac{5}{15} + \frac{6}{15} = \frac{11}{15}$$

Percent

A **percent** is a measure of a part to a whole, with the whole being equal to 100.

- To change a decimal to a percentage, move the decimal point two units to the right and add a percent symbol.

  Examples:

  $.45 = 45\%$ $.07 = 7\%$ $.9 = 90\%$

- To change a fraction to a percentage, first change the fraction to a decimal. To do this, divide the numerator by the denominator. Then, change the decimal to a percentage.

  Examples:

  $\frac{4}{5} = .80 = 80\%$

  $\frac{2}{5} = .4 = 40\%$

  $\frac{1}{8} = .125 = 12.5\%$

- To change a percentage to a decimal, simply move the decimal point two places to the left and eliminate the percent symbol.

  Examples:

  $64\% = .64$ $87\% = .87$ $7\% = .07$

- To change a percentage to a fraction, divide by 100 and reduce.

  Examples:

  $64\% = \frac{64}{100} = \frac{16}{25}$

  $75\% = \frac{75}{100} = \frac{3}{4}$

  $82\% = \frac{82}{100} = \frac{41}{50}$

- Keep in mind that any percentage that is 100 or greater will need to reflect a whole number or mixed number when converted.

  Examples:

  $125\% = 1.25$ or $1\frac{1}{4}$

  $350\% = 3.5$ or $3\frac{1}{2}$

Here are some conversions you should be familiar with.

Fraction	Decimal	Percentage
$\frac{1}{2}$	.5	50%
$\frac{1}{4}$	.25	25%
$\frac{1}{3}$	.333 . . .	$33.\overline{3}$%
$\frac{2}{3}$	.666 . . .	$66.\overline{6}$%
$\frac{1}{10}$	.1	10%
$\frac{1}{8}$	.125	12.5%
$\frac{1}{6}$	.1666 . . .	$16.\overline{6}$%
$\frac{1}{5}$	.2	20%

Algebra Review

Equations

An **equation** is solved by finding a number that is equal to an unknown variable.

Simple Rules for Working with Equations

1. The equal sign separates an equation into two sides.
2. Whenever an operation is performed on one side, the same operation must be performed on the other side.
3. Your first goal is to get all the variables on one side and all the numbers on the other.
4. The final step often will be to divide each side by the coefficient, leaving the variable equal to a number.

Checking Equations

To check an equation, substitute the number equal to the variable in the original equation.

Example:

To check the equation below, substitute the number 10 for the variable x.

$$\frac{x}{6} = \frac{x+10}{12}$$

$$\frac{10}{6} = \frac{10+10}{12}$$

$$\frac{10}{6} = \frac{20}{12}$$

$$1\frac{2}{3} = 1\frac{2}{3} \qquad \frac{10}{6} = \frac{10}{6}$$

Because this statement is true, you know the answer $x = 10$ must be correct.

Special Tips for Checking Equations

1. If time permits, be sure to check all equations.
2. Be careful to answer the question that is being asked. Sometimes this involves solving for a variable and then performing an operation.

Example:
If the question asks the value of $x - 2$, and you find $x = 2$, the answer is not 2, but $2 - 2$. Thus, the answer is 0.

Algebraic Fractions

Algebraic fractions are very similar to fractions in arithmetic.

Example:
Write $\frac{x}{5} - \frac{x}{10}$ as a single fraction.

Solution:
Just like in arithmetic, you need to find the LCD of 5 and 10, which is 10. Then, change each fraction into an equivalent fraction that has 10 as a denominator.

$$\frac{x}{5} - \frac{x}{10} = \frac{x(2)}{5(2)} - \frac{x}{10}$$
$$= \frac{2x}{10} - \frac{x}{10}$$
$$= \frac{x}{10}$$

Geometry Review

Area	the space inside a two-dimensional figure
Circumference	the distance around a circle
Perimeter	the distance around a figure
Radius	the distance from the center point of a circle to any point on the circle

Area

Area is the space inside of the lines defining the shape.

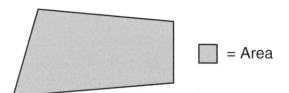

This geometry review will focus on the area formula for three main shapes: circles, rectangles/squares, and triangles.

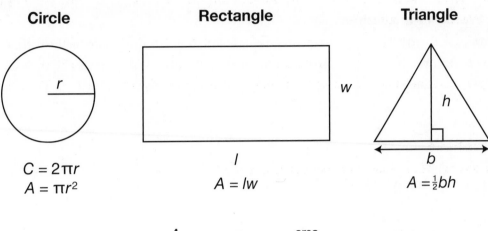

Circle	Rectangle	Triangle
$C = 2\pi r$		
$A = \pi r^2$	$A = lw$	$A = \frac{1}{2}bh$

A	=	area
r	=	radius
l	=	length
w	=	width
b	=	base
h	=	height
C	=	circumference
π	=	3.14

Perimeter

The **perimeter** of an object is simply the sum of all of its sides.

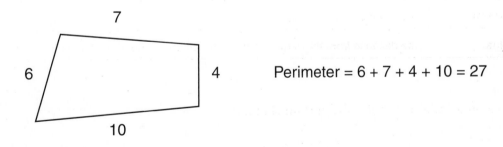

Perimeter = 6 + 7 + 4 + 10 = 27

The **circumference** is the perimeter of a circle.

$C = 2\pi r$

Word Problem Review

Because many of the math problems on the exam will be word problems, pay extra attention to the following review.

Translating Words into Numbers

The most important skill needed for word problems is being able to translate words into mathematical operations. The following will assist you by giving you some common examples of English phrases and their mathematical equivalents.

- "Increase" means add.

  Example:
  A number increased by five $= x + 5$

- "Less than" means subtract.

  Example:
  10 less than a number $= x - 10$

- "Times" or "product" means multiply.

  Example:
  Three times a number $= 3x$

- "Times the sum" means to multiply a number by a quantity.

  Example:
  Five times the sum of a number and three $= 5(x + 3)$

- Two variables are sometimes used together.

  Example:
  A number y exceeds 5 times a number x by 10
  $y = 5x + 10$

- "Of" means multiply.

  Example:
  10% of 100 is 10 $= 10\% \times 100 = 10$

- "Is" means equals.

Example:
15 is 14 plus 1
$15 = 14 + 1$

Assigning Variables in Word Problems

It may be necessary to create and assign variables in a word problem. To do this, first identify an unknown and a known. You may not actually know the exact value of the "known," but you will know at least something about its value.

Examples:
Max is three years older than Ricky.
Unknown = Ricky's age = x
Known = Max's age is three years older.
Therefore,
Ricky's age = x and Max's age = $x + 3$.

Heidi made twice as many cookies as Rebecca.
Unknown = number of cookies Rebecca made = x
Known = number of cookies Heidi made = $2x$

Jessica has five more than three times the number of books that Becky has.
Unknown = the number of books Becky has = x
Known = the number of books Jessica has = $3x + 5$

Percentage Problems

There is one formula that is useful for solving the three types of percentage problems:

$$\frac{\text{\# part}}{\text{whole}} = \frac{\% }{100}$$

When reading a percentage problem, substitute the necessary information into this formula based on the following:

- 100 is always written in the denominator of the percentage sign column.
- If given a percentage, write it in the numerator position of the number column. If you are not given a percentage, then the variable should be placed there.
- The denominator of the number column represents the number that is equal to the whole, or 100%. This number always follows the word *of* in a word problem.

- The numerator of the number column represents the number that is the percent.
- In the formula, the equal sign can be interchanged with the word *is*.

Examples:

- Finding a percentage of a given number:

What number is equal to 40% of 50?

$$\begin{array}{cc} \# & \% \\ \dfrac{x}{50} & = & \dfrac{40}{100} \end{array}$$

Cross multiply:

$$100(x) = (40)(50)$$
$$100x = 2{,}000$$
$$\frac{100x}{100} = \frac{2{,}000}{100}$$
$$x = 20 \quad \text{Therefore, 20 is 40\% of 50.}$$

- Finding a number when a percentage is given:

40% of what number is 24?

$$\begin{array}{cc} \# & \% \\ \dfrac{24}{x} & = & \dfrac{40}{100} \end{array}$$

Cross multiply:

$$(24)(100) = (40)(x)$$
$$2{,}400 = 40x$$
$$\frac{2{,}400}{40} = \frac{40x}{40}$$
$$60 = x \quad \text{Therefore, 40\% of 60 is 24.}$$

- Finding what percentage one number is of another:

What percentage of 75 is 15?

$$\begin{array}{cc} \# & \% \\ \dfrac{15}{75} & = & \dfrac{x}{100} \end{array}$$

$$\text{Rate} = \frac{x \text{ units}}{y \text{ units}}$$

A percentage problem simply means that *y* units is equal to 100. Remember that a percentage problem may be worded using the word *rate*.

Cross multiply:

$15(100) = (75)(x)$

$1,500 = 75x$

$\frac{1,500}{75} = \frac{75x}{75}$

$20 = x$ Therefore, 20% of 75 is 15.

Rate Problems

Rate is defined as a comparison of two quantities with different units of measure.

$$\text{Rate} = \frac{x \text{ units}}{y \text{ units}}$$

Examples: $\frac{\text{dollars}}{\text{square foot}}$, $\frac{\text{interest}}{\text{year}}$

Cost Per Unit

Some problems on your exam may require that you calculate the cost per unit.

Example:

If 100 square feet cost $1,000, how much does 1 square foot cost?

Solution:

$\frac{\text{total cost}}{\text{\# of square feet}} = \frac{\$1,000}{100} = \$10$ per square foot

Interest Rate

The formula for simple interest is Interest = Principal × Rate × Time, or $I = PRT$. If you know certain values but not others, you can still find the answer using algebra. In simple interest problems, the value of T is usually 1, as in one year. There are three basic kinds of interest problems, depending on which number is missing.

Here are some equivalencies you may need to use to complete some questions. Generally, any equivalencies you will need to know for your exam are provided to you.

Equivalencies

12 inches (in. or ") = 1 foot (ft. or ')

3 feet = 36 inches = 1 yard (yd.)

1,760 yards = 1 mile (mi.)

5,280 feet = 1 mile = approximately 0.6 kilometers (km)

144 square inches (sq. in. or in.^{2}) = 1 square foot (sq. ft. or ft.^{2})

9 square feet = 1 square yard

43,560 feet = 1 acre

640 acres = 1 square mile = 1 section (see illustration on page 155)

36 square miles = 36 sections = 1 township (see illustration on page 155)

Percents

You may be asked a basic percentage problem.

Example:
What is 86% of 1,750?

Solution:
Start by translating words into math terms.

$x = (86\%)(1,750)$

Change the percent into a decimal by moving the decimal point two spaces to the *left*.

86% = .86

Now you can solve.

$x = (.86)(1,750)$

$x = 1,505$

Other percentage problems you may find on the exam will come in the form of rate problems. Keep reading for more examples of these problems.

Interest Problems

Let's take a look at a problem in which you have calculate the interest rate (R). Remember, the rate is the same as the percentage.

Example:
Mary Valencia borrowed $5,000, for which she is paying $600 interest per year. What is the rate of interest being charged?

Solution:

Start with the values you know.

Principal = $5,000

Interest = $600

Rate = x

Time = 1 year

Using the formula $I = PRT$, insert the values you know and solve for x.

$600 = $5,000$(x)(1)$

$600 = $5,000$x$

$$\frac{\$600}{\$5,000} = \frac{x}{\$5,000}$$

$.12 = x$

To convert .12 to a percent, move the decimal point two places to the *right*.

$.12 = 12\%$

Principal and Interest

Sometimes, you will need to know the interest rate on a loan when the only information you have is the interest portion of the current payment and the principal balance. The formula is

$$\text{Principal Balance} \times \text{Interest Rate} = \text{Annual Interest Amount}$$

Example:

If the current principal balance is $300,000 and the amount of the payment applied to interest this month is $1,500, what is the interest rate?

Solution:

Move the variables in the equation around so that it reads:

$$\text{interest rate} = \frac{(\text{monthly interest} \times 12)}{\text{principal balance}}$$

$$\text{interest rate} = \frac{(\$1,500 \times 12)}{\$300,000}$$

$\text{interest rate} = .06$

So the interest rate is 6%.

Debt Service

You may be asked to calculate the total interest paid over the life of the mortgage.

Example:

If a mortgage loan is $150,000, the annual interest rate is 6.5%, the monthly payment is $948.10, and the term is 30 years, how much interest will the borrower pay over the life of the loan?

Solution:

First, calculate the total amount paid over the life of the mortgage.

term $\times$ 12 $\times$ monthly payment = total paid

$30 \times 12 \times \$948.10 = \$341,316$

Then, find the total interest paid.

total paid − principal = total interest paid

$\$341,316 − \$150,000 = \$191,316$

Private Mortgage Insurance (PMI)

Private mortgage insurance companies often charge an annual premium.

Example:

If the principal balance is $250,000 and the PMI company charges a .5% annual premium, what is the monthly PMI amount?

Solution:

The formula for the annual premium is principal balance $\times$ premium rate = annual premium.

$\$250,000 \times .005 = \$1,250$

To find the monthly PMI amount:

$$\frac{\text{annual premium}}{12} = \text{monthly PMI}$$

$$\frac{\$1,250}{12} = \$104.17$$

The monthly PMI portion of the payment is $104.17.

Discount Rate

The discount rate, or the internal rate of return, is the annual percentage increase in value of an investment.

Example:

Bob has been urged to buy a property for $150,000 because the expected value in seven years is $350,000. Bob wants to know what the annual increase will be.

Solution:

The formula for discount rate is:

$$r = \left(\frac{FV}{PV}\right)^{\frac{1}{n}} - 1$$

where

FV = future value

PV = present value

n = term

r = discount rate

So we set up the problem:

$$r = \left(\frac{\$350,000}{\$150,000}\right)^{\left(\frac{1}{7}\right)} - 1$$

$$r = (2.33)^{.1429} - 1$$

$$r = .1284$$

The return is 12.84% annually.

Area

Some of the problems on your exam may ask you to figure the area of a piece of land, a building, or some other figure. Here are some formulas and how to use them.

Rectangles

Remember the formula Area = (length)(width).

Example:

A man purchased a lot that is 50 feet by 10 feet for a garden. How many square feet of land does he have?

Solution:

Using the formula Area = (length)(width), you have

A = (50)(10) = 500 square feet

Example:

The Meyers family bought a piece of land for a summer home that was 2.75 acres. The lake frontage was 150 feet. What was the length of the lot?

Solution:

When you take your exam, you may be provided with certain equivalencies. You will need to refer to the "Equivalencies" list on page 136 to answer this question. First, find the area of the land in square feet.

$(2.75)(43,560) = 119,790$ square feet

In the previous example, you were given the length and the width. In this example, you are given the area and the width, so you are solving for the length. Because you know the area and the width of the lot, use the formula to solve.

Area = (length)(width)

$119,790 = (x)(150)$

Divide both sides by 150.

$\frac{119,790}{150} = \frac{(x)(150)}{150}$

$x = \frac{119,790}{150}$

$x = 798.6$ feet

Triangles

Although it may not be as common, you may be asked to find the area of a triangle. If you don't remember the formula, see page 131.

Example:

The Baron family is buying a triangular piece of land for a gas station. It is 200 feet at the base, and the side perpendicular to the base is 200 feet. They are paying $2 per square foot for the property. What will it cost?

Solution:

Start with the formula Area = $\frac{1}{2}$(base)(height).

Now, write down the values you know.

Area = x

Base = 200

Height = 200

If it's easier, you can change $\frac{1}{2}$ to a decimal.

$\frac{1}{2} = .5$

Now you can plug these values into the formula.

$x = (.5)(200)(200)$

$x = (.5)(40,000)$

$x = 20,000$ square feet

Don't forget that the question is not asking for the number of square feet, but for the *cost* of the property per square foot. This is a rate problem, so you need to complete one more step. (20,000 square feet)($2 per square foot) = $40,000.

Example:

Victor and Evelyn Robinson have an outlot that a neighbor wants to buy. The side of the outlot next to their property is 86 feet. The rear line is perpendicular to their side lot, and the road frontage is 111 feet. Their plat shows they own 3,000 square feet in the outlot. What is the length of the rear line of the outlot? Round your answer to the nearest whole number.

Solution:

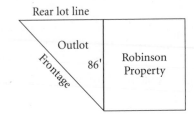

It helps to draw the figure to conceive shapes. The rear lot line is perpendicular to the side lot line. This makes the side lot line the base and the rear lot line the height (altitude).

Area = $\frac{1}{2}$(base)(height)

Area = 3,000 square feet

Base = 86 feet

Height = x

If it's easier, you can change $\frac{1}{2}$ to a decimal.

$\frac{1}{2} = .5$

Now you can plug these values into the formula.

$3,000 = (.5)(86)(x)$

$3,000 = (43)(x)$

Divide both sides by 43.

$\frac{3,000}{43} = \frac{(43)(x)}{43}$

$x = 69.767$ feet

Don't forget the question says to round your answer to the nearest whole number. The answer is 70 feet.

Circles

Remember the formula Area = πr^2.

Example:

Marie Brodman, a contractor, has been awarded the job to put up a circular bandstand in the town square. The radius of the circular area for the bandstand is 15 feet. What is the area of the bandstand? Use 3.14 for π.

Solution:

Area = πr^2

Start with the values you know.

Area = x

$\pi = 3.14$

radius = 15

Now plug these values into the formula.

Area = (3.14)(15)(15) = 706.5 sq. ft.

Property Tax

To solve property tax questions, you will be using percents and rates.

Example:

The tax rate in your county is $4.17 per hundred of assessed valuation, and Mr. Brown, a possible client, has told his broker that his taxes are $1,100. What is his property assessment? (Round your answer to the nearest 10 cents.)

Solution:

Start off with the values you know.

Taxes = $1,100

Assessment = x

Tax rate = $4.17 per hundred (%)

If you remember the definition of percent as being an amount per hundred, then $4.17 per hundred is actually 4.17%. To make this equation more manageable, convert this percent to a decimal by moving the decimal point two spaces to the *left*. Now the tax rate is .0417.

.0417 of the assessed value of the house is $1,100. Translate the words into math terms. This means: $(.0417)(x) = \$1,100$.

To solve the equation, divide both sides by .0417.

$$\frac{.0417x}{.0417} = \frac{\$1,100}{.0417}$$

$x = \$26,378.896$

Remember, the question asks you round to the nearest 10 cents. That means that .896 needs to be rounded up to 90. So the answer is $26,378.90.

Example:

Ms. Sassoon knew her own taxes were $975, and her property assessment was $17,000 for the house and $6,000 for the land. She wanted to know the tax rate (%).

Note that you may be asked for monthly amounts in certain problems. Most calculations are on an annual basis—unless you divide by 12.

Solution:

Start with the values you know.

Tax = $975

Assessment for house = $17,000 plus assessment for land = $6,000. Therefore, total = $23,000.

Rate (%) = x

According to the question, $23,000 at a rate of x is $975. Convert this statement into an equation.

($23,000)($x$) = $975.

Solve the equation by dividing both sides by $23,000.

$$\frac{\$23,000x}{\$23,000} = \frac{\$975}{\$23,000}$$

$x = .0423913$

To make this equation more simple, round the answer to .0424.

Remember that you are looking for the rate. Therefore, you need to convert this decimal to a percent by moving the decimal point two places to the *right*. The rate is 4.24%. (This can also be expressed as $4.24 per hundred.)

Loan-to-Value Ratios

These problems often deal with percentages.

Example:

A mortgage loan for 10% is at a 75% loan-to-value ratio. The interest on the original balance for the first year is $6,590. What is the value of the property securing the loan? Round to the nearest one cent.

Solution:

First, find out the loan amount.

$6,590 is 10% of the loan amount. Let x equal the loan amount. Now, translate these words into math terms.

$6,590 = (10%)($x$)

Change 10% into a decimal by moving the decimal point two places to the *left*.

10% = .1

Rewrite the equation with the decimal.

$6,590 = (.1)($x$)

Divide both sides by (.1).

$x = $65,900

Now that you know the loan amount ($65,900), use this information to find the value of the property.

Write down the values you know.

Loan amount = $65,900

Loan-to-value ratio = 75%

Value = x

We know that 75% of the value is $65,900.

Translate this into math terms.

$(75\%)(x) = \$65,900$

Change the percent into a decimal (75% = .75) and solve.

$(.75)(x) = \$65,900$

Divide both sides by .75.

$$\frac{(.75)(x)}{(.75)} = \frac{\$65,900}{(.75)}$$

$x = \$87,866.66666$

When rounded to the nearest one cent, the answer is $87,866.67.

Points

Loan discounts are often called **points**, or loan placement fees, one point meaning 1% of the face amount of the loan. The service fee of 1% paid by buyers of government-backed loans is called a **loan origination fee**.

Example:

A homebuyer may obtain a $50,000 FHA mortgage loan, provided the seller pays a discount of five points. What is the amount of the discount?

Solution:

The definition of one point is 1% of the face amount of the loan.

Therefore, five points = 5% of face of loan. First, change the percent to a decimal.

5% = .05

Now you can use these values to solve.

Amount of discount = x

Points = .05

Amount of loan = $50,000

So, $x = (.05)(\$50,000)$

$x = \$2,500$

Example:

A property is listed at $74,000. An offer is made for $72,000, provided the seller pays three points on a loan for 80% of the purchase price. The brokerage commission rate is 7%. How much less will the seller receive if she accepts the offer than she would have received if she sold at all cash at the original terms?

Solution:

Here are the values you know:

Sold for original terms—price	$74,000
Less 7% commission	− 5,180 (.07)($74,000) = $5,180
Seller's net	$68,820

This question becomes more difficult, because in order to find the seller's net on the offered price, you must calculate the discount. The provision is that the seller pays three points (or .03) on a loan for 80% (or .8) of the price.

Start by finding 80% of the price.

$(.8)($72,000) = $57,600$

Now, the points are applied to this amount. This means .03 of $57,600 is the discount.

So, $(.03)($57,600) = $ discount = $1,728.

You know these values:

Sold at offered terms—price	$72,000
Less 7% commission	− 5,040 (.07)($72,000) = $5,040
Less discount	− 1,728
Seller's net	$65,232

$72,000	Sales price		Net at original	$68,820
× .80	Loan-to-value ratio		Net at offered	− 65,232
$57,600	Loan amount		Difference	$ 3,588
× .03	Points			
$ 1,728	Discount			

Equity

Example:

If a homeowner has a first mortgage loan balance of $48,350, a second mortgage loan balance of $18,200, and $26,300 equity, what is the value of her home?

Solution:

In this case, the value of the home is determined by the total loan balance plus the equity. Add the three numbers to find the value of the home.

$48,350 loan balance + $18,200 loan balance + $26,300 = value of the home

$92,850 = value of the home

Qualifying Buyers

Example:

A buyer is obtaining a conventional loan that requires 29/33 ratios. He earns $66,000 a year and has a $1,350 monthly car payment. What is his maximum principle, interest, taxes, and insurance (PITI) payment?

a. $1,612.50

b. $1,812.50

c. $465

d. $2,475

Solution:

$66,000 divided by 12 = $5,500 monthly income

($5,500)(.29) = $1,595 front end qualifier

($5,500)(.33) = $1,815 − $1,350 debt = $465 back end qualifier

The maximum PITI is the lower of these two qualifiers, $465.

Prorations

At the time of settlement, there must be a reconciliation or adjustment of any monies owed by either party as of that date. The important fact to bear in mind is that *the party who used the service pays for it.* If you keep this firmly in mind, you will not have any difficulty deciding who to credit and who to debit.

Example:

Mr. Kim's taxes are $1,200 per year, paid in advance on a calendar year. He is settling on the sale of his house to Ms. Rasheed on August 1. Which of them owes how much to the other?

Solution:

Ask yourself some questions:

How many months has the seller paid for?	12	($1,200)
How many months has the seller used?	7	($700)
How many months should the seller be reimbursed for?	5	($500)
How many months will the buyer use?	5	($500)
How many months has the buyer paid for?	0	($0)
How many months should the buyer reimburse the seller for?	5	($500)

Credit Mr. Kim $500

Debit Ms. Rasheed $500

What would the answer be if the taxes were paid in arrears? In other words, the seller has used the service for seven months but hasn't paid anything. The buyer will have to pay it all at the end of the year. In that case, the seller owes the buyer for seven months, or $700.

In working proration problems, be sure you have the right dates when you subtract. Sometimes the termination date for the policy is not given, and the tendency is to subtract the date the policy was written from the date of settlement. This will not give you the unused portion. You must subtract the date of settlement from the date of termination of the policy, which will be exactly the same date one, three, or five years after written, depending on the term of the policy. Most problems use either a one- or three-year term.

Remember!

Use a 30-day month and a 360-day year in all calculations unless you are told otherwise. Assume a calendar year, unless a fiscal or school year is specified.

Commissions

Let's look at a commission problem. They are typically rate (percentage) problems.

Example:

Broker Roberts sold the Weisman house for $65,000. The total commission came to $4,000. What was Roberts's commission rate? Round to the nearest whole percent.

Solution:

You see the word *rate* and decide this is solved using percentages.

Start with the values you know.

Price of house = $65,000

Commission rate = x

Commission = $4,000

Now, translate the word problem into an equation.

$65,000x = $4,000

Divide both sides by $65,000.

$$x = \frac{\$4,000}{\$65,000}$$

$x = 0.061$

Convert the decimal to a percent by moving the decimal two places to the *right*. 0.061 becomes 6.1%.

Example:

An agent received a 3% commission on $\frac{1}{4}$ of her total sales. On the remainder, she received a 6% commission. What was her average commission for all of her sales?

Solution:

Start off by asking yourself: How many fourths (parts) were there? Four, naturally.

3%   6%   6%   6%

To find the average, you add up all the numbers, and divide by the number of items you add together. In this case, there are four numbers.

So, 3 + 6 + 6 + 6 = 21

And 21% ÷ 4 = 5.25%

Sale Proceeds

Example:

Broker Garcia was trying to list a house. The owner said he wanted to clear (net) $12,000 from the sale of the house. The balance of the mortgage was $37,000. It would cost about $1,200 to fix the house up to sell. How much would the owner have to sell the house for if 7% commission was included? (Round your answer to the nearest cent.)

Solution:

Use a chart to clarify the problem.

Expenses	In Dollars	In Percents
Seller's net	$12,000	
Loan balance	$37,000	
Repairs	$1,200	
Commission		%
	$50,200	7%

If the sales price is 100% and the commission is 7% of the sales price, all the remaining items added together must make 93% of the sales price. The place where most people go wrong is in not including the seller's net when adding the expenses. The seller's net has to come out of the sales price. (Where else would it come from?) Therefore, it is part of the remaining 93%. You now have a percentage problem. As always, convert your percents to decimals.

Start with the values you know:

Expenses = $50,200

Sales price = x

Seller's net, loan balance, repairs = .93 of sales price

.93 of the sales price is $50,200.

Convert this statement into an equation.

$(.93)(x) = \$50,200$

Divide both sides by .93.

$\frac{(.93)(x)}{.93} = \frac{\$50,200}{.93}$

$x = \frac{\$50,200}{.93}$

$x = \$53,978.4945$

Don't forget to round to the nearest cent!

$x = \$53,978.49$

Transfer Tax/Conveyance Tax/Revenue Stamps

Here is a transfer tax question.

Example:

A property is sold for \$135,800 in cash. The transfer tax is \$441.35. If transfer taxes are calculated per \$200 of value, what was the rate (per \$200) of the transfer tax?

Solution:

Start with the values you know.

Selling price = \$135,800

Transfer tax rate = x per \$200

Transfer tax = \$441.35

It's probably easiest to begin by dividing \$200 because the rate is calculated per \$200 of value.

So, $\frac{\$135,800}{\$200} = \$679$

You know that \$441.35 is some rate of \$679. Translate this into math terms.

$\$441.35 = (x)(\$679)$

Divide both sides by \$679.

$\frac{\$441.35}{(\$679)} = \frac{(x)(\$679)}{(\$679)}$

$.65 = x$

Therefore, the transfer tax rate is \$.65 per \$200.

Competitive Market Analyses (CMA)

To solve these problems, you will use measurements and other hypothetical features of the comparable property to arrive at a value. Remember, a CMA is not an appraisal.

Example:

If Building A measures 52' by 106' and Building B measures 75' by 85', how much will B cost if A costs \$140,000 and both cost the same per square foot to build?

Solution:

Area = (length)(width)

Area of Building A = (52)(106) = 5,512 square feet

Area of Building B = (75)(85) = 6,375 square feet

Cost of Building A per square foot = $\frac{\$140,000}{5,512}$ = $25.40

Cost of Building B = (6,375)($25.40) = $161,925

Example:

Carson's house (B), which is being appraised, is an exact twin of the houses on either side of it, built by the same builder at the same time. House A was appraised for $145,000, but it has a 14-by-20-foot garage, which was added at a cost of about $18 per square foot. House C recently sold for $143,000, with central air valued at $3,000. What would be a fair estimate of the value of Carson's house?

Solution:

Comparable C	$143,000
– Air Conditioning	– 3,000
	$140,000

Comparable A	$145,000	Garage: 14' × 20' = 280 sq. ft.
– Cost of Garage	– 5,040	280 sq. ft. × $18 = $5,040
	$139,960	

Answer: $140,000

Income Properties

Example:

An investor is considering the purchase of an income property generating a gross income of $350,000. Operating expenses constitute 70% of gross income. If the investor wants a return of 14%, what is the maximum she can pay?

Solution:

Gross income = $350,000

Expenses = 70% of gross income

Net income = Gross income – Expenses

Desired return = 14%

Maximum buyer can pay = x

This is a multistep problem. Start by calculating the expenses, but remember, you will need to stop to calculate the net income. First, change the percent to a decimal.

70% = .70

Now, you know that expenses are 70% of the gross income of $350,000. Change the words to mathematical terms.

Expenses = (.7)($350,000) = $245,000

Gross income – Expenses = Net income

$350,000 – $245,000 = $105,000

The buyer wants the net income ($105,000) to be 14% of what she pays for the property.

Change the percent to a decimal (14% = .14) and then convert this statement to an equation.

$150,000 = (.14)(x)

Divide both sides by .14.

$$\frac{\$150,000}{.14} = \frac{(.14)(x)}{.14}$$

$150,000 ÷ .14 = x

$750,000 = x

Depreciation

The straight-line method of depreciation spreads the total depreciation over the useful life of the building in equal annual amounts. It is calculated by dividing the replacement cost by the years of useful life left.

$$\frac{\text{replacement cost}}{\text{years of useful life}} = \text{annual depreciation}$$

The depreciation rate may be given or may have to be calculated by the straight-line method. This means dividing the total depreciation (100%) by the estimated useful life given for the building.

$$\frac{100\%}{\text{years of useful life}} = \text{depreciated rate}$$

If a building has 50 years of useful life left, the depreciation rate would be computed as follows:

$$\frac{100\%}{50} = 2\%$$

In other words, it has a 2% depreciation rate annually.

Example:

The replacement cost of a building has been estimated at $80,000. The building is 12 years old and has an estimated 40 years of useful life left. What can be charged to annual depreciation? What is the total depreciation for 12 years? What is the present value of this building?

Solution:

Calculate the annual depreciation.

$$\frac{\text{replacement cost}}{\text{years of useful life}} = \text{annual depreciation}$$

$$\frac{\$80,000}{40} = \$2,000$$

Find the total depreciation over 12 years.

Annual depreciation of $2,000 × 12 years = $24,000.

Find the current value: replacement − depreciation = current value

$80,000 − $24,000 = $56,000

▶ Compound Interest and Discount Factors

Before the era of spreadsheets and financial calculators, to solve many real estate problems, appraisers and other real estate professionals used published financial tables of compound interest, discount factors, and annuities, computed for different interest rates. On the next page you will find such a table, which you must use in conjunction with the following sections. These sections are a list and description of six of the basic financial functions of $1 and their formulas, computed for n years (1–30) years using and an annual interest rate i at 10%.

Future Value of $1 ($S^n$)

This function calculates the amount (FV) that a one-time investment (I_1) will grow to if the investment is allowed to compound at an interest rate, i, for n periods.

The formula is: $S^n = I_1(1 + i)^n$

Example:

What will an investment of $1,000 grow to if earning 10% per year for 15 years?

Solution:

Use the first column in the table and go to the row where $n = 15$, then take this number and multiply by $1,000: $4,177.248, or $4,177.25

Future Value Annuity of $1 Per Period

This function calculates the amount (FVA) that a series of regular investments (PMT) will grow to over a certain number of periods, n, if earning interest at a compound rate, i.

The formula is:

$$FVA = \frac{(1 + i)^n - 1}{i}$$

Example:

What will an investment of $10,000 ($PMT$) per year grow to in five years if the investment is earning 10% i per year compounded?

Annual Compound Interest Tables at 10% Annual Interest Rate

Years	Future Value of $1	Future Value Annuity of $1 Per Year	Sinking Fund Factor $1	Present Value or Reversion of $1	Present Value Annuity of $1	Payment to Fully Amortize $1
	Beginning	End	End	End	End	End
1	1.100000	1.000000	1.000000	0.909091	0.909091	1.100000
2	1.210000	2.100000	0.476190	0.826446	1.735537	0.576190
3	1.331000	3.310000	0.302115	0.751315	2.486852	0.402115
4	1.464100	4.641000	0.215471	0.683013	3.169865	0.315471
5	1.610510	6.105100	0.163797	0.620921	3.790787	0.263797
6	1.771561	7.715610	0.129607	0.564474	4.355261	0.229607
7	1.948717	9.487171	0.105405	0.513158	4.868419	0.205405
8	2.143589	11.435888	0.087444	0.466507	5.334926	0.187444
9	2.357948	13.579477	0.073641	0.424098	5.759024	0.173641
10	2.593742	15.937425	0.062745	0.385543	6.144567	0.162745
11	2.853117	18.531167	0.053963	0.350494	6.495061	0.153963
12	3.138428	21.384284	0.046763	0.318631	6.813692	0.146763
13	3.452271	24.522712	0.040779	0.289664	7.103356	0.140779
14	3.797498	27.974983	0.035746	0.263331	7.366687	0.135746
15	4.177248	31.772482	0.031474	0.239392	7.606080	0.131474
16	4.594973	35.949730	0.027817	0.217629	7.823709	0.127817
17	5.054470	40.544703	0.024664	0.197845	8.021553	0.124664
18	5.559917	45.599173	0.021930	0.179859	8.201412	0.121930
19	6.115909	51.159090	0.019547	0.163508	8.364920	0.119547
20	6.727500	57.274999	0.017460	0.148644	8.513564	0.117460
21	7.400250	64.002499	0.015624	0.135131	8.648694	0.115624
22	8.140275	71.402749	0.014005	0.122846	8.771540	0.114005
23	8.954302	79.543024	0.012572	0.111678	8.883218	0.112572
24	9.849733	88.497327	0.011300	0.101526	8.984744	0.111300
25	10.834706	98.347059	0.010168	0.092296	9.077040	0.110168
26	11.918177	109.181765	0.009159	0.083905	9.160945	0.109159
27	13.109994	121.099942	0.008258	0.076278	9.237223	0.108258
28	14.420994	134.209936	0.007451	0.069343	9.306567	0.107451
29	15.863093	148.630930	0.006728	0.063039	9.369606	0.106728
30	17.449402	164.494023	0.006079	0.057309	9.426914	0.106079

Solution:

Use the second column in the table and go to the row where $n = 5$, then take this number and multiply by $10,000: $61,051

Sinking Fund Factor of $1 Necessary to Produce a Required Amount in the Future

This function calculates how much money must be periodically invested or deposited (PMT) to achieve a specified amount in the future ($\frac{1}{S_n}$) given the interest rate, i, for a certain number of periods n.

The formula is: $\frac{1}{S_n} = \frac{i}{(1+i)^n - 1} = \frac{1}{FVA}$

Example:

How much must be deposited annually in an account earning compounding at a 10% i interest rate in order to have $20,000 at the end of 20 years?

Solution:

Use the third column in the table and go to the row where $n = 20$, then take this number and multiply by $20,000: $349.20

Present Value of $1

This function calculates today's present value (PV_n) for a single benefit (FV) in n periods in the future for a required interest (yield) rate, i.

The formula is: $PV_n = \frac{1}{(1+i)^n}$

Example:

How much must be paid for the right to receive $50,000 ($FV$) in 12 years if the required return is an annual yield, i, of 10%?

Solution:

Use the fourth column in the table and go to the row where $n = 12$, then take this number and multiply it by $50,000: $15,931.55

Present Value of $1 Per Period

This function calculates how much should be paid (PVA_n) for a series of benefits (an ordinary level annuity) to be received over a certain number of periods n in the future based on a required interest (yield) rate, i.

The formula is: $PVA_n = \dfrac{1 - \dfrac{1}{(1+i)^n}}{i}$

Example:

What is the present value PVA_n of an income stream of $5,000 per year for 20 years, n, worth today if the investor requires a 10% (i) annual yield?

Solution:

Use the fifth column in the table and go to the row where $n = 20$, then take this number and multiply it by $5,000: $42,567.82

Payments to Amortize $1

This function calculates how much must be periodically paid (*PMT*) to amortize a loan (*PV*) over n periods at a given interest rate, i.

The formula is: $PMT = \dfrac{i}{1 - \dfrac{1}{(1 + i)^n}} = \dfrac{1}{PVA_n}$

Example:

What annual mortgage payment (*PMT*) is required to amortize a $200,000 loan over 30 years (*n*) at an annual interest rate (*i*) of 10%?

Solution:

Use the sixth column in the table and go to the row where $n = 30$, then take this number and multiply by $200,000: $21,215.80

▶ Using a Rectangular Survey

The following list contains some important appraisal math constants to remember.

43,560 square feet = 1 acre

640 acres = 1 mile × 1 mile (1 square mile) = 1 section. See illustration that follows.

6 miles × 6 miles (36 square miles) contains 36 sections = 1 township. See illustration that follows.

**U.S. GOVERNMENT SURVEY
TOWNSHIP DIVIDED INTO SECTIONS**

6	5	4	3	2	1
7	8	9	10	11	12
18	17	16	15	14	13
19	20	21	22	23	24
30	29	28	27	26	25
31	32	33	34	35	36

6 miles

← 6 miles →

Example:

What is the section number due north of section number 16?

Solution:

The answer is section 9. The sections are numbered as if you were plowing a field—start in the upper-most right box and go left. When you get to the end of the field, go down and then go back to the right to the end of this row and so on.

Example:

What is the section number due east of section number 24?

The answer is section 19. Remember, the adjacent township is next to this section.

Example:

How many acres is the NW quarter of the SE quarter of section 16?

Solution:

You are given that each section comprises 640 acres, so first figure how many acres the SE quarter of the section would be.

.25 × 640 = 160 acres

Now figure out what the NW quarter of that section would be.

.25 × 160 = 40 acres

Example:

The following illustration is a more in-depth look at section 16, broken into 16 sections, labeled A–P. In which box would you find the 40 acres you solved for in the previous example and solution?

North

A	B	C	D
E	F	G	H
I	J	K	L
M	N	O	P

West   East

South

Solution:

You must locate this portion of the section by going backward. The SE quarter of this section contains portions K, L, O, P. The NW quarter portion of this group is K.

▶ Appraisal Statistics

Appraisers are often faced with the analysis of data. Following are five terms used in statistics of data. These terms measure the central tendency of the data analyzed.

Mean

The **mean** (average) of a group of numbers is the sum of these numerical values divided by the sample size (how many are in the population).

Example:

The values are as follows:

5, 10, 15, 20, 25

Solution:

Add the values:

(5 + 10 + 15 + 20 + 25) = 75

There are five values in the population, so divide by that number to find the mean:

$\frac{75}{5} = 15$

The mean, or average, is 15.

Mode

The **mode** of a group of numbers is the number that appears most often.

Example:

The values are as follows:

10, 15, 15, 15, 20, 25, 30

Solution:

The mode is 15 because in the set of values, it appears most often, or three times.

Example:

The values are as follows:

10, 15, 20, 20, 25, 25, 30

Solution:

The modes are 20 and 25. Because this particular set of values has two modes, it is known as **bimodal**.

Example:

The values are as follows:

5, 10, 15, 20, 25, 30, 35

Solution:

There is no mode; therefore, all numbers are equally likely.

Median

The **median** of a sample is the number or numbers where half the population is above and half is below in the value set.

Example:

The values are as follows:

10, 20, 40, 50, 30, 70, 60

Solution:

To find the median, first rearrange the numbers in numerical order:

10, 20, 30, **40**, 50, 60, 70

The median is 40.

Example:

The values are as follows:

10, 20, 40, 50, 30, 60

Solution:

First, rearrange the numbers in numerical order:

10, 20, **30**, **40**, 50, 60

If the sample size is even as it is here, take the average of the two middle numbers:

$$\frac{40 + 30}{2} = 35$$

The median is 35.

Range

The range of the data set is the difference between the largest and smallest numbers in the set.

> *Example:*
> The values are as follows:
> **10**, 20, 30, 40, 50, 60, **70**

> *Solution:*
> To find the range, subtract the smallest number from the largest.
> $70 - 10 = 60$
> The range is 60.

Standard Deviation

The standard deviation is the root mean square (RMS) deviation of the values from their arithmetic mean.

> *Example:*
> The values are as follows:
> 10, 20, 30

> *Solution:*
> First, find the mean:
> $(10 + 20 + 30) \div 3 = 60 \div 3 = 20$
> Then, plug the values into the standard deviation formula:
> Standard deviation = Square root of $[(10 - 20)^2 + (20 - 20)^2 + (30 - 20)^2]$
> = Square root of $[(10)^2 + (0)^2 + (10)^2]$
> = Square root of $[200] = 14.142$

▶ Summary

Hopefully, with this review, you have realized that real estate math is not as bad as you might have imagined. If you feel you need more practice, check out LearningExpress's *Practical Math Success in 20 Minutes a Day, 3rd Edition* or *1,001 Math Problems, 2nd Edition*. Use the exams in those books to practice even more real estate math.

7 ▶ Real Estate Glossary

CHAPTER SUMMARY

One of the most basic components in preparing for your appraisal exam is making sure you know all the terminology. This glossary provides a list of the most commonly used real estate terms and their definitions.

THESE TERMS WILL help you not only as you study for your appraisal exam, but also after you pass your exam and are on the job every day. The terms are listed in alphabetical order for easy reference.

▶ **A**

abandonment the voluntary surrender of a right, claim, or interest in a piece of property without naming a successor as owner or tenant.

absorption rate an estimate of the rate at which a particular classification of properties for sale or lease can be successfully marketed in a given area; it is often requested in a feasibility study or an appraisal in connection with a request for financing.

abstract of title a certified summary of the history of a title to a particular parcel of real estate that includes the original grant and all subsequent transfers, encumbrances, and releases.

abstraction sometimes known as the *extraction* or *allocation* method; a method of valuing land in which the appraiser estimates ratios of land values to total property value. This ratio is typically determined from comparable sales data.

abutting sharing a common boundary; adjoining.

acceleration clause a clause in a note, mortgage, or deed of trust that permits the lender to declare the entire amount of principal and accrued interest due and payable immediately in the event of default.

acceptance the indication by a party receiving an offer that they agree to the terms of the offer. In most states, the offer and acceptance must be reduced to writing when real property is involved.

access the means of physical entrance into or upon a property.

accessibility the ease with which a person can enter or exit a particular tract of land.

accession the transfer of ownership of fixtures or land as a result of the attachment of those fixtures or land to another property.

accretion the increase or addition of land resulting from the natural deposit of sand or soil by streams, lakes, or rivers.

accrued depreciation the difference between an improvement's reproduction or replacement cost and its market value as of the date of appraisal. It represents the total depreciation accumulated since the improvement was constructed.

accrued items a list of expenses that have been incurred but have not yet been paid, such as interest on a mortgage loan, that are included on a closing statement.

accumulated depreciation see *accrued depreciation*.

acknowledgment a formal declaration before a public official, usually a notary public, by a person who has signed a deed, contract, or other document that the execution was a voluntary act.

acre a measure of land equal to 43,560 square feet or 4,840 square yards. There are 640 acres of land in a section.

actual age also known as *chronological* or *historical age*; the number of years that have elapsed since construction was completed.

actual eviction the result of legal action brought by a landlord against a defaulted tenant, whereby the tenant is physically removed from rented or leased property by a court order.

actual notice the actual knowledge that a person has of a particular fact.

addendum any provision added to a contract, or an addition to a contract that expands, modifies, or enhances the clarity of the agreement. To be a part of the contract and legally enforceable, an addendum must be referenced within the contract.

adjacent lying near but not necessarily in actual contact with.

adjacent land land physically located close to or near another parcel of land.

adjoining contiguous or attached; in actual contact with.

adjustable-rate mortgage (ARM) a mortgage in which the interest changes periodically, according to corresponding fluctuations in an index. All ARMs are tied to indexes. For example, a seven-year, adjustable-rate mortgage is a loan in which the rate remains fixed for the first seven years, and then fluctuates according to the index to which it is tied.

adjusted basis the original cost of a property, plus acquisition costs, plus the value of added improvements to the property, minus accrued depreciation.

adjusted sales price the estimated sales price of a comparable property after additions and/or subtractions have been made to the actual sales price to allow for differences between the comparable and the subject property.

adjustment date the date the interest rate changes on an adjustable-rate mortgage.

adjustments the dollar value or percentage amounts added to or subtracted from the sales price of a comparable property, to arrive at an indicated value for the property being appraised (subject property). Real estate elements of comparison are typically adjusted in the following order: property rights, financing terms, conditions of sale, market conditions, location, and physical characteristics.

administrator a person appointed by a court to settle the estate of a person who has died without leaving a will.

ad valorem tax tax in proportion to the value of a property. Real property tax is an *ad valorem* tax based on the assessed valuation of the property.

adverse possession a method of acquiring title to another person's property through court action after taking actual, open, hostile, and continuous possession for a statutory period of time; may require payment of property taxes during the period of possession.

advocacy the act of supporting an idea, cause, or interest of another.

affidavit a written statement made under oath and signed before a licensed public official, usually a notary public.

after-tax cash flow (ATCF) the cash flow remaining after debt service and ordinary income tax on operations are subtracted from net operating income.

Age Discrimination in Employment Act of 1967 a law that protects individuals 40 years of age and older from discrimination.

agency the legal relationship between principal and agent that arises out of a contract wherein an agent is employed to do certain acts on behalf of the principal, who has retained the agent to deal with a third party.

agent one who has been granted the authority to act on behalf of another.

agreement of sale a written agreement between a seller and a purchaser whereby the purchaser agrees to buy a certain piece of property from the seller for a specified price.

air rights the right to use the open space above a particular property.

alienation the transfer of ownership of a property to another, either voluntarily or involuntarily.

alienation clause the clause in a mortgage or deed of trust that permits the lender to declare all unpaid principal and accrued interest due and payable if the borrower transfers title to the property.

allocation a method to determine site value by treating the land as a percent of the total property value (site value to total property value ratio). See *abstraction*.

allodial system a system of land ownership in the United States in which land is held free and clear of any rent or services due to the government; commonly contrasted with the feudal system, in which ownership is held by a monarch.

amendment the process of changing one zoning classification to another.

amenities features or benefits of a particular property that enhance the property's desirability and value, such as a scenic view or a pool.

Americans with Disabilities Act (ADA) federal legislation designed to integrate people with disabilities fully into the mainstream of American life.

amortization the method of repaying a loan or debt by making periodic installment payments composed of both principal and interest. When all principal has been repaid, it is considered fully amortized.

amortization schedule a table that shows how much of each loan payment will be applied toward principal and how much toward interest over the lifespan of the loan. It also shows the gradual decrease of the outstanding loan balance until it reaches zero.

amortize to repay a loan through regular payments that consist of principal and interest.

anchor tenant the major tenant in a shopping center that attracts or generates foot traffic. In a neighborhood center, the anchor is usually the supermarket and/or drugstore, while in a regional mall, the anchor is a regional or national major chain or department store.

annual debt service the total mortgage payments required in one year in regard to a particular loan.

annual loan constant the ratio of annual debt service or yearly loan payment to the original principal on the loan.

annual percentage rate (APR) the total or effective amount of interest charged on a loan, expressed as a percentage, on a yearly basis. This value is created according to a government formula intended to reflect the true annual cost of borrowing.

annuity a series of periodic equal cash flows.

anticipation the appraisal principle that states that value is created by the expectation of benefits to be received in the future and is the basis of the income approach.

anti-deficiency laws laws used in some states to limit the claim of a lender on default on payment of a purchase money mortgage on owner-occupied residential property to the value of the collateral.

anti-trust laws laws designed to protect free enterprise and the open marketplace by prohibiting certain business practices that restrict competition. In reference to real estate, these laws would prevent such practices as price fixing or agreements by brokers to limit their areas of trade.

apportionments adjustment of income, expenses, or carrying charges related to real estate, usually computed to the date of closing so that the seller pays all expenses to date, and then the buyer pays all expenses beginning on the closing date.

appraisal an estimate or opinion of the value of an adequately described property, as of a specific date.

appraisal practice valuation services conducted by a qualified real estate appraiser.

appraisal principles concepts that provide the rationale of market behavior, which affects value. Appraisal principles include anticipation, change, supply and demand, substitution, and balance.

appraisal process the step-by-step analysis undertaken by an appraiser for the purpose of accurately estimating an opinion of value.

appraisal report a report, written or oral, that contains the results of an appraisal assignment. See the USPAP Standard 10.

appraisal review the act or process of developing and communicating an opinion about the quality of another appraiser's work. The subject of an appraisal review assignment may be all or part of a report, workfile, or a combination of these.

appraiser a professional who conducts valuation services in a competent, ethical, and impartial manner.

appreciation an increase in the market value of a property.

approaches to value various methods typically used by an appraiser in preparing an appraisal report. Of the three traditional approaches to value, the *cost approach* bases value on the reproduction or replacement cost of improvements, less depreciation, plus the value of the land. The *income approach* bases value on the capitalization of future cash flows, from a property, at an acceptable market rate. The *market approach* (or sale comparison) bases value on a comparative analysis of recent sales prices of similar properties, after making adjustments for seller concessions, time, and any difference in properties.

appurtenances items that have been affixed to a property and thus have become an inherent part of the property. Such items usually pass with the property when title is transferred, even though they are not part of the property (e.g., easements, water rights, condominium parking stalls).

arbitration the process of settling a dispute in which the parties submit their differences to an impartial third party, whose decision on the matter is binding.

ARELLO the Association of Real Estate License Law Officials.

arm's-length transaction a transaction occurring in a competitive market, with reasonable exposure, under conditions requisite to a fair sale with a willing buyer and seller each acting prudently, knowledgeably, and for self-interest. An arm's-length transaction assumes that neither buyer nor seller is under undue duress or is related.

asking price the price at which the owner offers to sell the property.

assemblage in appraising real property, the combining of parcels, usually but not necessarily contiguous, into one ownership or use. When appraising personal property, the combining of properties (e.g., items or components) into units, sets, or groups. When appraising business enterprises, the integration or combination under unified control of business entities.

assessed value the value or worth of a property on which *ad valorem* taxes are based. Assessed value times rate equals the property tax.

assessment the process of assigning value on property for taxation purposes.

assessment ratio the ratio of the assessed value to full market value as set by the taxing authority.

assessor a public official who establishes the value of a property for taxation purposes.

asset an item of value owned by an individual. Assets that can be quickly converted into cash are considered liquid assets, such as bank accounts and stock portfolios. Other assets include real estate, personal property, and debts owed.

assignment (1) a valuation service provided by an appraiser for a client. (2) The transfer of all the lessee's rights to another party. The assignor is still liable for the performance of the agreement, unless the lessor releases him or her.

assignment result the opinions and conclusions reached by an appraiser for an assignment.

assumption a written agreement in which the buyer will pay the mortgage and is obligated to the seller. The seller may still be liable to the lender.

assumption of mortgage the act of acquiring the title to a property that has an existing mortgage and agreeing to be liable for the payment of any debt still existing on that mortgage. However, the lender must accept the transfer of liability for the original borrower to be relieved of the debt.

attachment the process whereby a court takes custody of a debtor's property until the creditor's debt is satisfied.

attest to bear witness by providing a signature.

attorney-in-fact a person who is authorized under a power of attorney to act on behalf of another.

avulsion the removal of land from one owner to another when a stream or other body of water suddenly changes its channel.

▶ **B**

balance the appraisal principle that states that property value is a function of contrasting, opposing, or interacting elements and their state of equilibrium.

balloon mortgage a loan in which the periodic payments do not fully amortize the loan, so that a final payment (a balloon payment) is substantially larger than the amount of the periodic payments that must be made to satisfy the debt.

balloon payment the final, lump-sum payment that is due at the termination of a balloon mortgage.

band of investment an appraisal technique used in the income approach, where the overall rate is derived from the weighted-average rates attributable to the components of the capital investment. The technique can be based on mortgage-equity components or land-building components. *Note*: The term is often used to refer only to the mortgage-equity approach. In this case, the overall rate is found by a weighted average of the mortgage loan constant and the equity dividend rate.

bankruptcy an individual or individuals can restructure or relieve themselves of debts and liabilities by filing in federal bankruptcy court. There are many types of bankruptcies, and the most common for an individual is Chapter 7 No Asset, which relieves the borrower of most types of debt.

bargain and sale deed a deed that conveys title, but does not necessarily carry warranties against liens or encumbrances.

base rent the minimum rent stipulated in the lease. Many times, it is the initial rent in the lease.

baseline one of the imaginary east-west lines used as a reference point when describing property with the rectangular or government survey method of property description.

basis point one-hundredth of 1%; used to indicate a change in the interest rate. Hence, if the interest increases from 8% to 8.5%, this is an increase in 50 basis points.

before-tax cash flow (BTCF) also referred to as *pretax cash flow*; the cash flow remaining after deduction of debt service (principal and interest) and any other cash outflows from net operating income. BTCF considers all cash flows that could affect the investor, except federal income tax. For example, leasing commissions and the cost of tenant improvements would be subtracted when calculating BTCF.

benchmark a permanently marked point with a known elevation, used as a reference by surveyors to measure elevations.

beneficiary (1) one who benefits from the acts of another; (2) the lender in a deed of trust.

bequest personal property given by provision of a will.

betterment an improvement to property that increases its value.

bias a prejudicial partiality or inclination that obstructs objective consideration of an appraisal question.

bilateral contract a contract in which each party promises to perform an act in exchange for the other party's promise to also perform an act.

bill of sale a written instrument that transfers ownership of personal property. A bill of sale cannot be used to transfer ownership of real property, which is passed by deed.

binder an agreement, accompanied by an earnest money deposit, for the purchase of a piece of real estate to show the purchaser's good faith intent to complete a transaction.

biweekly mortgage a mortgage in which payments are made every two weeks instead of once a month. Therefore, instead of making 12 monthly payments during the year, the borrower makes the equivalent of 13 monthly payments. The extra payment reduces the principal, thereby reducing the time it takes to pay off a 30-year mortgage.

blanket mortgage a mortgage in which more than one parcel of real estate is pledged to cover a single debt.

blockbusting the illegal and discriminatory practice of inducing homeowners to sell their properties by suggesting or implying the introduction of members of a protected class into the neighborhood.

bona fide in good faith, honest.

bond evidence of personal debt secured by a mortgage or other lien on real estate.

book depreciation the amount of capital recapture charged on an owner's books.

book value the amount at which property is carried on the books of a company. Usually equal to the original cost, less accounting depreciation, plus any addition to the capital.

boot money or property provided to make up a difference in value or equity between two properties in an exchange.

branch office a place of business secondary to a principal office. The branch office is a satellite office generally run by a licensed broker, for the benefit of the broker running the principal office, as well as the associate broker's convenience.

breach of contract violation of any conditions or terms in a contract without legal excuse.

broker the term *broker* can mean many things, but in terms of real estate, it is the owner-manager of a business that brings together the parties to a real estate transaction for a fee. The roles of brokers and brokers' associates are defined by state law. In the mortgage industry, *broker* usually refers to a company or individual who does not lend the money for the loans directly, but that brokers loans to larger lenders or investors.

brokerage the business of bringing together buyers and sellers or other participants in a real estate transaction.

broker's price opinion (BPO) a broker's opinion of value based on a comparative market analysis, rather than a certified appraisal.

buffer zone geographic areas used to physically separate two incompatible uses.

building capitalization rate (R_B) the ratio of the building income to the building value. In the income approach to value, the rate is used in both the band of investment and residual techniques to convert income into estimated value.

building codes rules and ordinances created by a municipal government to regulate the design, construction, quality, use, occupancy, location, and maintenance of buildings to provide minimum standards to safeguard the public's welfare. Building codes are a part of a state's police power and are enforced by inspection and the issuance of building permits and certificates of occupancy.

building line the distance from the front, rear, or sides of a building lot beyond which no structures may extend.

building ratio the ratio of building value to total property value; used in band of investment techniques in the income approach to appraisal.

building residual technique a method used to find property value in the income approach, when the value of land and net operating income are known. The income attributable to land is subtracted from the net operating income. This figure is then capitalized and added to the land value to estimate the property value.

building restrictions limitations listed in zoning ordinances or deed restrictions on the size and type of improvements allowed on a property.

bundle of rights the concept that ownership of a property includes certain rights regarding the property, such as possession, enjoyment, control of use, and disposition.

buydown usually refers to a fixed-rate mortgage where the interest rate is bought down for a temporary period, usually one to three years. After that time and for the remainder of the term, the borrower's payment is calculated at the note rate. In order to buy down the initial rate for the temporary payment, a lump sum is paid and held in an account used to supplement the borrower's monthly payment. These funds usually come from the seller as a financial incentive to induce someone to buy their property.

buyer's broker real estate broker retained by a prospective buyer; this buyer becomes the broker's client to whom fiduciary duties are owed.

bylaws rules and regulations adopted by an association—for example, a condominium association.

► **C**

cancellation clause a provision in a lease that confers on one or all parties to the lease the right to terminate the parties' obligations, should the occurrence of the condition or contingency set forth in the clause happen.

canvassing the practice of searching for prospective clients by making unsolicited phone calls and/or visiting homes door to door.

cap the limit on fluctuation rates regarding ARMs. Limitations, or caps, may apply to how much the loan may adjust over a six-month period, an annual period, and the life of the loan. There is also a limit on how much that payment can change each year.

cap rate abbreviation for capitalization rate.

capital money used to create income, or the net worth of a business as represented by the amount by which its assets exceed its liabilities.

capital expenditure the cost of a betterment to a property.

capital gains tax a tax charged on the profit gained from the sale of a capital asset.

capitalization a technique used in the income approach to convert income into an estimate of value. See *direct capitalization* and *yield capitalization*.

capitalization rate a rate used in the income approach to convert income to value.

capitalize in appraisal, the process of determining an estimate of value based on the income produced by the property. The value can be estimated by yield capitalization, or by direct capitalization.

cash equivalency analysis the procedure in which the sales prices of comparable properties with atypical financing terms are adjusted to reflect typical market terms.

cash flow the net income produced by an investment property, calculated by deducting operating and fixed expenses from gross income.

cash flow analysis a study of the anticipated movement of cash into or out of an investment.

cash-on-cash return (RE) see *equity dividend rate*.

caveat emptor a Latin phrase meaning "let the buyer beware."

CC&R covenants, conditions, and restrictions of a cooperative or condominium development.

central business district (CBD) a city's downtown area, which contains business and governmental activities (e.g., City Hall) of the area.

certificate of discharge a document used when the security instrument is a mortgage.

certificate of eligibility a document issued by the Veterans Administration (VA) that certifies a veteran's eligibility for a VA loan.

certificate of reasonable value (CRV) a document issued by the VA once the appraisal has been performed on a property being bought with a VA loan.

certificate of sale the document given to a purchaser of real estate that is sold at a tax foreclosure sale.

certificate of title a report stating an opinion on the status of a title, based on the examination of public records.

chain of title the recorded history of conveyances and encumbrances that affect the title to a parcel of land.

change the appraisal principle that states that the cause and effect of economic and social forces are constantly causing property values to be in transition.

chattel mortgage a loan in which personal property is pledged to secure the debt.

chattels real all interests in real estate that do not constitute a freehold estate in land, such as a leasehold estate.

chronological age the actual or true age of an item.

city a large municipality governed under a charter and granted by the state.

Civil Rights Act of 1964 (Title VII) law that prohibits employment discrimination based on race, color, sex, or national origin.

Civil Rights Act of 1991 law that provides monetary damages for intentional employment discrimination.

clear title a title that is free of liens and legal questions as to ownership of a property that is a requirement for the sale of real estate; sometimes referred to as *just title*, *good title*, or *free and clear*.

client a person or group that uses the services of an appraiser for an assignment.

closing the point in a real estate transaction when the purchase price is paid to the seller and the deed to the property is transferred from the seller to the buyer.

closing costs there are two kinds: (1) nonrecurring closing costs and (2) prepaid items. Nonrecurring closing costs are any items paid once as a result of buying the property or obtaining a loan. Prepaid items are items that recur over time, such as property taxes and homeowners insurance. A lender makes an attempt to estimate the amount of nonrecurring closing costs and prepaid items on the good faith estimate, which is issued to the borrower within three days of receiving a home loan application.

closing date the date on which the buyer takes over the property.

closing statement a written accounting of funds received and disbursed during a real estate transaction. The buyer and seller receive separate closing statements.

cloud on the title an outstanding claim or encumbrance that can affect or impair the owner's title.

clustering the grouping of home sites within a subdivision on smaller lots than normal, with the remaining land slated for use as common areas.

codicil a supplement or addition to a will that modifies the original instrument.

coinsurance clause a clause in an insurance policy that requires the insured to pay a portion of any loss experienced.

collateral something of value hypothecated (real property) or pledged (personal property) by a borrower as security for a debt.

collection when a borrower falls behind, the lender contacts the borrower in an effort to bring the loan current.

collection loss a loss in income when payment from tenants is not collected.

color of title an instrument that gives evidence of title, but may not be legally adequate to convey title.

Commercial Mortgage Backed Securities (CMBS) securities issued to investors backed by pools of commercial mortgages.

commercial property property used to produce income, such as an office building or a restaurant.

commingling the illegal act of an agent mixing a client's monies, which should be held in a separate escrow account, with the agent's personal monies; in some states, commingling also means placing funds that are separate property in an account containing funds that are community property.

commission the fee paid to a broker for services rendered in a real estate transaction.

commitment letter a pledge in writing affirming an agreement.

common areas portions of a building, land, and amenities owned (or managed) by a planned unit development or condominium project's homeowners association or a cooperative project's cooperative corporation. These areas are used by all of the unit owners, who share in the common expenses of their operation and maintenance. Common areas may include swimming pools, tennis courts, and other recreational facilities, as well as common corridors of buildings, parking areas, and lobbies.

common elements the part of the land and buildings in a condominium form of ownership that is jointly owned and used with other unit owners.

common law the body of laws derived from local custom and judicial precedent.

community property a system of property ownership in which each spouse has equal interest in property acquired during the marriage; recognized in nine states.

comparable also known as *comps*; properties used to determine an estimate of value for a subject property. Such properties have been recently sold or leased and are similar to the property being evaluated. The comparable need not be identical to the subject, but should be similar or relatively easy to adjust for differences in comparison.

comparable sales recent sales of similar properties in nearby areas that are used to help estimate the current market value of a property.

comparative unit method method used to estimate building costs in which components of the building are summed on a unit basis, such as dollars per square foot or cubic foot of area, and are based on known costs of similar structures adjusted for time and physical differences.

competent parties people who are legally qualified to enter a contract, usually meaning that they are of legal age, of sound mind, and not under the influence of drugs or other mind-altering substances.

competition an appraisal principle that states that competition is a function of supply and demand.

competitive market analysis (CMA) an analysis intended to assist a seller or buyer in determining a property's range of value.

concessions service or discount given to prospective tenants to induce them to lease the property. Concession includes things such as tenant improvements paid by the landlord or free rent.

condemnation the judicial process by which the government exercises its power of eminent domain.

condition of sale element of comparison in the sales comparison approach that refers to the motivation of the buyer and seller in a sales transaction. Examples include the relationship between buyer and seller, financial needs of the buyer and seller (a "quick" sale), and lack of exposure on the market.

conditional use, or special use permission granted for special or conditional land use (e.g., church, hospital) in specific zones. These uses require special permits.

condominium a form of ownership in which an individual owns a specific unit in a multiunit building and shares ownership of common areas with other unit owners.

condominium conversion changing the ownership of an existing building (usually a multi-dwelling rental unit) from single ownership to condominium ownership.

conformity an appraisal principle that asserts that property achieves its maximum value when a neighborhood is homogeneous in its use of land; the basis for zoning ordinances.

consideration something of value that induces parties to enter into a contract, such as money or services.

consistent use principle that states land must be valued for the same use as its improvements.

construction mortgage a short-term loan used to finance the building of improvements to real estate.

constructive eviction action or inaction by a landlord that renders a property uninhabitable, forcing a tenant to move out with no further liability for rent.

constructive notice notice of a fact given by making the fact part of the public record. All persons are responsible for knowing the information, whether or not they have actually seen the record.

consumer price index (CPI) a statistical measure of the change in price levels of a predetermined mix of consumer goods and services. The CPI is often used as a means for annual rental adjustments to the lease from the initial base rent.

consumer price index (CPI) adjustment an adjustment used in leases in which the rent payment is periodically adjusted by a percentage increase in the CPI. These adjustments are used to protect the lessor (landlord) from inflation increases.

contingency a condition that must be met before a contract is legally binding. A satisfactory home inspection report from a qualified home inspector is an example of a common type of contingency.

contiguous lots lots that are touching.

contract an agreement between two or more legally competent parties to do or to refrain from doing some legal act in exchange for a consideration.

contract for deed a contract for the sale of a parcel of real estate in which the buyer makes periodic payments to the seller and receives title to the property only after all, or a substantial part, of the purchase price has been paid, or regular payments have been made for one year or longer.

contract rent the actual rent specified in a lease.

contractor's overhead direct costs other than the costs of materials and labor (job supervision costs, contractors insurance, and worker's compensation).

contribution appraisal principle that states the worth of a particular component is measured by the amount it contributes to the value of the whole property, regardless of the actual cost of the component; the value of the component may be measured as the amount by which its absence would detract from the entire property value.

conventional loan a loan that is neither insured nor guaranteed by an agency of government.

conversion transformation of an income-producing property into another use, or changing from an apartment complex to a condominium.

conversion option an option in an adjustable-rate mortgage to convert it to a fixed-rate mortgage.

convertible ARM an adjustable-rate mortgage that allows the borrower to change the ARM to a fixed-rate mortgage at a specific time.

conveyance the transfer of title from the grantor to the grantee.

cooperative a form of property ownership in which a corporation owns a multiunit building and stockholders of the corporation may lease and occupy individual units of the building through a proprietary lease.

corner influence corner sites may have higher or lower value. Corner influence tables will determine the effect on value.

corporation a type of company with multiple ownership governed by a corporate charter. Two types of corporations are C-corporations and S-corporations.

cost approach one of three traditional approaches to value in appraisal theory. In the cost approach, value is based on the estimated land value plus the current cost to reproduce or replace the existing structure, deducting for all accrued depreciation in the property.

cost service index an adjustment in the subject improvement cost from the original cost to the current cost.

counteroffer an offer submitted in response to an offer. It has the effect of overriding the original offer.

credit an agreement in which a borrower receives something of value in exchange for a promise to repay the lender.

credit history a record of an individual's repayment of debt.

cul-de-sac a dead-end street that widens at the end, creating a circular turnaround area.

curable functional obsolescence a defect caused by a flaw in the structure, material, or design in which the cost to cure the item is less than or the same as the anticipated increase in value after the item is cured.

curable physical deterioration an item in need of repair; deferred maintenance. To be curable, the cost of curing the item must be reasonable and economically feasible.

curtesy the statutory or common law right of a husband to all or part of real estate owned by his deceased wife, regardless of will provisions, recognized in some states.

curtilage area of land occupied by a building, its outbuildings, and yard, either actually enclosed or considered enclosed.

▶ **D**

damages the amount of money recoverable by a person who has been injured by the actions of another.

date of the report date of the transmittal letter of a written report or the date a written report lacking a transmittal letter is prepared by the appraiser. The date of an oral report is the date it is communicated to or for the client. The date of the report may or may not be the same as the effective date of the appraisal.

date of value date at which the value of the property is estimated in the appraisal report. *It is not always the same as the date of the report* and can be retrospective (past), current, or prospective (future).

datum a specific point used in surveying.

DBA the abbreviation for "doing business as."

debt an amount owed to another.

debt coverage ratio (DCR) the annual net operating income divided by the annual debt service; often used as a criterion in underwriting income property loans.

debt equity ratio the relationship between the total amount of the loan and the invested capital (equity) of the owner(s).

debt service the dollar amount of the annual loan payment.

decedent a person who dies.

dedication the donation of private property by its owner to a governmental body for public use.

deed a written document that, when properly signed and delivered, conveys title to real property from the grantor to the grantee.

deed in lieu a foreclosure instrument used to convey title to the lender when the borrower is in default and wants to avoid foreclosure.

deed of trust a deed in which the title to property is transferred to a third party trustee to secure repayment of a loan; three-party mortgage arrangement.

deed restriction an imposed restriction for the purpose of limiting the use of land, such as the size or type of improvements to be allowed. Also called a restrictive covenant.

default the failure to perform a contractual duty.

defeasance clause a clause in a mortgage that renders it void where all obligations have been fulfilled.

deferred maintenance items in need of repair because the maintenance has been postponed resulting in physical depreciation or loss in value of a building; this type of depreciation is usually curable.

deficiency judgment a personal claim against a borrower when mortgaged property is foreclosed and sale of the property does not produce sufficient funds to pay off the mortgage. Deficiency judgments may be prohibited in some circumstances by anti-deficiency protection.

delinquency failure to make mortgage or loan payments when payments are due.

demand quantity of real property desired at a certain price or rent at a specific time in a given market.

density zoning a zoning ordinance that restricts the number of houses or dwelling units that can be built per acre in a particular area, such as a subdivision.

depreciation loss in property value from any cause; the difference between reproduction cost or replacement cost and market value. In appraisal, depreciation is divided into three classes: physical deterioration, functional obsolescence, and external obsolescence. The term *depreciation* is also used to refer to tax depreciation, which is a deduction from NOI (see *net operating income*) when calculating taxable income. Tax depreciation is a function of the current tax law and is not necessarily related to actual depreciation in the value of the asset.

descent the transfer of property to an owner's heirs when the owner dies intestate.

developer's profit sum of money a developer expects to receive in addition to the costs for the time and effort, coordination, and risks involved to develop real estate. The portion associated with the creation of the real estate by a developer is referred to as the developer's profit. See *entrepreneurial profit*.

devise the transfer of title to real estate by will.

devisee one who receives a bequest of real estate by will.

devisor one who grants real estate by will.

direct capitalization in the income approach, the method used to convert a single year's income into an estimate of property value (*V*). This can be accomplished by dividing the net operating income (NOI) by a market-derived overall capitalization rate (OAR), or by multiplying the income by a market-derived income multiplier. $V = NOI \div OAR$

direct costs Also known as *hard cost*; cost for labor and materials, including contractor's overhead and profit.

directional growth the direction toward which certain residential sections of a city are expected to grow.

discount (1) fee paid at the origination of a debt for the use of capital during the period, and commonly deducted from the principal when the funds are advanced; (2) Conversion of future payments to a present value with the use of a discount rate. See *discounted cash flow analysis*.

discount point 1% of the loan amount charged by a lender at closing to increase a loan's effective yield and lower the fare rate to the borrower.

discount rate the rate that lenders pay for mortgage funds—a higher rate is passed on to the borrower.

discounted cash flow analysis in general, the use of discounting in appraisal or investment analysis to calculate a present value, net present value, internal rate of return (IRR), or other measures that consider the time value of money. A procedure in which anticipated future cash flows are discounted to a net present value by the appropriate yield rate based on the assumption that benefits received in the future is worth less than benefits received now, due to the time value of money.

dispossess to remove a tenant from property by legal process.

dominant estate (tenement) property that includes the right to use an easement on adjoining property.

dower the right of a widow to the property of her husband upon his death in noncommunity property states.

down payment the part of the purchase price that the buyer pays in cash and is not financed with a mortgage or loan.

dual agency an agent who represents both parties in a transaction.

due-on-sale clause a provision in a mortgage that allows the lender to demand repayment in full if the borrower sells the property that serves as security for the mortgage.

duress the use of unlawful means to force a person to act or to refrain from an action against his or her will.

dwelling units a room or rooms containing a single kitchen and constituting an independent unit for living space of a single-family dwelling. Motel and hotel units are not considered dwelling units.

▶ E

earnest money down payment made by a buyer of real estate as evidence of good faith.

easement the right of one party to use the land of another for a particular purpose, such as to lay utility lines.

easement by necessity an easement, granted by law and requiring court action that is deemed necessary for the full enjoyment of a parcel of land. An example would be an easement allowing access from landlocked property to a road.

easement by prescription a means of acquiring an easement by continued, open, and hostile use of someone else's property for a statutorily defined period of time.

easement in gross a personal right granted by an owner with no requirement that the easement holder own adjoining land.

economic age-life method method of estimating accrued depreciation in which the ratio of effective age to total economic life is multiplied by the reproduction or replacement cost to calculate the accrued depreciation.

economic base economic activity of a community that allows local businesses to generate income from markets outside the community's borders. Economic base analysis is a survey of the industries and businesses that generate employment and income in a community.

economic depreciation loss of value from all causes outside the boundaries of the property itself.

economic life the period of time over which an improved property will generate sufficient income to justify its continued existence.

economic obsolescence see *external obsolescence.*

effective age an appraiser's estimate of the physical condition of a building. The actual age of a building may be different from its effective age.

effective date the date at which the analyses, opinions, and advice in an appraisal, review, or consulting service apply.

effective date of the appraisal the date at which the value opinion in an appraisal applies, which may or may not be the date of inspection; the date of the market conditions that provide the context for the value opinion.

effective gross income (EGI) potential gross income less vacancy and collection losses.

effective gross income multiplier (EGIM) the sales price or value divided by the effective gross income.

effective rate (investment yield) rate of return on an investment. The higher effective rate has the shortest compounding periods.

elements of comparison a categorization of property characteristics that cause real estate prices to vary. Examples include property rights, financing terms, conditions of sale, date of sale (or market conditions), location, and physical characteristics.

elevation views of the front, back, and sides of a property.

emblements cultivated crops; generally considered to be personal property.

eminent domain the right of a government to take private property for public use upon payment of its fair market value. Eminent domain is the basis for condemnation proceedings.

encroachment a trespass caused when a structure, such as a wall or fence, invades another person's land or air space.

encumbrance anything that affects or limits the title to a property, such as easements, leases, mortgages, or restrictions.

entrepreneurial profit sum of money an entrepreneur expects to receive in addition to costs for time, effort, and risk required to create a project or operate a business. It is associated with "going-concern value" or a business property. The going-concern value includes inventory, fixtures, and goodwill.

environmental forces in appraisal theory, one of four categories of forces that affect property value; environmental forces include climate, location, topography, natural barriers, and transportation systems.

Environmental Protection Agency (EPA) enforces environmental laws.

Equal Employment Opportunity Commission federal agency that enforces antidiscrimination laws governing employment.

Equal Pay Act of 1963 (EPA) law that requires that men and women who perform the same work receive the same pay.

equitable title the interest in a piece of real estate held by a buyer who has agreed to purchase the property, but has not yet completed the transaction; the interest of a buyer under a contract for deed.

equity the difference between the current market value of a property and the outstanding indebtedness due on it.

equity capitalization rate see *equity dividend rate.*

equity dividend rate (R_E) also known as *equity capitalization rate* and *cash on cash return*; ratio of before-tax cash flow to the equity investment.

equity of redemption the right of a borrower to stop the foreclosure process.

equity yield rate (Y_E) rate of return on equity capital; the equity investor's internal rate of return based on before-tax cash flows and the equity investment.

erosion the gradual wearing away of land by wind, water, and other natural processes.

escalation clause a clause in a lease allowing the lessor to charge more rent based on an increase in costs; sometimes called a *pass-through clause*.

escheat the claim to property by the state when the owner dies intestate and no heirs can be found.

escrow the deposit of funds and/or documents with a disinterested third party for safekeeping until the terms of the escrow agreement have been met.

escrow account a trust account established to hold escrow funds for safekeeping until disbursement.

escrow analysis annual report to disclose escrow receipts, payments, and current balances.

escrow disbursements money paid from an escrow account.

estate an interest in real property. The sum total of all the real property and personal property owned by an individual.

estate for years a leasehold estate granting possession for a definite period of time.

estate tax federal tax levied on property transferred upon death.

estoppel certificate a document that certifies the outstanding amount owed on a mortgage loan, as well as the rate of interest.

et al abbreviation for the Latin phrase *et alius,* meaning "and another."

et ux abbreviation for Latin term *et uxor,* meaning "and wife."

et vir Latin term meaning "and husband."

evaluation an analysis of a parcel of real estate in which a value estimate is not necessarily required. The study may be based on the nature, quality, or utility of an interest in the parcel or entire parcel.

eviction the lawful expulsion of an occupant from real property.

evidence of title a document that identifies ownership of property.

examination of title a review of an abstract to determine current condition of title.

excess land on an unimproved site, land that is not needed to accommodate a site's highest and best use. On an improved site, the surplus land that is not needed to serve or support the existing improvement.

excess rent the amount of contract rent over market rent; probably created by a favorable lease with a locational advantage, unusual management, or lease origination in a stronger market.

exchange a transaction in which property is traded for another property rather than sold for money or other consideration.

exclusive agency listing a contract between a property owner and one broker that gives the broker the right to sell the property for a fee within a specified period of time but does not obligate the owner to pay the broker a fee if the owner produces his or her own buyer without the broker's assistance. The owner is barred only from appointing another broker within this period.

exclusive right to sell a contract between a property owner and a broker that gives the broker the right to collect a commission regardless of who sells the property during the specified period of time of the agreement.

execution the signing of a contract.

executor/executrix a person named in a will to administer an estate. The court will appoint an administrator if no executor is named. "Executrix" is the feminine form.

executory contract a contract in which one or more of the obligations have yet to be performed.

executed contract a contract in which all obligations have been fully performed.

express contract an oral or written contract in which the terms are expressed in words.

extension agreement an agreement between mortgagor and mortgagee to extend the maturity date of the mortgage after it is due.

external obsolescence a loss in value of a property because of factors outside the property, such as a change in surrounding land use.

externality appraisal principle that states that forces outside a property's boundaries may have a positive or negative effect on its value.

extraction variation of allocation; estimate the total contribution of improvements and deduct improvement value from the total value.

extraordinary assumption a presumption that, if discovered to be inaccurate, may change the opinions or conclusions of an appraiser.

▶ F

Fair Credit Reporting Act (FCRA) federal legislation protecting consumers from the reporting of inaccurate credit information to credit reporting agencies.

Fair Housing law a term used to refer to federal and state laws prohibiting discrimination in the sale or rental of residential property.

fair market value the highest price that a buyer, willing but not compelled to buy, would pay, and the lowest a seller, willing but not compelled to sell, would accept.

feasibility analysis a study of the cost-benefit relationship of an economic endeavor.

Federal Emergency Management Agency (FEMA) federal agency that identifies flood-prone areas.

Federal Fair Housing Act (Title VIII of the Civil Rights Act of 1968) federal legislation that makes it illegal to discriminate on the basis of race, color, religion, sex, or national origin in connection with the sale or rental of housing or vacant land offered for residential construction or use.

Federal Home Loan Mortgage Corporation (FHLMC) (also known as *Freddie Mac*) independent agency that purchases conventional mortgages from S&Ls and commercial banks.

Federal Housing Administration (FHA) an agency within the U.S. Department of Housing and Urban Development (HUD) that insures mortgage loans by FHA-approved lenders to make loans available to buyers with limited cash.

Federal Interstate Land Sales Full Disclosure Act federal legislation requiring land developers to register subdivisions of 100 or more nonexempt lots with HUD and to provide each purchaser with a disclosure document called a property report.

Federal National Mortgage Association (FNMA) also known as *Fannie Mae*; independent agency that purchases mortgages from the primary markets and issues long-term debentures and short-term discount notes.

Federal Reserve System the central banking system of the United States that controls the monetary policy and, therefore, the money supply, interest rates, and availability of credit.

fee appraiser person who charges a fee for rendering an opinion of value rather than basing compensation on the derived value.

fee simple absolute the most complete form of ownership of real estate.

fee simple defeasible (qualified fee) freehold estate that is subject to a condition that, if it occurs, automatically reverts the estate back to the grantor or his or her heirs.

fee simple estate ownership of a property that is unencumbered by any other interest or estate.

FHA-insured loan a loan insured by the Federal Housing Administration.

fiduciary relationship a legal relationship with an obligation of trust, as that of agent and principal.

financial management rate of return (FMRR) variant of the internal rate of return in which negative cash flows are discounted to a present value at a safe rate and positive cash flows are compounded forward to the end of the holding period at a reinvestment rate. The FMRR is the rate that equates the present value to the future value of the positive cash flows.

finder's fee a fee or commission paid to a mortgage broker for finding a mortgage loan for a prospective borrower.

first mortgage a mortgage that has priority to be satisfied over all other mortgages.

fixed expenses expenses that don't vary with occupancy (e.g., property taxes, casualty insurance).

fixed-rate loan a loan with an interest rate that does not change during the entire term of the loan.

fixity characteristic of a real estate market that says each parcel of land is unique and fixed in its location.

fixture an article of personal property that has been permanently attached to the real estate so as to become an integral part of the real estate.

flat lease a lease with rents that are constant; doesn't compensate landlord for inflation.

floor area ratio (FAR) ratio of floor space to land area.

forecast an estimate of outcome of future occurrences based on market research.

foreclosure the legal process by which a borrower in default of a mortgage is deprived of interest in the mortgaged property. This usually involves a forced sale of the property at public auction, where the proceeds of the sale are applied to the mortgage debt.

forfeiture the loss of money, property, rights, or privileges because of a breach of legal obligation.

Foreign Investment in Real Property Tax Act (FIRPTA) federal legislation requiring that a buyer withhold 10% of the gross sales price and send it to the IRS if the seller is a "foreign person."

fractional ownership the form of ownership that results when a group of individuals pool their resources to buy a property.

franchise in real estate, an organization that lends a standardized trade name, operating procedures, referral services, and supplies to member brokerages.

fraud a deliberate misstatement of material fact or an act or omission made with deliberate intent to deceive (active fraud) or gross disregard for the truth (constructive fraud).

freehold estate an estate of ownership in real property.

frontage linear distance of land that abuts a lake, river, street, or highway.

front-foot a measurement of property taken by measuring the frontage of the property along the street line.

functional obsolescence a loss in value of a property because of causes within the property, such as faulty design, outdated structural style, or inadequacy to function properly.

functional utility ability of a property or building to be useful and to perform the function for which it is intended, according to current market tastes and standards, as well as the efficiency of a building's use in terms of architectural style, design and layout, traffic patterns, and sizes and types of rooms.

future interest ownership interest in property that cannot be enjoyed until the occurrence of some event; sometimes referred to as a household or equitable interest.

▶ **G**

general agent an agent who is authorized to act for and obligate a principal in a specific range of matters, as specified by their mutual agreement.

general lien a claim on all property, real and personal, owned by a debtor.

general partnership (GP) a type of company in which two or more persons share profits and liabilities.

general warranty deed an instrument in which the grantor guarantees the grantee that the title being conveyed is good and free of other claims or encumbrances.

gentrification process of renewal and rebuilding accompanying the influx of middle class or highly affluent people into deteriorating areas that displaces poorer residents.

going-concern value the value created by a proven business operation; includes an intangible value that is not considered as a part of the real estate.

government-backed mortgage a mortgage that is insured by the Federal Housing Administration (FHA) or guaranteed by the Department of Veterans Affairs (VA) or the Rural Housing Service (RHS). Mortgages that are not government loans are identified as conventional loans.

Government National Mortgage Association (GNMA) also known as *Ginnie Mae*; a government-owned corporation within the U.S. Department of Housing and Urban Development (HUD). Ginnie Mae manages and liquidates government-backed loans and assists HUD in special lending projects.

government rectangular survey legal description of land that divides land into townships by range lines (north-south lines) and tier lines (east-west lines). These lines are based on true east-west lines (baselines) and true north-south lines (principle meridians). Townships are six miles square, each containing 36 sections, which are one mile square, or 640 acres. See Real Estate Math Review.

graduated lease a lease that calls for periodic, stated changes in rent during the term of the lease.

graduated-payment mortgage (GPM) loan in which payments start low and increase over the term of the loan. It is designed to help borrowers match payments with projected increases in income.

graduated rental rent that graduates (usually increases) periodically during a lease term based on changes specified in the lease.

grant the transfer of title to real property by deed.

grant deed a deed that includes three warranties: (1) that the owner has the right to convey title to the property, (2) that there are no encumbrances other than those noted specifically in the deed, and (3) that the owner will convey any future interest that he or she may acquire in the property.

grantee one who receives title to real property.

grantor one who conveys title to real property; the present owner.

gross building area (GBA) total floor area of a building measured from the exterior of the walls.

gross income the total income received from a property before deducting expenses.

gross income multiplier (GIM) also known as *gross rent multiplier*; ratio of sales price to gross income at the time of sale.

gross lease a lease in which a tenant pays only a fixed amount for rental and the landlord pays all operating expenses and taxes.

gross leasable area (GLA) total floor area designed for the occupancy of tenants; it does not include common areas.

gross living area (GLA) residential space measured by finished and habitable above-grade areas.

gross rent multiplier similar to *gross income multiplier*, except that it looks at the relationship between sales price and monthly gross rent.

ground lease a lease of land only, on which a tenant already owns a building or will construct improvements.

guaranteed sale plan an agreement between a broker and a seller that the broker will buy the seller's property if it does not sell within a specified period of time.

guardian one who is legally responsible for the care of another person's rights and/or property.

▶ H

habendum clause the clause in a deed, beginning with the words *to have and to hold*, that defines or limits the exact interest in the estate granted by the deed.

hamlet a small village.

heir one who is legally entitled to receive property when the owner dies intestate.

highest and best use the legally permitted use of a parcel of land that will yield the greatest return to the owner in terms of money or amenities.

holdover tenancy a tenancy in which a lessee retains possession of the property after the lease has expired, and the landlord, by continuing to accept rent, agrees to the tenant's continued occupancy.

holographic will a will that is entirely handwritten, dated, and signed by the testator.

home equity conversion mortgage (HECM) often called a *reverse-annuity mortgage*; instead of making payments to a lender, the lender makes payments to you. It enables older homeowners to convert the equity they have in their homes to cash, usually in the form of monthly payments. Unlike traditional home equity loans, a borrower does not qualify on the basis of income but on the value of his or her home. In addition, the loan does not have to be repaid until the borrower no longer occupies the property.

home equity line of credit a mortgage loan that allows the borrower to obtain cash drawn against the equity of his or her home, up to a predetermined amount.

home inspection a thorough inspection by a professional that evaluates the structural and mechanical condition of a property. A satisfactory home inspection is often included as a contingency by the purchaser.

homeowners insurance an insurance policy specifically designed to protect residential property owners against financial loss from common risks such as fire, theft, and liability.

homeowners warranty an insurance policy that protects purchasers of newly constructed or pre-owned homes against certain structural and mechanical defects.

homestead the parcel of land and improvements legally qualifying as the owner's principal residence.

HUD an acronym for the Department of Housing and Urban Development, a federal agency that enforces federal fair housing laws and oversees agencies such as FHA and GNMA.

hypothetical condition that which is contrary to what exists but is supposed for the purpose of analysis. Hypothetical conditions assume conditions contrary to known facts about physical, legal, or economic characteristics of the subject property; or about conditions external to the property, such as market conditions or trends; or about the integrity of data used in an analysis.

▶ **I**

implied contract a contract by which the agreement of the parties is created by their conduct.

improvement human-made addition to real estate.

income approach also called the *income capitalization approach*; one of three approaches to value in appraisal theory; property value is estimated based on the property's anticipated future benefits.

income capitalization approach a method of estimating the value of income-producing property by dividing the expected annual net operating income of the property by a capitalization rate.

income property real estate developed or improved to produce income.

incorporeal right intangible, non-possessory rights in real estate, such as an easement or right-of-way.

incurable functional obsolescence defect that is caused by a deficiency or super-adequacy in the structure, materials, or design and layout of a structure; the defect is deemed incurable if the cost to cure the defect is greater than the anticipated increase in value after the defect is cured.

incurable physical deterioration defect caused by physical wear and tear on the building that is considered unreasonable or uneconomic to correct.

independent contractor one who is retained by another to perform a certain task and is not subject to the control and direction of the hiring person with regard to the end result of the task. Individual contractors receive a fee for their services but pay their own expenses and taxes and receive no employee benefits.

index a number used to compute the interest rate for an adjustable-rate mortgage (ARM). The index is a published number or percentage, such as the average yield on U.S. Treasury bills. A margin is added to the index to determine the interest rate to be charged on the ARM. This interest rate is subject to any caps that are associated with the mortgage.

industrial property buildings and land used for the manufacture and distribution of goods, such as a factory.

inflation an increase in the amount of money or credit available in relation to the amount of goods or services available, which causes an increase in the general price level of goods and services.

initial interest rate the beginning interest rate of the mortgage at the time of closing. This rate changes for an adjustable-rate mortgage (ARM).

installment the regular, periodic payment that a borrower agrees to make to a lender, usually in relation to a loan.

installment contract see *contract for deed.*

installment loan borrowed money that is repaid in periodic payments, known as installments.

installment sale a transaction in which the sales price is paid to the seller in two or more installments over more than one calendar year.

insurable value portion of asset value recognized under the provisions of a loss insurance policy.

insurance a contract that provides indemnification from specific losses in exchange for a periodic payment. The individual contract is known as an insurance policy, and the periodic payment is known as an insurance premium.

insurance binder a document that states that temporary insurance is in effect until a permanent insurance policy is issued.

insured mortgage a mortgage that is protected by the Federal Housing Administration (FHA) or by private mortgage insurance (PMI). If the borrower defaults on the loan, the insurer must pay the lender the insured amount.

interest a fee charged by a lender for the use of the money loaned; or a share of ownership in real estate.

interest accrual rate the percentage rate at which interest accrues on the mortgage.

interest rate the rent or rate charged to use funds belonging to another.

interest rate buydown plan an arrangement in which the property seller (or any other party) deposits money to an account so that it can be released each month to reduce the mortgagor's monthly payments during the early years of a mortgage. During the specified period, the mortgagor's effective interest rate is bought down below the actual interest rate.

interest rate ceiling the maximum interest rate that may be charged for an adjustable-rate mortgage (ARM), as specified in the mortgage note.

interest rate floor the minimum interest rate for an adjustable-rate mortgage (ARM), as specified in the mortgage note.

interim financing a short-term loan made during the building phase of a project; also known as a *construction mortgage.*

interim use temporary use until the property is ready for future highest and best use (e.g., farmland waiting for subdivision approval).

internal rate of return (IRR) annualized rate of return on capital that equates the value of cash returns over time with the cash invested; the discount rate that makes the net present value of an investment equal to zero.

interval ownership see *time-sharing*.

intestate the state of having died without having authored a valid will.

invalid not legally binding or enforceable.

investment property a property not occupied by the owner.

investment value the value of the property to a particular investor.

investment yield rate of return on an investment (effective rate). The highest investment yield will have the shortest compounding periods.

▶ J

joint tenancy co-ownership that gives each tenant equal interest and equal rights in the property, including the right of survivorship.

joint venture an agreement between two or more parties to engage in a specific business enterprise.

judgment a decision rendered by court determining the rights and obligations of parties to an action or lawsuit.

judgment lien a lien on the property of a debtor resulting from a court judgment.

judicial foreclosure a proceeding that is handled as a civil lawsuit and conducted through court; used in some states.

jumbo loan a loan that exceeds Fannie Mae's mortgage amount limits. Also called a *non-conforming loan*.

junior mortgage any mortgage that is inferior to a first lien and that will be satisfied only after the first mortgage; also called a *secondary mortgage*.

jurisdictional exception a law or regulation that may supersede USPAP. If a part or parts of USPAP (not USPAP as a whole) is against a particular area's law or public policy, only that part or parts of USPAP is voided.

just compensation fair and reasonable compensation to both the private owner of the property and the public when the property is taken for public use through condemnation.

▶ L

laches a doctrine used by a court to bar the assertion of a legal claim or right, based on the failure to assert the claim in a timely manner.

land the earth from its surface to its center, and the air space above it.

land building ratio the ratio between the total land space and the gross building area.

land capitalization rate (R_L) land income divided by land value; it is used in the income approach in residual techniques to convert income into estimated value.

land ratio the ratio of land value to total property value.

land residual technique a technique used to find property value in the income approach when the value of the building and net operating income are known. The income attributable to the building is subtracted from the net operating income to find the income attributable to the land. This figure is then capitalized and added to the building value to find the total property value.

landlocked property surrounded on all sides by property belonging to another.

landlord also called *lessor*; one who leases a property to another.

lease a contract between a landlord and a tenant wherein the landlord grants the tenant possession and use of the property for a specified period of time and for a consideration.

leased fee estate the landlord's interest in a parcel of leased property.

lease option a financing option that allows homebuyers to lease a home with an option to buy. Each month's rent payment may consist of rent, plus an additional amount that can be applied toward the down payment on an already specified price.

leasehold estate a tenant's right to occupy a parcel of real estate for the term of a lease.

legal description a description of a parcel of real estate that is specific and complete enough for an independent surveyor to locate and identify it.

lessee the one who receives that right to use and occupy the property during the term of the leasehold estate.

lessor the owner of the property who grants the right of possession to the lessee.

leverage the use of borrowed funds to purchase an asset.

levy to assess or collect a tax.

license (1) a revocable authorization to perform a particular act on another's property; (2) authorization granted by a state to act as a real estate broker or salesperson.

lien a legal claim against a property to secure payment of a financial obligation.

life estate a freehold estate in real property limited in duration to the lifetime of the holder of the life estate or another specified person.

life tenant one who holds a life estate.

limited common elements items in a multiunit project that are available for use by one or more, but not all units (e.g., parking stalls or storage units).

limited liability company (LLC) a type of company that has the limited liability advantage of a corporation with the tax status of a sole proprietor or partnership.

limited partnership ownership arrangement that is passive; limited partners are liable only to the extent of their own capital contributions. Limited partnerships are managed by a general partner, who is individually liable for financial operations.

liquidation value the value based on a quick sale or less than adequate exposure in the open market.

liquidity the ability to convert an asset into cash.

lis pendens a Latin phrase meaning "suit pending"; a public notice that a lawsuit has been filed that may affect the title to a particular piece of property.

listing agreement a contract between the owner and a licensed real estate broker wherein the broker is employed to sell real estate on the owner's terms within a given time, for which service the owner agrees to pay the broker an agreed-upon fee.

listing broker a broker who contracts with a property owner to sell or lease the described property; the listing agreement typically may provide for the broker to make property available through a multiple-listing system.

littoral rights landowner's claim to use water in large, navigable lakes and oceans adjacent to property; ownership rights to land-bordering bodies of water up to the high-water mark.

loan a sum of borrowed money, or principal, that is generally repaid with interest.

loan officer (or lender) serves several functions and has various responsibilities, such as soliciting loans; a loan officer both represents the lending institution and represents the borrower to the lending institution.

loan-to-value ratio (LTV) the ratio of the current loan balance to the property value.

lock-in an agreement in which the lender guarantees a specified interest rate for a certain period of time.

lock-in period the time period during which the lender has guaranteed an interest rate to a borrower.

lot and block description a method of describing a particular property by referring to a lot and block number within a subdivision recorded in the public record.

▶ M

management agreement a contract between the owner of an income property and a firm or individual who agrees to manage the property.

margin the difference between the interest rate and the index on an adjustable-rate mortgage. The margin remains stable over the life of the loan, while the index fluctuates.

market approach one of three approaches to value in appraisal theory; value is estimated by comparing sales of similar properties recently sold to the subject property and adjusting the comparable sales for differences in characteristics to indicate a final value estimate for the subject property.

market conditions characteristics of the market such as vacancy rates, interest rates, employment levels, and so forth.

market rent the rent income a property would most probably command if offered in the competitive market.

market segmentation analysis of submarkets within a larger market.

marketable title title to property that is free from encumbrances and reasonable doubts and that a court would compel a buyer to accept.

mass appraisal estimate of value for a large number of properties as of a given date; similar properties are valued in a uniform manner by property types with standard methodology.

mean the average in a set of numbers.

mechanic's lien a statutory lien created to secure payment for those who supply labor or materials for the construction of an improvement to land.

median middle figure in a numerically ordered set of data, such that an equal number of values lie above and below the middle figure.

meridian a vertical (north-south) dividing line used in the rectangular survey method of land description.

metes and bounds method legal description of land in which land boundaries are referred to by a point of beginning (POB), a line in a specified direction from this point (metes), and a point of change in direction in the boundary (bounds), until the line has returned to the point of beginning.

mil or mill one-tenth of one cent; used by some states to express or calculate property tax rates.

mill rate calculated by dividing the tax rate by the assessed value of a property.

millage a tax rate on property, often expressed as mills per dollar value of the property.

minor a person who has not attained the legal age of majority.

misrepresentation a misstatement of fact, either deliberate or unintentional.

mode the most frequent value in a set of numbers.

modification the act of changing any of the terms of the mortgage.

modified economic age-life method a method of estimating accrued depreciation in which the ratio of effective age to total economic life is multiplied by the reproduction or replacement cost minus curable physical and functional obsolescence.

money judgment a court order to settle a claim with a monetary payment rather than specific performance.

money market often referred to as the *safe rate* or *risk free rate of return*; investments in short-term debt securities such as CDs, government securities, and Treasury bills.

month-to-month tenancy tenancy in which the tenant rents for only one month at a time.

monument a fixed, visible marker used to establish boundaries for a survey.

mortgage a written instrument that pledges property to secure payment of a debt obligation as evidenced by a promissory note. When duly recorded in the public record, a mortgage creates a lien against the title to a property.

mortgage banker an entity that originates, funds, and services loans to be sold into the secondary money market.

mortgage broker an entity that, for a fee, brings borrowers together with lenders.

mortgage constant or mortgage capitalization rate annual debt service divided by the loan amount.

mortgage lien an encumbrance created by recording a mortgage.

mortgagee the lender who benefits from the mortgage.

mortgagor the borrower who pledges the property as collateral.

most probable selling price most likely price at which a property would sell if exposed in a competitive market for a reasonable period of time, under the market conditions at the date of the appraisal. See *market value*.

multi-dwelling units properties that provide separate housing units for more than one family that secure only a single mortgage. Apartment buildings are also considered multi-dwelling units.

multiple-listing system (MLS; also multiple-listing service) the method of marketing a property listing to all participants in the MLS.

mutual rescission an agreement by all parties to a contract to release one another from the obligations of the contract.

► N

National Environmental Policy Act (NEPA) provides environmental impact statements.

negative amortization occurs when an adjustable-rate mortgage is allowed to fluctuate independently of a required minimum payment. A gradual increase in mortgage debt happens when the monthly payment is not large enough to cover the entire principal and interest due. The amount of the shortfall is added to the remaining balance to create negative amortization.

negative leverage when the cost of borrowed money is more than the property yields.

neighborhood group of similar land uses within accepted geographical boundaries.

net income the income produced by a property, calculated by deducting operating expenses from gross income.

net income multiplier (NIM) property value or sales price divided by its net operating income for a given year. It is the reciprocal of the overall capitalization rate.

net lease a lease that requires the tenant to pay maintenance and operating expenses, as well as rent.

net listing a listing in which the broker's fee is established as anything above a specified amount to be received by the seller from the sale of the property.

net operating income (NOI) effective gross income (EGI) minus operating expenses (OE).

net worth the value of all of a person's assets.

no cash out refinance a refinance transaction in which the new mortgage amount is limited to the sum of the remaining balance of the existing first mortgage.

non-conforming use a use of land that is permitted to continue, or grandfathered, even after a zoning ordinance is passed that prohibits the use.

nonliquid asset an asset that cannot easily be converted into cash.

notarize to have a document certified by a notary public.

notary public a person who is authorized to administer oaths and take acknowledgments.

note a written instrument acknowledging a debt, with a promise to repay, including an outline of the terms of repayment.

note rate the interest rate on a promissory note.

notice of default a formal written notice to a borrower that a default has occurred on a loan and that legal action may be taken.

novation the substitution of a new contract for an existing one; the new contract must reference the first and indicate that the first is being replaced and no longer has any force and effect.

▶ **O**

obligee person on whose favor an obligation is entered.

obligor person who is bound to another by an obligation.

obsolescence a loss in the value of a property because of functional or external factors.

offer to propose as payment; to place a bid on property.

offer and acceptance two of the necessary elements for the creation of a contract.

open-end mortgage a loan containing a clause that allows the mortgagor to borrow additional funds from the lender, up to a specified amount, without rewriting the mortgage.

open listing a listing contract given to one or more brokers in which a commission is paid only to the broker who procures a sale. If the owner sells the house without the assistance of one of the brokers, no commission is due.

operating expense ratio (OER) total operating expenses divided by effective gross income (EGI).

operating expenses expenses incurred to maintain the property plus an allowance for replacing certain items.

opinion of title an opinion, usually given by an attorney, regarding the status of a title to property.

opportunity cost represents the cost of passing up an opportunity.

option an agreement that gives a prospective buyer the right to purchase a seller's property within a specified period of time for a specified price.

optionee one who receives or holds an option.

optionor one who grants an option; the property owner.

ordinance a municipal regulation.

original cost actual cost of a property to its present owner.

original principal balance the total amount of principal owed on a loan before any payments are made; the amount borrowed.

origination fee the amount charged by a lender to cover the cost of assembling the loan package and originating the loan.

overage rent amount paid over and above the minimum rent (e.g., percentage lease).

overall capitalization rate (OAR) net operating income from a single year or average of several years divided by the sales price or property value.

owner financing a real estate transaction in which the property seller provides all or part of the financing.

ownership the exclusive right to use, possess, control, and dispose of property.

▶ **P**

package mortgage a mortgage that pledges both real and personal property as collateral to secure repayment of a loan.

paired sales analysis procedure used in the sales comparison approach to estimate values of specific property characteristics to find a value of the subject property; property sales are paired by similar property characteristics. Ideally, the properties are exactly the same except for one characteristic; the difference in sale price can then be attributed to the difference in this characteristic. However, several adjustments are usually made to paired sales to isolate the effect of one characteristic.

parcel a lot or specific portion of a large tract of real estate.

partial release mortgage clause in a blanket mortgage in which the lender agrees to release certain parcels from the mortgage lien upon payment by the mortgagor; frequently found in tract development construction loans.

partial taking in eminent domain, when only a portion of a parcel of land is taken.

participation mortgage a type of mortgage in which the lender receives a certain percentage of the income or resale proceeds from a property, as well as interest on the loan.

partition the division of property held by co-owners into individual shares.

partnership an agreement between two parties to conduct business for profit. In a partnership, property is owned by the partnership, not the individual partners, so partners cannot sell their interest in the property without the consent of the other partners.

party wall a common wall used to separate two adjoining properties.

payee one who receives payment from another.

payor one who makes payment to another.

percentage lease a lease in which the rental rate is based on a percentage of the tenant's gross sales. This type of lease is most often used for retail space.

periodic estate tenancy that automatically renews itself until either the landlord or tenant gives notice to terminate it.

personal property (hereditaments) all items that are not permanently attached to real estate; also known as chattels.

physical age-life method a method of estimating incurable physical deterioration in which the deterioration is calculated by multiplying the ratio of effective age divided by the total physical life of the item by the reproduction or replacement cost of the item minus any curable physical deterioration already charged. See *incurable physical deterioration*.

physical deterioration a loss in the value of a property because of impairment of its physical condition.

PITI principal, interest, taxes, and insurance—components of a regular mortgage payment.

planned unit development (PUD) a type of zoning that provides for residential and commercial uses within a specified area.

plat a map of subdivided land showing the boundaries of individual parcels or lots.

plat book a group of maps located in the public record showing the division of land into subdivisions, blocks, and individual parcels or lots.

plat number a number that identifies a parcel of real estate for which a plat has been recorded in the public record.

plottage increment of value that results when extra utility is created by combining two or more sites under a single ownership.

point 1% of the loan.

point of beginning the starting point for a survey using the metes and bounds method of description.

police power the right of the government to enact laws, ordinances, and regulations to protect the public health, safety, welfare, and morals.

population complete set of all items in a specific category.

positive leverage when the cost of borrowed money is less than the property yield.

potential gross income (PGI) total operating income produced by a real property, assuming full occupancy and before operating expenses are deducted, including vending, garage fees, washer/dryers, etc.

potential gross income multiplier (PGIM) ratio of sales price or value to the potential gross income.

pottage combining two or more parcels to make them more valuable for a particular purpose.

power of attorney a legal document that authorizes someone to act on another's behalf. A power of attorney can grant complete authority or can be limited to certain acts and/or certain periods of time.

preapproval condition where a borrower has completed a loan application and provided debt, income, and savings documentation that an underwriter has reviewed and approved. A preapproval is usually done at a certain loan amount, making assumptions about what the interest rate will actually be at the time the loan is actually made, as well as estimates for the amount that will be paid for property taxes, insurance, and so on.

prepayment amount paid to reduce the outstanding principal balance of a loan before the due date.

prepayment penalty a fee charged to a borrower by a lender for paying off a debt before the term of the loan expires.

prequalification a lender's opinion on the ability of a borrower to qualify for a loan, based on furnished information regarding debt, income, and available capital for down payment, closing costs, and prepaids. Prequalification is less formal than preapproval.

prescription a method of acquiring an easement to property by prolonged, unauthorized use.

present value (PV) current worth of a payment or payments based on the time value of money; future payments are discounted to an equivalent current value by a discount rate based on the premise that cash flows received sooner are more valuable than cash flows received later.

pre-tax cash flow net operating income minus the debt service.

price the sum or amount of money for which property can be offered, bought, or sold.

primary mortgage market the financial market in which loans are originated, funded, and serviced.

prime rate the short-term interest rate that banks charge to their preferred customers. Changes in prime rate are used as the indexes in some adjustable-rate mortgages, such as home equity lines of credit.

principal (1) one who authorizes another to act on his or her behalf; (2) one of the contracting parties to a transaction; (3) the amount of money borrowed in a loan, separate from the interest charged on it.

principal curtailment an off-schedule mortgage payment applied only to the principal balance.

principal meridian one of the 36 longitudinal lines used in the rectangular survey system method of land description.

private mortgage insurance (PMI) mortgage insurance offered by private companies to mitigate the risk of the first 20–25% of the mortgage amount.

probate the judicial procedure of proving the validity of a will.

procuring cause the action that brings about the desired result. For example, if a broker takes actions that result in a sale, the broker is the procuring cause of the sale.

profit also known as *profit 'a prendre*; right to remove items such as topsoil or minerals from land belonging to another.

progression economic principle in which the value of under-improved property increases toward its surroundings.

promissory note the debt instrument that details the terms of the loan.

property management the operating of an income property for another.

property tax a tax levied by the government on property, real or personal.

property value worth of a property; may have several different values depending on the interest or use involved. See *market value, investment value, insurable value, assessed value*, and *going-concern value*.

proprietary lease in a cooperative building, the lease a corporation provides to the stockholders that allows them to use a specific unit under the conditions specified.

prorate to divide ongoing property costs such as taxes or maintenance fees proportionately between buyer and seller at closing.

pur autre vie a Latin phrase meaning "for the life of another." In a life estate *pur autre vie*, the term of the estate is measured by the life of a person other than the person who holds the life estate.

purchase agreement a written contract signed by the buyer and seller stating the terms and conditions under which a property will be sold.

purchase money mortgage a mortgage given by a buyer to a seller to secure repayment of any loan used to pay part or all of the purchase price.

▶ Q

qualifying ratio a calculation to determine whether a borrower can qualify for a mortgage. There are two ratios. The top ratio is a calculation of the borrower's monthly housing costs (principal, taxes, insurance, mortgage insurance, homeowner's association fees) as a percentage of monthly income. The bottom ratio includes housing costs as well as all other monthly debt.

quantity survey method most comprehensive method of estimating building costs in which the quantity and quality of all materials and labor are estimated on a unit cost basis to arrive at a total cost estimate; it duplicates the contractor's method of developing a bid.

quitclaim deed a conveyance whereby the grantor transfers without warranty or obligations whatever interest or title he or she may have.

▶ R

range (1) an area of land six miles wide, numbered east or west from a principal meridian in the rectangular survey system. (2) An interval of numbers ordered sequentially from lowest to highest value.

range lines in the rectangular survey system, the north-south lines, spaced six miles apart, used to define a township.

range of value in an appraisal report, the confidence interval in which the final estimate of a property's value may lie.

ready, willing, and able the state of being able to pay the asking price for a property and being prepared to complete the transaction.

real estate land, the earth below it, the air above it, and anything permanently attached to it.

real estate agent a real estate broker who has been appointed to market a property for and represent the property owner (listing agent), or a broker who has been appointed to represent the interest of the buyer (buyer's agent).

real estate board an organization whose members consist primarily of real estate sales agents, brokers, and administrators.

real estate broker a licensed person, association, partnership, or corporation who negotiates real estate transactions for others for a fee.

real estate market interaction of buyers and sellers exchanging real property rights for money. It is not an efficient or perfect market.

Real Estate Settlement Procedures Act (RESPA) a consumer protection law that requires lenders to give borrowers advance notice of closing costs and prohibits certain abusive practices against buyers using federally related loans to purchase their homes.

real property the rights of ownership to land and its improvements.

REALTOR® a registered trademark for use by members of the National Association of REALTORS® and affiliated state and local associations.

reconciliation in the sales comparison approach, the reviewing of each sale and judging the comparability to the subject property.

recorded plat (lot, block, subdivision system) legal method of land description.

recording entering documents, such as deeds and mortgages, into the public record to give constructive notice.

rectangular survey system a method of land description based on principal meridians (lines of longitude) and baselines (lines of latitude). Also called the *government survey system*.

redemption period the statutory period of time during which an owner can reclaim foreclosed property by paying the debt owed, plus court costs and other charges established by statute.

redlining the illegal practice of lending institutions refusing to provide certain financial services, such as mortgage loans, to property owners in certain areas.

refinance transaction the process of paying off one loan with the proceeds from a new loan using the same property as security or collateral.

regression economic principle in which the value of over-improved property declines toward its surroundings.

regression analysis mostly used for mass appraisals of single-family residences to determine assessed value.

Regulation Z a Federal Reserve regulation that implements the federal Truth-in-Lending Act.

release clause a clause in a mortgage that releases a portion of the property upon payment of a portion of the loan.

remainder estate a future interest in an estate that takes effect upon the termination of a life estate.

remaining balance in a mortgage, the amount of principal that has not yet been repaid.

remaining economic life estimated time period during which operating income will be greater than operating expenses; the period over which improvements will continue to contribute to property value.

remaining term the original amortization term minus the number of payments that have been applied to it.

renewal options a lease clause that allows the lessee to extend the lease under specified terms for a certain period of time.

rent a periodic payment paid by a lessee to a landlord for the use and possession of leased property.

replacement cost the estimated current cost to replace an asset similar or equivalent to the one being appraised.

replacement reserve money set aside to replace certain items in the future (e.g., roof replacement, carpeting, kitchen appliances).

reproduction cost the cost to construct an exact duplicate of a building at current prices using the same materials, standards, design, layout, and quality, and embodying all the subject's deficiencies, super-adequacies, and obsolescence.

rescission canceling or terminating a contract by mutual consent or by the action of one party on default by the other party.

reserve for replacement accounting allowance to provide for the maintenance and replacement of short-lived items (carpets, drapes, blinds, roof, etc.).

residual value or income attributable to a component, such as financial, physical, or legal estate components, after deducting an amount necessary to meet a required return on the other component.

residual techniques processes used in the income approach in which the unknown income from one component is derived by subtracting the known income from another component from the net operating income. The derived (residual) income is then capitalized to find the value of the corresponding component. Can be used for land-building or mortgage-equity components.

restriction (restrict covenant) a limitation on the way a property can be used.

reverse annuity mortgage when a homeowner receives monthly checks or a lump sum with no repayment until property is sold; usually an agreement between mortgagor and elderly homeowners.

reversion a lessor's right to possess leased property at the termination of a lease. Also refers generally to sale of a property at the end of a holding period.

review appraiser an appraiser who inspects the reports of other appraisers to determine the validity of the conclusions and data given in the report.

revision a revised or new version, as in a contract.

rezoning change or amendment to a zoning map.

right of egress (or ingress) the right to enter or leave designated premises.

right of first refusal the right of a person to have the first opportunity to purchase property before it is offered to anyone else.

right of redemption the statutory right to reclaim ownership of property after a foreclosure sale.

right of survivorship in joint tenancy, the right of survivors to acquire the interest of a deceased joint tenant.

riparian rights the rights of a landowner whose property is adjacent to a flowing waterway, such as a river, to access and use the water.

risk principle that deals with the uncertainty of outcomes.

▶ S

safety clause a contract provision that provides a time period following expiration of a listing agreement, during which the agent will be compensated if there is a transaction with a buyer who was initially introduced to the property by the agent.

sale-leaseback a transaction in which the owner sells improved property and, as part of the same transaction, signs a long-term lease to remain in possession of its premises, thus becoming the tenant of the new owner.

sale price the amount of money paid or asked for in a specific transaction; the sale price may include non-realty items such as personal property or a financing premium.

sales comparison approach one of three approaches to value in appraisal theory; value is estimated by comparing similar properties that have sold recently to the subject property.

sales contract a contract between a buyer and a seller outlining the terms of the sale.

salesperson one who is licensed to sell real estate in a given territory.

salvage value the value of a property at the end of its economic life.

sandwich lease sublease that occurs when a lessee leases a property to another and becomes a lessor.

satisfaction an instrument acknowledging that a debt has been paid in full.

scope of work amount and type of information researched and the analysis applied in an assignment. See *USPAP section, scope of work rule.*

secondary mortgage a mortgage that is in less than first lien position; see *junior mortgage.*

secondary mortgage market a market that exists for the sale and purchase of existing mortgages; it provides more liquidity for the mortgage market.

section in the rectangular survey method of legally describing land, it equals one square mile, or 640 acres, or $\frac{1}{36}$ of a township.

secured loan a loan that is backed by property or collateral.

security property that is offered as collateral for a loan.

selling broker the broker who secures a buyer for a listed property; the selling broker may be the listing agent, a subagent, or a buyer's agent.

separate property property owned individually by a spouse, as opposed to community property.

sequence of adjustments in the sales comparison approach, adjustments to comparable characteristics should be made in the following order to find the appropriate value of the subject property: property rights, financing terms, conditions of sale, market conditions, location, and physical characteristics.

servient tenement a property on which an easement or right-of-way for an adjacent (dominant) property passes.

setback the amount of space between the lot line and the building line, usually established by a local zoning ordinance or restrictive covenants; see *deed restrictions*.

setback, side yard, or rear yard restrictions on the amount of land required surrounding improvements; the amount of space required between the building and lot line.

settlement statement (HUD-1) the form used to itemize all costs related to closing of a residential transaction covered by RESPA regulations.

severalty the ownership of a property by only one legal entity.

shared appreciation mortgage loan made upon the security of an interest in real property that may obligate the borrower to pay to the lender a contingent deferred interest.

sinking fund account in which equal installments of funds are deposited periodically to accumulate enough money to replace an asset or reach a specified target sum. See real estate math review, compound interest tables.

site plot of land improved to the extent it is ready to be used for the purpose it was intended.

site description detailed listing of factual data, including a legal description, title and record data, and information on pertinent characteristics.

six functions of a dollar refers to compound interest and present value factors. See real estate math review, compound interest tables.

social forces in appraisal theory, one of four forces thought to influence property value; refers to population characteristics such as population age and distribution.

sole proprietorship a type of company that has one owner who assumes all responsibilities.

special assessment a tax levied against only the specific properties that will benefit from a public improvement, such as a street or sewer; an assessment by a homeowners association for a capital improvement to the common areas for which no budgeted funds are available.

special use see *conditional use*.

special warranty deed a deed in which the grantor guarantees the title only against the defects that may have occurred during the grantor's ownership and not against any defects that occurred prior to that time.

specific date data collected dealing with the subject property and the comparable properties.

specific lien a lien, such as a mortgage, that attaches to one defined parcel of real estate.

specific performance a legal action in which a court compels a defaulted party to a contract to perform according to the terms of the contract, rather than awarding damages.

speculative use property held primarily for future sale; value based on the future highest and best use.

spot zoning result by which one parcel is zoned differently than surrounding parcels.

standard payment calculation the method used to calculate the monthly payment required to repay the remaining balance of a mortgage in equal installments over the remaining term of the mortgage at the current interest rate.

statute of frauds the state law that requires certain contracts to be in writing to be enforceable.

statute of limitations the state law that requires that certain actions be brought to court within a specified period of time.

statutory lien a lien imposed on property by statute, such as a tax lien.

steering the illegal practice of directing prospective homebuyers to or away from particular areas.

straight-line capitalization method of developing an overall capitalization rate; the cap rate is calculated by adding an allowance for return of capital to the discount rate (return on capital). The allowance for return of capital assumes the capital is recaptured evenly over the holding period or economic life of the property. For example, if the economic life of the property is 50 years, the allowance for return of capital will be $\frac{1}{50}$, or 2%. With a 10% discount rate, the overall cap rate is 12%. This method, which is not commonly used today, implicitly assumes that the property's income is declining each year.

straight-line depreciation a method of computing depreciation by decreasing value by an equal amount each year during the useful life of the property.

strip center commercial use of real estate, such as a neighborhood shopping center, in which the buildings are adjoining and narrow in depth relative to the length.

subdivision large plot of land divided into small lots for sale or lease.

subject property the property being appraised.

sublease agreement in which the tenant (lessee) leases the property or part of the property to a third party, thus becoming a lessor.

sublet the act of a lessee transferring part or all of his or her lease to a third party while maintaining responsibility for all duties and obligations of the lease contract.

subordinate to accept, voluntarily, a lower priority lien position than that to which one would normally be entitled.

subrogation the substitution of one party into another's legal role as the creditor for a particular debt.

substitution the principle in appraising that a buyer will be willing to pay no more for the property being appraised than the cost of purchasing an equally desirable property.

suit for possession a lawsuit filed by a landlord to evict a tenant who has violated the terms of the lease or retained possession of the property after the lease has expired.

suit for specific performance a lawsuit filed for the purpose of compelling a party to perform particular acts rather than pay monetary damages to settle a dispute.

super-adequacy features that are not fully valued by the marketplace (e.g., 24-carat gold faucets).

supplemental standards additional requirements that add to the development and reporting requirements of USPAP.

supply and demand in appraisal, a principle that states that the value of a property depends on the quantity and price of the property type available in the market and on the number of market participants and the price they are willing to pay.

surplus productivity the net income that remains after the costs of labor, capital, and coordination have been deducted from total income.

survey a map that shows the exact legal boundaries of a property, the location of easements, encroachments, improvements, rights-of-way, and other physical features.

syndicate a group formed by a syndicator to combine funds for real estate investment.

▶ T

tax deed in some states, an instrument given to the purchaser at the time of sale.

tax lien a charge against a property created by law or statue. Tax liens take priority over all other types of liens.

tax rate the rate applied to the assessed value of a property to determine the property taxes.

tax sale the court-ordered sale of a property after the owner fails to pay *ad valorem* taxes owed on the property.

tenancy at sufferance the tenancy of a party who unlawfully retains possession of a landlord's property after the term of the lease has expired.

tenancy at will an indefinite tenancy that can be terminated by either the landlord or the tenant at any time by giving notice to the other party one rental period in advance of the desired termination date.

tenancy by the entirety ownership by a married couple of property acquired during the marriage with right of survivorship; not recognized by community property states.

tenancy in common a form of co-ownership in which two or more persons hold an undivided interest in property without the right of survivorship.

tenant one who holds or possesses the right of occupancy title.

tenant improvements in construction projects, the installation of finished tenant space by lessee or lessor; also may refer to fixed improvements installed and paid for by a lessee.

tenement the space that may be occupied by a tenant under the terms of a lease.

testate the state of dying after having created a valid will directing the testator's desires with regard to the disposition of the estate.

"time is of the essence" language in a contract that requires strict adherence to the dates listed in the contract as deadlines for the performance of specific acts.

time-sharing Also called *interval owning*; undivided ownership of real estate for only an allotted portion of a year.

title a legal document that demonstrates a person's right to, or ownership of, a property. *Note*: Title is *not* an instrument. The instrument, such as a deed, gives evidence of title or ownership.

title insurance an insurance policy that protects the holder from defects in a title, subject to the exceptions noted in the policy.

title search a check of public records to ensure that the seller is the legal owner of the property and that there are no liens or other outstanding claims.

Torrens system a system of registering titles to land with a public authority, who is usually called a registrar.

township a division of land, measuring 36 square miles, in the government survey system.

township lines in the rectangular survey system, the east-west lines, spaced six miles apart, used to define a township.

topography contour, grade, soil conditions, and physical usability of a site.

trade fixtures an item of personal property installed by a commercial tenant and removable upon expiration of the lease.

transfer tax a state or municipal tax payable when the conveyancing instrument is recorded.

trend series of related changes brought about by a chain of causes and effects.

trust an arrangement in which title to property is transferred from a grantor to a trustee, who holds title but not the right of possession for a third party, the beneficiary.

trustee a person who holds title to property for another person designated as the beneficiary.

Truth-in-Lending Law also known as *Regulation Z*; requires lenders to make full disclosure regarding the terms of a loan.

▶ U

underwriting the process of evaluating a loan application to determine the risk involved for the lender.

undivided interest the interest of co-owners to the use of an entire property despite the fractional interest owned.

uniform residential appraisal report (URAR) appraisal form requested by many federal agencies to value residential properties in a consistent manner.

Uniform Standards of Professional Appraisal Practice (USPAP) a manual of professional standards of practice for appraisers; contains ethical principals and codes of conduct for appraisers.

unilateral contract a one-sided contract in which one party is obligated to perform a particular act completely before the other party has any obligation to perform.

unit-in-place method also known as *segregated cost method*; a method of estimating building cost in which total building cost is estimated by summing prices for various building components as installed, based on specific units of use such as square footage or cubic footage.

units of comparison physical or economic measure that can be divided into the property's price to provide a more standardized comparison of the properties. The measure should be one that accounts for differences in the price typically paid for the properties, such as price per square foot (office building), price per seat (theater), or price per gallon of gas pumped (gas station). Income can also be a unit of comparison, such as when price is divided by effective gross income to obtain an effective gross income multiplier.

unsecured loan a loan that is not backed by collateral or security.

useful life the period of time a property is expected to have economic utility.

usury the practice of charging interest at a rate higher than that allowed by law.

utility also known as *functional utility*; measure of usefulness of a property.

▶ V

vacancy and collection loss the loss of income due to vacancy and nonpayment of rent.

VA-guaranteed loan a mortgage loan made to a qualified veteran that is guaranteed by the Department of Veterans Affairs.

valid contract an agreement that is legally enforceable and binding on all parties.

valuation process of estimating a defined value of an identified interest in a specific parcel of real estate as of a given date.

value in exchange value of a property in a typical market; market value.

value in use value of a property based on a specific use. This may differ from market value when the use is specialized and there is a limited market for the property based on that use.

variable expense expenses that vary depending on the level of occupancy (e.g., utilities, garbage removal).

variance permission obtained from zoning authorities to build a structure that is not in complete compliance with current zoning laws. A variance does not permit a non-conforming use of a property.

vendee a buyer.

vendor a seller; the property owner.

village an incorporated minor municipality usually larger than a hamlet and smaller than a town.

void contract a contract that is not legally enforceable; the absence of a valid contract.

voidable contract a contract that appears to be valid but is subject to cancellation by one or both of the parties.

▶ W

waiver the surrender of a known right or claim.

warranty deed a deed in which the grantor fully warrants a good, clear title to the property.

waste the improper use of a property by a party with the right to possession, such as the holder of a life estate.

wear and tear physical deterioration of property due to weathering, aging, and use.

will a written document that directs the distribution of a deceased person's property, real and personal.

wraparound mortgage a mortgage that includes the remaining balance on an existing first mortgage, plus an additional amount. Full payments on both mortgages are made to the wraparound mortgagee, who then forwards the payments on the first mortgage to the first mortgagee.

writ of execution a court order to the sheriff or other officer to sell the property of a debtor to satisfy a previously rendered judgment.

► Y

yield rate of return on an investment. Could be an overall yield for the property (y_o), a yield for the equity investor (y_e), or a yield for the lender (y_m) mortgage component.

yield capitalization method used in the income approach to determine property value by discounting future cash flows at an appropriate discount rate (yield rate) that reflects the rate of return required by investors. The approach may or may not explicitly consider financing. See *discounted cash flow analysis*.

► Z

zone an area reserved by authorities for specific use that is subject to certain restrictions.

zoning ordinance the exercise of regulating and controlling the use of a property in a municipality.

zoning restrictions restrictions may be placed on issues such as height, density, use, or development of properties.

8 ▶ Residential Appraisal Practice Exam 2

CHAPTER SUMMARY

This is the second of the two practice tests in this book based on the Appraisal Qualifications Board's (AQB) National Uniform Exam Content Outlines for state-licensed real estate appraisers and state-certified residential appraisers. Take this exam to see how far you have come since your first practice exam.

THIS IS THE second residential appraiser practice exam in this book, but it is not designed to be any harder than the first; it is simply another representation of what you might expect on the real test. Just as when you take the real test, there should not be anything here that surprises you. In fact, you probably already know what is in a lot of it! That will be the case with the real test, too.

For this exam, pull together all the tips you have been practicing since the first practice exam. Give yourself the time and space to work. Find out what the time limit is for the actual exam in your state, and try to complete this test in that time frame. Time limits vary between states, but in general, they are between one and three hours. Because you won't be taking the real test in your living room, you might take this one in an unfamiliar location such as a library. In addition, use what you have learned from reading the answer explanations on the previous practice test. Remember the types of questions that caused problems for you in the past, and when you are unsure, try to consider how those answers were explained. Once again, use the answer explanations at the end of the exam to understand questions you may have missed.

After you have taken this written exam, you should try the free online practice test offered with this book—that way, you will be familiar with taking exams on a computer. You'll find instructions on how to access this online exam at the back of this book.

▶ Residential Appraisal Practice Exam 2 Answer Sheet

1.	ⓐ	ⓑ	ⓒ	ⓓ	36.	ⓐ	ⓑ	ⓒ	ⓓ	71.	ⓐ	ⓑ	ⓒ	ⓓ
2.	ⓐ	ⓑ	ⓒ	ⓓ	37.	ⓐ	ⓑ	ⓒ	ⓓ	72.	ⓐ	ⓑ	ⓒ	ⓓ
3.	ⓐ	ⓑ	ⓒ	ⓓ	38.	ⓐ	ⓑ	ⓒ	ⓓ	73.	ⓐ	ⓑ	ⓒ	ⓓ
4.	ⓐ	ⓑ	ⓒ	ⓓ	39.	ⓐ	ⓑ	ⓒ	ⓓ	74.	ⓐ	ⓑ	ⓒ	ⓓ
5.	ⓐ	ⓑ	ⓒ	ⓓ	40.	ⓐ	ⓑ	ⓒ	ⓓ	75.	ⓐ	ⓑ	ⓒ	ⓓ
6.	ⓐ	ⓑ	ⓒ	ⓓ	41.	ⓐ	ⓑ	ⓒ	ⓓ	76.	ⓐ	ⓑ	ⓒ	ⓓ
7.	ⓐ	ⓑ	ⓒ	ⓓ	42.	ⓐ	ⓑ	ⓒ	ⓓ	77.	ⓐ	ⓑ	ⓒ	ⓓ
8.	ⓐ	ⓑ	ⓒ	ⓓ	43.	ⓐ	ⓑ	ⓒ	ⓓ	78.	ⓐ	ⓑ	ⓒ	ⓓ
9.	ⓐ	ⓑ	ⓒ	ⓓ	44.	ⓐ	ⓑ	ⓒ	ⓓ	79.	ⓐ	ⓑ	ⓒ	ⓓ
10.	ⓐ	ⓑ	ⓒ	ⓓ	45.	ⓐ	ⓑ	ⓒ	ⓓ	80.	ⓐ	ⓑ	ⓒ	ⓓ
11.	ⓐ	ⓑ	ⓒ	ⓓ	46.	ⓐ	ⓑ	ⓒ	ⓓ	81.	ⓐ	ⓑ	ⓒ	ⓓ
12.	ⓐ	ⓑ	ⓒ	ⓓ	47.	ⓐ	ⓑ	ⓒ	ⓓ	82.	ⓐ	ⓑ	ⓒ	ⓓ
13.	ⓐ	ⓑ	ⓒ	ⓓ	48.	ⓐ	ⓑ	ⓒ	ⓓ	83.	ⓐ	ⓑ	ⓒ	ⓓ
14.	ⓐ	ⓑ	ⓒ	ⓓ	49.	ⓐ	ⓑ	ⓒ	ⓓ	84.	ⓐ	ⓑ	ⓒ	ⓓ
15.	ⓐ	ⓑ	ⓒ	ⓓ	50.	ⓐ	ⓑ	ⓒ	ⓓ	85.	ⓐ	ⓑ	ⓒ	ⓓ
16.	ⓐ	ⓑ	ⓒ	ⓓ	51.	ⓐ	ⓑ	ⓒ	ⓓ	86.	ⓐ	ⓑ	ⓒ	ⓓ
17.	ⓐ	ⓑ	ⓒ	ⓓ	52.	ⓐ	ⓑ	ⓒ	ⓓ	87.	ⓐ	ⓑ	ⓒ	ⓓ
18.	ⓐ	ⓑ	ⓒ	ⓓ	53.	ⓐ	ⓑ	ⓒ	ⓓ	88.	ⓐ	ⓑ	ⓒ	ⓓ
19.	ⓐ	ⓑ	ⓒ	ⓓ	54.	ⓐ	ⓑ	ⓒ	ⓓ	89.	ⓐ	ⓑ	ⓒ	ⓓ
20.	ⓐ	ⓑ	ⓒ	ⓓ	55.	ⓐ	ⓑ	ⓒ	ⓓ	90.	ⓐ	ⓑ	ⓒ	ⓓ
21.	ⓐ	ⓑ	ⓒ	ⓓ	56.	ⓐ	ⓑ	ⓒ	ⓓ	91.	ⓐ	ⓑ	ⓒ	ⓓ
22.	ⓐ	ⓑ	ⓒ	ⓓ	57.	ⓐ	ⓑ	ⓒ	ⓓ	92.	ⓐ	ⓑ	ⓒ	ⓓ
23.	ⓐ	ⓑ	ⓒ	ⓓ	58.	ⓐ	ⓑ	ⓒ	ⓓ	93.	ⓐ	ⓑ	ⓒ	ⓓ
24.	ⓐ	ⓑ	ⓒ	ⓓ	59.	ⓐ	ⓑ	ⓒ	ⓓ	94.	ⓐ	ⓑ	ⓒ	ⓓ
25.	ⓐ	ⓑ	ⓒ	ⓓ	60.	ⓐ	ⓑ	ⓒ	ⓓ	95.	ⓐ	ⓑ	ⓒ	ⓓ
26.	ⓐ	ⓑ	ⓒ	ⓓ	61.	ⓐ	ⓑ	ⓒ	ⓓ	96.	ⓐ	ⓑ	ⓒ	ⓓ
27.	ⓐ	ⓑ	ⓒ	ⓓ	62.	ⓐ	ⓑ	ⓒ	ⓓ	97.	ⓐ	ⓑ	ⓒ	ⓓ
28.	ⓐ	ⓑ	ⓒ	ⓓ	63.	ⓐ	ⓑ	ⓒ	ⓓ	98.	ⓐ	ⓑ	ⓒ	ⓓ
29.	ⓐ	ⓑ	ⓒ	ⓓ	64.	ⓐ	ⓑ	ⓒ	ⓓ	99.	ⓐ	ⓑ	ⓒ	ⓓ
30.	ⓐ	ⓑ	ⓒ	ⓓ	65.	ⓐ	ⓑ	ⓒ	ⓓ	100.	ⓐ	ⓑ	ⓒ	ⓓ
31.	ⓐ	ⓑ	ⓒ	ⓓ	66.	ⓐ	ⓑ	ⓒ	ⓓ					
32.	ⓐ	ⓑ	ⓒ	ⓓ	67.	ⓐ	ⓑ	ⓒ	ⓓ					
33.	ⓐ	ⓑ	ⓒ	ⓓ	68.	ⓐ	ⓑ	ⓒ	ⓓ					
34.	ⓐ	ⓑ	ⓒ	ⓓ	69.	ⓐ	ⓑ	ⓒ	ⓓ					
35.	ⓐ	ⓑ	ⓒ	ⓓ	70.	ⓐ	ⓑ	ⓒ	ⓓ					

► Residential Appraisal Practice Exam 2

1. A fee simple estate or freehold estate of inheritance might NOT include which of the following?
   a. the right to use and possess the land
   b. the right to use the adjacent land (an easement)
   c. the right to exclude others from the land
   d. the right to dispose of the land

2. Which of the following variable combinations are all demand variables?
   a. households, mortgage interest rate, and construction material prices
   b. household income, mortgage interest rate, and prices of substitute housing units
   c. prices of construction materials and the number of builders
   d. construction wages, expected profits, prices of substitute housing units

3. Each of the following is a characteristic of market value EXCEPT
   a. the buyer and seller are motivated for an immediate sale.
   b. the buyer and seller are well informed.
   c. the buyer and seller act in their own best interest.
   d. the buyer and seller make financial arrangements at the market rates.

4. Each of the following is a critical issue in defining the appraisal problem EXCEPT
   a. identifying the client and intended users.
   b. identifying the data collection requirements.
   c. identifying the purpose of the appraisal.
   d. identifying the scope of work.

5. Which of the following legal description methods uses distances and directions?
   a. government rectangular survey
   b. lot and block
   c. metes and bounds
   d. plat map

6. Each of the following factors directly affects financial feasibility calculations EXCEPT
   a. development costs of the site.
   b. zoning and subdivision restrictions.
   c. operating expenses.
   d. vacancy losses.

7. An appraisal is an opinion of value. Which of the following adjective(s) is NOT associated with that opinion of value?
   a. unbiased
   b. informed, knowledgeable, learned, educated
   c. undocumented, unsupported by evidence
   d. all of the above

8. When the appraiser estimates the relative age of the structure based on the level of maintenance and repair, compared to the level of maintenance of the comparable properties in the market, which of the following items is being measured?
   a. effective age
   b. remaining economic life
   c. physical age
   d. age by reconciliation

9. Which of the following calculations yields a present value of $792.09?

    a. $900 due at the end of two years, at a discount rate of 9%

    b. $900 due at the end of three years, at a discount rate of 7%

    c. $1,000 due at the end of four years, at a discount rate of 6%

    d. $1,100 due at the end of four years, at a discount rate of 8%

10. Which principle states that the price of land will change as economic and demographic variables in the market change?

    a. anticipation

    b. supply and demand

    c. conformity

    d. substitution

11. Which of the following is an example of a social influence on real estate?

    a. population density

    b. per capita income

    c. a zoning ordinance

    d. street patterns

12. Which of the following principles states that interaction among participants in the property market can influence real property value?

    a. change

    b. competition

    c. conformity

    d. contribution

13. What part of the Ethics Rule states that the appraiser cannot be an advocate?

    a. conduct

    b. confidentiality

    c. management

    d. record keeping

14. Which one of the following factors does NOT affect financial feasibility?

    a. sales prices of comparable properties

    b. rents in comparable properties

    c. operating expenses of the subject and comparable properties

    d. development costs of the site

15. If a single-family house with a fully equipped kitchen is leased to a tenant for $1,500 per month, and if the owner must make annual payments of $1,600 for repairs, $2,000 for an improvement, $400 for property insurance, $1,200 for property tax, and reserves for replacement are $400, what is the net operating income?

    a. $16,400

    b. $14,800

    c. $14,400

    d. $12,400

16. Which of the following variable combinations are all supply variables?

    a. households, mortgage interest rate, and construction material prices

    b. household income, mortgage interest rate, and prices of substitute units

    c. prices of construction materials and the number of builders

    d. construction wages, expected profits, and prices of substitute housing units

17. If the subject property has a fireplace that costs $3,000 to place in the house during construction and adds $4,000 to the market value in the market, but the comparable property does not have a fireplace, what is the correct adjustment?
   a. Add $3,000 to the comparable property.
   b. Add $4,000 to the comparable property.
   c. Subtract $3,000 from the comparable property.
   d. Subtract $4,000 from the comparable property.

18. An appraiser may be an advocate for
   a. assignment results.
   b. the client.
   c. himself/herself.
   d. all of the above

19. Which of the following statements describes the process of direct capitalization to value an income-earning property?
   a. Sale price is divided by the market rent.
   b. Sale price is divided by the capitalization rate.
   c. Net operating income is divided by the capitalization rate.
   d. Net operating income is divided by market rent.

20. The combining of two or more parcels, usually (but not necessarily) contiguous, into one ownership or use is known as
   a. assemblage.
   b. frontage.
   c. plottage.
   d. salvage.

21. Mr. Smith has the right to use Mr. Brown's property for a specific purpose. What is Mr. Smith's right called?
   a. a time-share
   b. a life estate
   c. a leasehold
   d. an easement

22. Which of the following government building projects is funded by special assessments?
   a. an elementary school
   b. a government administrative building
   c. a paved street and sanitation sewer line on a previously unimproved road
   d. a fire station

23. Which of the following principles states that the net income to the land is the remainder after the costs of labor, capital, and entrepreneurial ability have been paid?
   a. balance
   b. externalities
   c. substitution
   d. surplus productivity

24. Which statement does not meet the market value requirements?
   a. The buyer and seller know the good and bad attributes of the property.
   b. The buyer and seller are related, and act as agents.
   c. The buyer and seller expect the loan to be at market terms and conditions.
   d. The buyer and seller are represented by agents.

25. What part of the Ethics Rule states that the appraiser must act in good faith with regard to the client?
a. conduct
b. confidentiality
c. management
d. record keeping

26. If the comparable property sold eight months ago for $200,000 in a market that has experienced 2% appreciation per year over the last few years, what is the adjustment to the comparable property?
a. Add $2,680 to the comparable property.
b. Add $4,000 to the comparable property.
c. Subtract $2,680 from the comparable property.
d. Subtract $4,000 from the comparable property.

27. Which of the following best describes interim use?
a. use of land that is not needed to serve or support the existing improvement, but can be separated and have a higher and better use of its own
b. use to which a site or improved property is put until it is ready to be its future highest and best use
c. use of land not necessary to support the highest and best use of the existing improvement but, because of physical limitations, building placement, or neighborhood norms, cannot be sold off separately
d. use of land valued for a different use than the improvement

28. Which of the following techniques for site valuation is based on developing the gross sales price of a building lot and then deducting all development costs?
a. allocation
b. extraction
c. land residual
d. land development

29. The difference between effective gross income and net operating income is caused by
a. appreciation.
b. capitalization.
c. operating expenses.
d. vacancy.

30. What part of the Ethics Rule states that it is unethical for the appraiser to accept an assignment or compensation contingent upon a stipulated result?
a. conduct
b. confidentiality
c. management
d. record keeping

31. Which of the following is a loan in which there exists negative amortization?
a. a graduated-payment mortgage
b. a fixed-rate mortgage
c. a shared-appreciation mortgage
d. a 1-2-3 buydown mortgage

32. Which of the following is an example of a social determinant of value?
a. smaller household sizes
b. land use restrictions
c. a view of a park
d. the closing of a production facility

33. Which of the following value definitions refers to the depreciable value of the property?
   a. assessed value
   b. insurance value
   c. investment value
   d. market value

34. The process of removing items of value from properties is known as
   a. assemblage.
   b. frontage.
   c. plottage.
   d. salvage.

35. When the owner of a property is analyzing the relationship between the property's current market value and its current net operating income (NOI), he or she is considering the property's
   a. capitalization rate.
   b. operating expense ratio.
   c. vacancy rate.
   d. all of the above

36. Which of the following items is NOT an indirect cost of construction?
   a. architect fees
   b. permits and inspection fees
   c. construction worker wages
   d. profit for the contractor

37. What part of the Ethics Rule states that the appraiser cannot tie compensation to the value estimate for the property?
   a. conduct
   b. confidentiality
   c. management
   d. record keeping

38. Each of the following statements about disclosure of the scope of work is correct EXCEPT
   a. the appraiser can disclose only the planned scope of work.
   b. the appraiser can disclose only the scope of work performed in the assignment.
   c. the appraiser can disclose the research and analysis performed.
   d. the appraiser can disclose the research and analysis that was not performed.

39. When the planning department of a county tells a property owner that the house under construction is too close to the street, which of the following ordinances is being considered?
   a. subdivision regulations
   b. zoning ordinances
   c. construction codes
   d. restrictive covenants

40. Each of the following statements about the "intended user," that is, the client, is correct EXCEPT
   a. the client may be identified as a person or as an entity.
   b. users other than the client are provided the appraisal report.
   c. the client's identity may be omitted from the report if anonymity is sought.
   d. intended users other than the client must be identified by name or type.

41. Which of the following calculations yields a future value of $857.53?
   a. $800 at 5% for three years
   b. $800 at 4% for five years
   c. $700 at 7% for three years
   d. $700 at 6.5% for four years

42. Which of the Standard Rules deals with review appraisals?
a. Standard 1
b. Standard 3
c. Standard 4
d. Standard 6

43. Which technique for site valuation is based on developing the portion of the property's NOI that can be allocated to the land and uses this NOI to estimate land value?
a. allocation
b. extraction
c. land residual
d. land development

44. A mortgage note is a document that
a. makes a property the security or collateral for a debt.
b. identifies the money the seller owes the lender.
c. notifies the buyer of a foreclosure sale.
d. serves as evidence of the borrower's debt.

45. How many square feet does this site have?

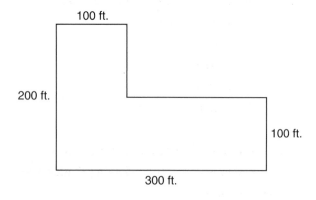

a. 30,000
b. 40,000
c. 50,000
d. 60,000

46. Which of the following is the most commonly used and reliable land valuation technique?
a. allocation
b. extraction
c. land development
d. sales comparison

Use the following information to answer questions 47–51 about cash flow analysis.

The appraiser obtains the following income and expense data for the subject property.

Market rent per unit per month	$1,600
Units	2
Market vacancy	10%
Operating expenses per unit per year	$4,200
Market value of the property	$205,000

47. When the appraiser develops the cash flow statement, the figure $34,560 is the
a. potential gross income.
b. net operating income.
c. effective gross income.
d. before-tax cash flow.

48. When the appraiser develops the cash flow statement, the figure $26,160 is the
a. potential gross income.
b. net operating income.
c. effective gross income.
d. before-tax cash flow.

49. When the appraiser develops the cash flow statement, the figure $8,400 is the
a. total operating expenses.
b. potential gross income.
c. net operating income.
d. effective gross income.

50. When the appraiser develops the cash flow statement, the figure 24.31% is the
   a. operating expense ratio.
   b. vacancy rate.
   c. discount rate.
   d. overall property capitalization rate.

51. When the appraiser develops the cash flow statement, the figure 12.76% is the
   a. operating expense ratio.
   b. vacancy rate.
   c. discount rate.
   d. overall property capitalization rate.

52. Which of the Standard Rules deals with mass appraisals?
   a. Standard 1
   b. Standard 3
   c. Standard 4
   d. Standard 6

53. A subdivision of a neighborhood is downwind from a waste treatment plant. What type of determinant of value is this?
   a. economic
   b. governmental
   c. physical/environmental
   d. social

54. Which of the following value definitions refers to the value of the property as an operating business to a specific individual who is considering its purchase?
   a. acquisition value
   b. going-concern value
   c. investment value
   d. liquidation value

55. What does amortization mean?
   a. The loan term is long, i.e., 30 years.
   b. The loan is paid back over the term of the loan.
   c. The loan payment is constant over the term of the loan.
   d. The loan-to-value ratio is high, i.e., 80% or more.

56. When the appraiser estimates the cost of the materials and labor, he or she is considering
   a. indirect cost.
   b. direct cost.
   c. replacement cost.
   d. reproduction cost.

57. Which of the following principles states that property value is created and sustained when opposing market forces are in a state of equilibrium?
   a. balance
   b. externalities
   c. substitution
   d. surplus productivity

58. Which of the Standard Rules deals with appraisal consulting?
   a. Standard 1
   b. Standard 3
   c. Standard 4
   d. Standard 6

59. A cash equivalency adjustment is an activity related to which of the following elements of comparison?
   a. condition of sale
   b. financing
   c. date of sale
   d. economic characteristics

60. How many square feet is the following site?

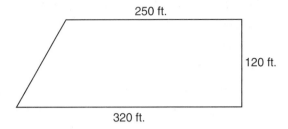

- **a.** 30,000
- **b.** 34,200
- **c.** 38,400
- **d.** 46,800

61. In order to perform a direct capitalization valuation technique on the subject property using property market data, all the following information might be needed EXCEPT
- **a.** operating expenses for the subject and comparable properties.
- **b.** market rent for the comparable properties.
- **c.** appreciation for the subject property.
- **d.** sales prices for the comparable properties.

62. Each of the following statements about the capitalization rate is true EXCEPT
- **a.** adjacent properties must have the same capitalization rate.
- **b.** a property's cap rate can change over time.
- **c.** similar properties in different neighborhoods can have different cap rates.
- **d.** all property types in the same neighborhood can have different cap rates.

63. When the appraiser uses information about land values and accrued depreciation to form the opinion of value, he or she is using the
- **a.** cost approach.
- **b.** income approach.
- **c.** sales comparison approach.
- **d.** direct capitalization approach.

64. An increase in the number of households desiring to live in a certain neighborhood would be
- **a.** an economic determinant of value.
- **b.** a governmental determinant of value.
- **c.** a physical/environmental determinant of value.
- **d.** a social determinant of value.

65. Standard 1 has six associated rules. Which of these Standard Rules discusses the need to identify the client and the intended users?
- **a.** Standard Rule 1–1
- **b.** Standard Rule 1–2
- **c.** Standard Rule 1–3
- **d.** Standard Rule 1–4

66. Which of the following choices contains a pair of loans that both have constant payments over the entire term of the loan?
- **a.** graduated payment and buydown
- **b.** interest only and graduated payment
- **c.** buydown and shared appreciation
- **d.** shared appreciation and graduated payment

67. Which of the following terms describes land that is not needed for the current use, cannot be separated from the full site, and cannot be sold?
- **a.** excess
- **b.** functional
- **c.** salvageable
- **d.** surplus

68. Standard 1 has six associated rules. Which of these Standard Rules discusses the three valuation approaches?
- **a.** Standard Rule 1–1
- **b.** Standard Rule 1–2
- **c.** Standard Rule 1–3
- **d.** Standard Rule 1–4

69. Standard 1 has six associated rules. Which of these Standard Rules discusses the issue of reconciliation?
a. Standard Rule 1–3
b. Standard Rule 1–4
c. Standard Rule 1–5
d. Standard Rule 1–6

70. Adjustments to property attributes are used in which of the following appraisal techniques?
a. cost approach
b. income approach
c. sales comparison approach
d. highest and best use approach

71. Which of the following loans is based on an index that the lender can control?
a. adjustable-rate
b. buydown
c. graduated payment
d. none of the above

72. The capitalization rate (R) and the discount rate (d) are related by the following formula, in which g represents the growth in revenue.
a. $R = d + g$
b. $R = g - d$
c. $R = d - g$
d. $d = R - g$

73. Property appreciation adjustments are related to which of the following elements of comparison?
a. condition of sale
b. financing
c. date of sale
d. economic characteristics

74. Which legal description system uses baselines, townships, and sections to identify real property?
a. lot and block
b. plat map
c. government survey
d. metes and bounds

75. Which of the following principles states that the comparable property with the lowest price will attract the most potential buyers?
a. balance
b. externalities
c. substitution
d. surplus productivity

76. In the appraisal process, which of the following statements is a correct sequence of actions?
a. scope of work, data collection, highest and best use
b. data collection, highest and best use, scope of work
c. highest and best use, scope of work, data collection
d. scope of work, highest and best use, data collection

77. When several similar properties are available in the market, the property with the lowest price will attract the greatest level of demand. What appraisal principle supports this premise?
a. competition
b. conformity
c. market
d. substitution

78. Each of the following is a critical issue in defining the appraisal problem EXCEPT
   a. identifying the legal description of the property and ownership rights.
   b. identifying the effective date of the appraisal.
   c. identifying the site attributes.
   d. identifying the scope of work.

79. When the appraiser uses the age-life method to obtain an estimate of accrued depreciation, which of the following concepts is used in the calculation?
   a. actual age of the structure and the time period since its last major renovation or modernization
   b. actual age and effective age
   c. effective age and the remaining economic life of the structure
   d. the time period since the last major renovation and the remaining economic life of the structure

80. Which of the following statements about reserves for replacement is correct?
   a. maintenance and repairs
   b. appliances, floor covering, roof covering, etc.
   c. improvements to the structure
   d. renovations of the structure

81. The promises made by the borrower to protect the property securing the loan against any form of loss are contained in the
   a. promissory note.
   b. nonuniform covenants.
   c. uniform covenants.
   d. sales contract.

82. Which of the following pieces of information is NOT necessary to know in order to undertake the cost approach for estimating the current market value of the subject property?
   a. the availability of market data for estimating site value
   b. the availability of data on property tax
   c. the availability of market data for estimating sales price of the improved property
   d. the availability of market data to estimate functional and external obsolescence

83. Which of the area measurements is most important in evaluating housing units?
   a. gross building area
   b. gross leasable area
   c. gross living area
   d. usable area

84. An arm's-length transaction is related to which of the following elements of comparison?
   a. condition of sale
   b. financing
   c. real property ownership
   d. economic characteristics

85. When the seller of a property limits the buyer's use of the land, which of the following is taking place?
   a. easement appurtenant
   b. easement in gross—commercial
   c. specific lien
   d. restrictive covenant

86. All of the following actions can occur in the reconciliation section of the appraisal report EXCEPT
  a. evaluating the applicability of the appraisal approaches used in the report.
  b. adjusting value estimates from various approaches to minimize differences.
  c. checking the accuracy of all calculations.
  d. evaluating the relative dependability of the appraisal approaches used.

87. Which appraisal approach does NOT use comparable properties in the analysis?
  a. the cost approach
  b. the income approach
  c. the sales comparison approach
  d. Choices **a**, **b**, and **c** all use comparable properties.

88. When the appraiser discusses the position of the site relative to the street system and its surface characteristics, the general term for this discussion is
  a. plottage.
  b. topography.
  c. soil analysis.
  d. accessibility.

Use the following to answer questions 89–92.

An appraiser discovers the following information about the acreage of seven land parcels. The appraiser calculates the descriptive statistics for this data set. (Rounded to one decimal.)

	# of Acres
Parcel 1	9
Parcel 2	5
Parcel 3	15
Parcel 4	4
Parcel 5	10
Parcel 6	8
Parcel 7	19

89. Parcel 1 represents the
  a. average (mean) number of acres.
  b. median number of acres.
  c. range of acreage.
  d. standard deviation.

90. Ten acres represents the
  a. average (mean) size of the parcels.
  b. median size of the parcels.
  c. range in size of the parcels.
  d. standard deviation.

91. 15 acres represents the
  a. average (mean) size of the parcels.
  b. median size of the parcels.
  c. range in size of the parcels.
  d. standard deviation.

92. 5.4 acres represents the
  a. average (mean) size of the parcels.
  b. median size of the parcels.
  c. range in size of the parcels.
  d. standard deviation.

93. Which of the following statements about a real estate appraisal is NOT true?
  a. A real estate appraisal is an opinion of the value of real property.
  b. A real estate appraisal is an orderly, step-by-step process.
  c. A real estate appraisal focuses on both the physical property and legal aspects.
  d. A real estate appraisal must exhibit the appraiser's preferences.

94. A physically deteriorated item in the structure is considered to be incurable if
   a. the item can easily be repaired.
   b. the cost of the repair is not excessive.
   c. the repair cost is less than the increase in value due to the repair.
   d. the resulting value increase is less than the repair bill.

95. A neighborhood has high-quality public schools. What type of determinant of value is this?
   a. economic
   b. governmental
   c. physical/environmental
   d. social

96. Which of the following principles states that off-site facilities can affect property value?
   a. balance
   b. externalities
   c. substitution
   d. surplus productivity

97. Which of the following legal description methods uses baselines, meridians, and townships?
   a. government rectangular survey
   b. lot and block
   c. metes and bounds
   d. plat map

98. Which of the following statements is correct?
   a. Land is the surface of the earth not covered by oceans, seas, and large lakes, while a site is land in a specific location.
   b. Land exists in its unaltered natural condition, while a site is land that has been made ready for development.
   c. Land is the surface of the earth made ready for development, while a site is land that is of particular interest in the valuation assignment.
   d. Land and site are synonyms.

99. John buys a house for $220,000. What is the monthly payment for an 80% loan with a 30-year term and a 7% interest rate?
   a. $1,463.67
   b. $1,283.33
   c. $1,170.93
   d. $1,026.67

100. Which of the following value definitions refers to the value of the property that is offered for an immediate sale?
   a. assisted value
   b. going-concern value
   c. investment value
   d. liquidation value

▶ Answers

1. **b.** An easement is not a right that is defined as part of fee simple ownership.

2. **b.** Household income, mortgage interest rate, and prices of substitute housing units are all demand variables. Construction costs (prices) and materials are supply variables, which make the other three choices incorrect.

3. **a.** An immediate sale is not reasonable exposure and is not a characteristic of market value.

4. **b.** Identifying the data collection requirements occurs *after* the problem is identified.

5. **c.** The metes and bounds system is defined as a system for the legal description of land that refers to the property's boundaries, which are formed by the point of beginning (POB) and all intermediate points. It uses the distances and angles of each point.

6. **b.** Zoning and subdivision regulations can have an indirect affect on financial feasibility by affecting development costs and/or operating costs.

7. **c.** Appraisal opinions must be documented by using at least two of the appraisal methods.

8. **a.** Effective age is a judgment that is based on the condition of the subject property relative given its level of maintenance and repair.

9. **c.** The math solution is as follows, using a Hewlett Packard 12c:
   Keystrokes: 1000 FV, 4 n, 6 i/Yr, then press PV to get −792.09 (ignore the minus sign).

10. **b.** Supply and demand is the principle that states that the price of real property is directly influenced by the demand for it, further influenced by its availability (supply); in other words, a need or a desire for property in a particular community, coupled with a scarce availability, will drive up the prices. Conversely, little interest and a high availability of real property will drive the prices down.

11. **a.** Population density is a social influence on real estate. Per capita income is an economic influence. A zoning ordinance is a governmental influence, and street patterns are a physical influence.

12. **b.** Competition between and among market participants and between and among similar properties affects the value of the subject property.

13. **a.** The "Conduct" section of the "Ethics Rule" in USPAP states that an appraiser cannot act as an advocate under any circumstance or for any party.

14. **a.** Sales prices of comparable properties are the important items in the sales comparison technique. They are used in the direct capitalization approach to calculate the capitalization rate.

15. **c.** PGI = EGI = $1,500 × 12 = $18,000
    Operating Expenses = $1,600 + $400 + $1,200 + $400 = $3,600
    Improvement expenditures are not part of NOI.
    NOI = $18,000 − $3,600 = $14,400

16. **c.** Households, household income, and the price of substitute housing are demand variables and make the other three options incorrect.

17. **b.** The comparable property is adjusted to the subject property.

18. **a.** An appraiser must remain unbiased and therefore must not allow advocacy for any party associated with the appraisal.

19. **c.** The valuation formula is $V = NOI \div Ro$.

20. **a.** Assemblage is the process that creates plottage (choice **c**) value; it is the combining into one ownership or use of at least two parcels that are normally—but not necessarily—contiguous. Plottage is the increment of value that is created when at least two sites are combined to produce greater utility.

21. **d.** An easement is one person's right to use another person's land for a specific purpose.

22. **c.** The paved street is an off-site public improvement that directly benefits a particular property or properties. The other projects benefit the whole community or a big part of it.

23. **d.** Surplus productivity is the net income to the land or site that remains after the costs of various agents of production (labor, capital, and entrepreneurship) have been paid.

24. **b.** Buyers and sellers who are related are not assumed to be acting in their own best interest.

25. **b.** The "Confidentiality" section of the "Ethics Rule" in USPAP states that the appraiser must act in good faith with regard to the client.

26. **a.** The comparable property is adjusted to the subject property, so you must adjust the price of the comparable by adding the value of eight months of appreciation.
First, find the annual appreciation (2% of $200,000):
$.02 \times \$200,000 = \$4,000$
Remember, you must adjust for only eight months of appreciation, not a full year, so solve to find what percentage of a year is eight months:
$\frac{8}{12} = .67$, or 67%
Apply that percentage to annual appreciation to find your answer:
67% of $4,000 = $2,680

27. **b.** An interim use is defined as the use to which a site or improved property is put until it is ready to be put to its future highest and best use.

28. **d.** Land development technique considers the improvement of land with utilities, roads, and services, which makes the land suitable for resale as developable plots for housing or other purposes. The revenue from the sale of the lots is matched against the cost of the development to estimate the value of the land.

29. **c.** EGI − OE = NOI.

30. **c.** The "Management" section of the "Ethics Rule" in USPAP states that it is unethical for the appraiser to accept an assignment or compensation contingent on a stipulated result.

31. **a.** Negative amortization is a key element of the graduated-payment mortgage (GPM) in its early years (typically five years). The other three choices all have positive amortization.

32. a. Smaller household sizes are a social determinant of value. Land use restrictions (choice **b**) are a government determinant of value; a view of a park (choice **c**) is a physical determinant of value; the closing of a production facility (choice **d**) is an economic determinant of value.

33. b. Insurance can be obtained only on the depreciable base of the property.

34. d. Salvage value is the price expected for a whole property or a part of a property, e.g., a plumbing fixture that is removed from the premises usually for use elsewhere.

35. a. The capitalization rate formula is the current NOI divided by current market value or sales price.

36. c. Construction worker wages are a direct cost of construction. Architect fees (choice **a**), permits and inspection fees (choice **b**), and profit for the contractor (choice **d**) are all indirect costs.

37. c. The "Management" section of the "Ethics Rule" in USPAP states that the appraiser cannot tie compensation to the value estimate for the property.

38. a. The "Scope of Work" in the subsection on "Scope of Work Acceptability" in USPAP states that determining the scope of work is an ongoing process in an assignment. Information or conditions discovered during the course of an assignment might cause the appraiser to reconsider the scope of work. The other three disclosures are required.

39. b. The area regulations of a zoning ordinance state the required setback from the street.

40. b. The client and intended users other than the client must be identified by name or type in the report. Any other individuals are not given the report. See the definition of *intended user* in the "Definitions" section of USPAP.

41. c. The math solution is as follows, using a Hewlett Packard 12c:
Keystrokes: 700 FV, 3 n, 7 i/Yr, then press FV to get –857.53 (ignore the minus sign).

42. b. Review appraisals are discussed in Standard 3.

43. c. Land residual technique is a method of estimating land value in which the net operating income attributable to the land is estimated and then capitalized to produce an estimate of the land's contribution to the total property.

44. d. A key element of a note is that it serves as evidence of the borrower's debt. The mortgage makes a property the security or collateral for a debt (choice **a**). A closing balance on a loan identifies the money the seller owes the lender (choice **b**). A public advertisement notifies the buyer of a foreclosure sale (choice **c**).

45. b. For this problem, you can either split the shape into two rectangles that are 200 ft. by 100 ft. each and add their areas ((200 × 100) + (200 × 100)), or split the shape into a 300-by-100 (300 × 100) ft. rectangle and a 100-by-100 ft. square and then add their areas ((300 × 100) + (100 × 100)).

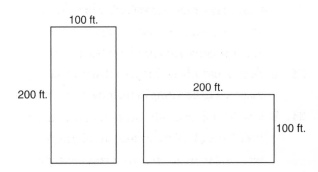

or

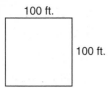

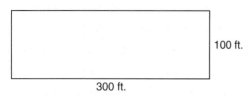

In both cases, the total is 40,000.

46. d. The sales comparison technique is the most preferred for valuing residential sites, and thus, it is the most used land valuation technique.

47. c. PGI = $1,600 × 2 × 12 = $38,400
PGI less Vacancy = EGI
$38,400 − ($38,400 × 10%) = $38,400
− $3,840 = $34,560

48. b. NOI = EGI − OE = $34,560 − $8,400
= $26,160.

49. a. Total operating expenses = 2 units × $4,200
= $8,400.

50. a. The operating expense ratio is $8,400
÷ $34,560 = 24.31%.

51. d. The overall property capitalization rate is
NOI / Property Value = $\frac{\$26,160}{\$205,000}$ = 12.76%.

52. d. Mass appraisals are discussed in Standard 6.

53. c. The waste treatment plant is a physical/environmental determinant of value.

54. b. Going-concern value is the value of an operating business on the real property.

55. b. Amortization is the method of repaying a loan or debt by making periodic payments composed of both principal and interest. When the entire principal has been repaid, it is considered fully amortized.

56. b. Labor and materials and their wages and costs are direct costs.

57. a. Balance is the principle that real property value is created and sustained when contrasting, opposing, or interacting elements are in a state of equilibrium.

58. c. Appraisal consulting is discussed in Standard 4.

59. b. Cash equivalency is typically an adjustment for different interest rates on the loan; therefore, it is a financing issue.

60. b. The easiest way to do this is to simply split the figure into a rectangle and a triangle.

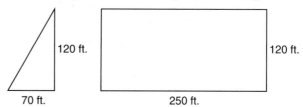

The rectangle portion is 250 × 120 = 30,000 square feet. The triangle portion is 120-feet high with a 70-foot base. The formula for the area of a triangle is $\frac{1}{2}bh$ (*b* for base, *h* for height). Plug in the numbers:
$\frac{1}{2}(70) × 120 = 35 × 120 = 4,200$ square feet
Add the total square feet of the two portions together:
30,000 + 4,200 = 34,200

61. c. Appreciation is a variable in the capitalization rate formula for a calculation using financial market data.

62. a. This answer is incorrect because adjacent properties could have different uses and thus different cap rates. Adjacent properties could have the same use (retail) but serve different markets.

63. a. In the cost approach, value is based on the estimated land value plus the current cost to reproduce or replace the existing structure, deducting for all accrued depreciation in the property.

64. **a.** Households desiring to live in the neighborhood is an economic determinant of value.

65. **b.** Standard Rule 1–2 discusses the need to identify the client and the intended users.

66. **c.** The graduated-payment mortgage (GPM), with its increasing payments in the early years, makes the other choices incorrect.

67. **d.** Surplus land is the portion of a site not necessary to support the highest and best use of the existing improvement but, because of physical limitations, building placement, or neighborhood norms, cannot be sold off separately.

68. **d.** Standard Rule 1–4 discusses the three valuation approaches.

69. **d.** Standard Rule 1–6 discusses the issue of reconciliation.

70. **c.** In the sales comparison approach, value is estimated by comparing (often using adjustments) similar properties that have sold recently to the subject property.

71. **d.** Choice **a** is incorrect because the lender does not control the index in an adjustable-rate mortgage (ARM); buydown loans (choice **b**) and graduated-payment mortgages (choice **c**) do not use an index.

72. **c.** The cap rate (R) is less than the discount rate (d) if the property has the potential for increasing value.

73. **c.** Date of sale adjustments focus on the time adjustment.

74. **c.** The government survey system is a land survey system used in Florida, Alabama, Mississippi, and all states north of the Ohio River or west of the Mississippi River (except Texas). It starts with the intersection of lines of longitude (meridians) and latitude (baselines) and then divides land around these intersections into townships approximately six miles square. Each township contains 36 sections of 640 acres each.

75. **c.** Substitution is the principle that states that when several similar commodities, goods, or services are available, the one with the lowest price will attract the greatest demand and widest distribution. It is also stated as a prudent buyer will not pay more for an item than he or she will pay for a similar item. Substitution is the primary principle upon which the cost and sales comparison approaches are based.

76. **a.** In the appraisal process, the scope of work occurs before the data collection and analysis.

77. **d.** As market participants make comparisons among similar properties, they substitute one property for another as they make their buying decisions.

78. **c.** Identifying the site attributes occurs *after* the problem is identified.

79. **c.** The age-life method for calculating a depreciation percentage is based on the following relationship: effective age (EA) divided by the sum of EA plus remaining economic life (REL).

80. **b.** The reserves for replacement are the funds set aside to replace short-lived components of the structure such as appliances, floor coverings, wall coverings, roof coverings, HVAC systems, windows, etc.

81. **c.** The protection of the collateral is a key element of the uniform covenants.

82. **b.** The property tax bill is used in the income approach as an operating expense.

83. **c.** Gross living area is the only choice that refers to a dwelling unit. The other area measures are commercial space measures.

84. a. Arm's-length is a catch phrase for *free of condition of sale violations*.

85. d. A restrictive covenant is a private agreement between the seller and the buyer that restricts the use and occupancy of real estate that is part of a deed and is binding on all subsequent purchasers. It can control the use of the property, the lot size, setbacks, and placement of buildings, the number and size of improvements, architecture, or cost of improvements.

86. b. Reconciliation does not call for adjustments to the value estimates for any reason, especially to minimize differences in those value estimates.

87. d. The cost approach (choice **a**) uses comparables in land valuation. The income approach (choice **b**) uses comparable properties to obtain market rent and vacancy as well as operating expenses. In the sales comparison approach (choice **c**), value is estimated by comparing similar properties that have sold recently to the subject property.

88. b. Topography is the general term for features or surface configurations of a property of an area (e.g., hills, valleys, slopes, lakes, rivers). Surface gradations are classified as compound slope, gently sloping land, hilly land, rolling land, undulating land, and very steep land. It can also relate the site to the street system (i.e., at grade, below grade).

Refer to the following for questions 89–92.

The numbers in the table have to be rearranged from high to low or low to high. They are arranged here from low to high and high to low.

	# of Acres	Low to high	High to low
Parcel 1	9	4 (Parcel 4)	19 (Parcel 7)
Parcel 2	5	5 (Parcel 2)	15 (Parcel 3)
Parcel 3	15	8 (Parcel 6)	10 (Parcel 5)
Parcel 4	4	9 (Parcel 1)	9 (Parcel 1)
Parcel 5	10	10 (Parcel 5)	8 (Parcel 6)
Parcel 6	8	15 (Parcel 3)	5 (Parcel 2)
Parcel 7	19	19 (Parcel 7)	4 (Parcel 4)

89. b. Parcel 1, which is 9 acres, represents the median number of acres.

90. a. Ten acres represents the average size of all the parcels. The total sum acreage of the seven parcels is 70. Divide that sum acreage by the number of parcels, 7, to get the average parcel size, 10 acres.

91. c. Fifteen acres represents the range of the parcels. To find the range, subtract the small parcel size from the largest.
$$19 - 4 = 15$$

92. d. 5.4 acres represent the standard deviation. A calculator with statistical capability is needed to find this answer.

93. d. A real estate appraisal must be an unbiased opinion, so it cannot exhibit the appraiser's preferences.

94. d. The increase in value needs to be equal to or greater than the cost to repair a physically deteriorated item in a structure or else that item is considered incurable.

95. b. Public schools are a governmental determinant of value.

96. b. Externalities is the principle that economies outside a property have a positive effect on its value, while diseconomies outside a property have a negative effect on its value.

97. **a.** The government survey system is a land survey system used in Florida, Alabama, Mississippi, and all states north of the Ohio River or west of the Mississippi River, except Texas. It starts with the intersection of lines of longitude (meridians) and latitude (baselines) and then divides land around these intersections into townships approximately six miles squared. Each township contains 36 sections of 640 acres each.

98. **b.** These definitions of land and site are both correct.

99. **c.** $220,000 \times 80\% = \$176,000$, which is the loan amount.
Keystrokes: 176,000 PV, 30 times 12 n, 7%/12 i/YR, then PMT = $1,170.93.

100. **d.** Liquidation value is related to an immediate or quick sale.

▶ Scoring

Once again, in order to evaluate how you did on this last exam, find the number of questions you answered correctly. The passing score for this practice exam is 75 correct (75%), but just as on the real test, you should be aiming for something higher than that on these practice exams. If you haven't reached a passing score on both practice tests, look at the suggestions for improvement in Chapter 2. Look at the following table to see what problem areas remain.

The key to success in almost any pursuit is complete preparation. By taking the practice exams in this book, you have prepared more than many other people who may be taking the exam with you. You have diagnosed where your strengths and weaknesses lie and learned how to deal with the various kinds of questions that will appear on the test. So go into the exam with confidence, knowing that you are ready and equipped to do your best!

Residential Appraisal Practice Exam 2 for Review

Topic	Corresponding Question Numbers
Influences on Real Estate	11, 32, 53, 64, 95
Legal Considerations in Appraisal	1, 22, 39, 74, 85
Types of Value	3, 24, 33, 54, 100
Economic Principles	12, 23, 57, 75, 77, 96
Real Estate Markets and Analysis	2, 16, 31, 44, 55, 66, 71, 81, 99
Valuation Process	4, 26, 63, 70, 76, 78, 86, 87
Property Description	5, 20, 34, 45, 60, 67, 83, 88, 97
Highest and Best Use Analysis	6, 14, 27, 47, 48, 49, 50, 51
Appraisal Math and Statistics	9, 41, 89, 90, 91, 92
Sales Comparison Approach	7, 17, 59, 73, 84, 93
Site Value	10, 28, 43, 46, 98
Cost Approach	8, 36, 56, 79, 82, 94
Income Approach	15, 19, 29, 35, 61, 62, 72, 80
Valuation of Partial Interests	21
Appraisal Standards and Ethics	13, 18, 25, 30, 37, 38, 40, 42, 52, 58, 65, 68, 69

9 ▶ Certified General Appraisal Practice Exam 2

CHAPTER SUMMARY

This is the second of the two practice tests in this book based on the Appraiser Qualifications Board's (AQB) National Uniform Exam Content Outlines for certified general appraisers. Take this exam to see how far you have come since your first practice exam.

THIS IS THE second certified general appraisal practice exam in this book, but it is not designed to be any harder than the first; it is simply another representation of what you might expect on the real test. Just as when you take the real test, there should not be anything here that surprises you. In fact, you probably already know what is in a lot of it! That will be the case with the real test, too.

For this exam, pull together all the tips you have been practicing since the first practice exam. Give yourself the time and space to work. Find out what the time limit is for the actual exam in your state, and try to complete this test in that time frame. Time limits vary between states, but in general, they are between one and three hours. Because you won't be taking the real test in your living room, you might take this one in an unfamiliar location such as a library. In addition, use what you have learned from reading the answer explanations on the previous practice test. Remember the types of questions that caused problems for you in the past, and when you are unsure, try to consider how those answers were explained. Once again, use the answer explanations at the end of the exam to understand questions you may have missed.

After you have taken this written exam, you should try the free online practice test offered with this book—that way you will be familiar with taking exams on a computer. You'll find instructions on how to access this online exam at the back of this book.

▶ Certified General Appraisal Practice Exam 2 Answer Sheet

#						#						#				
1.	ⓐ	ⓑ	ⓒ	ⓓ		46.	ⓐ	ⓑ	ⓒ	ⓓ		91.	ⓐ	ⓑ	ⓒ	ⓓ
2.	ⓐ	ⓑ	ⓒ	ⓓ		47.	ⓐ	ⓑ	ⓒ	ⓓ		92.	ⓐ	ⓑ	ⓒ	ⓓ
3.	ⓐ	ⓑ	ⓒ	ⓓ		48.	ⓐ	ⓑ	ⓒ	ⓓ		93.	ⓐ	ⓑ	ⓒ	ⓓ
4.	ⓐ	ⓑ	ⓒ	ⓓ		49.	ⓐ	ⓑ	ⓒ	ⓓ		94.	ⓐ	ⓑ	ⓒ	ⓓ
5.	ⓐ	ⓑ	ⓒ	ⓓ		50.	ⓐ	ⓑ	ⓒ	ⓓ		95.	ⓐ	ⓑ	ⓒ	ⓓ
6.	ⓐ	ⓑ	ⓒ	ⓓ		51.	ⓐ	ⓑ	ⓒ	ⓓ		96.	ⓐ	ⓑ	ⓒ	ⓓ
7.	ⓐ	ⓑ	ⓒ	ⓓ		52.	ⓐ	ⓑ	ⓒ	ⓓ		97.	ⓐ	ⓑ	ⓒ	ⓓ
8.	ⓐ	ⓑ	ⓒ	ⓓ		53.	ⓐ	ⓑ	ⓒ	ⓓ		98.	ⓐ	ⓑ	ⓒ	ⓓ
9.	ⓐ	ⓑ	ⓒ	ⓓ		54.	ⓐ	ⓑ	ⓒ	ⓓ		99.	ⓐ	ⓑ	ⓒ	ⓓ
10.	ⓐ	ⓑ	ⓒ	ⓓ		55.	ⓐ	ⓑ	ⓒ	ⓓ		100.	ⓐ	ⓑ	ⓒ	ⓓ
11.	ⓐ	ⓑ	ⓒ	ⓓ		56.	ⓐ	ⓑ	ⓒ	ⓓ		101.	ⓐ	ⓑ	ⓒ	ⓓ
12.	ⓐ	ⓑ	ⓒ	ⓓ		57.	ⓐ	ⓑ	ⓒ	ⓓ		102.	ⓐ	ⓑ	ⓒ	ⓓ
13.	ⓐ	ⓑ	ⓒ	ⓓ		58.	ⓐ	ⓑ	ⓒ	ⓓ		103.	ⓐ	ⓑ	ⓒ	ⓓ
14.	ⓐ	ⓑ	ⓒ	ⓓ		59.	ⓐ	ⓑ	ⓒ	ⓓ		104.	ⓐ	ⓑ	ⓒ	ⓓ
15.	ⓐ	ⓑ	ⓒ	ⓓ		60.	ⓐ	ⓑ	ⓒ	ⓓ		105.	ⓐ	ⓑ	ⓒ	ⓓ
16.	ⓐ	ⓑ	ⓒ	ⓓ		61.	ⓐ	ⓑ	ⓒ	ⓓ		106.	ⓐ	ⓑ	ⓒ	ⓓ
17.	ⓐ	ⓑ	ⓒ	ⓓ		62.	ⓐ	ⓑ	ⓒ	ⓓ		107.	ⓐ	ⓑ	ⓒ	ⓓ
18.	ⓐ	ⓑ	ⓒ	ⓓ		63.	ⓐ	ⓑ	ⓒ	ⓓ		108.	ⓐ	ⓑ	ⓒ	ⓓ
19.	ⓐ	ⓑ	ⓒ	ⓓ		64.	ⓐ	ⓑ	ⓒ	ⓓ		109.	ⓐ	ⓑ	ⓒ	ⓓ
20.	ⓐ	ⓑ	ⓒ	ⓓ		65.	ⓐ	ⓑ	ⓒ	ⓓ		110.	ⓐ	ⓑ	ⓒ	ⓓ
21.	ⓐ	ⓑ	ⓒ	ⓓ		66.	ⓐ	ⓑ	ⓒ	ⓓ		111.	ⓐ	ⓑ	ⓒ	ⓓ
22.	ⓐ	ⓑ	ⓒ	ⓓ		67.	ⓐ	ⓑ	ⓒ	ⓓ		112.	ⓐ	ⓑ	ⓒ	ⓓ
23.	ⓐ	ⓑ	ⓒ	ⓓ		68.	ⓐ	ⓑ	ⓒ	ⓓ		113.	ⓐ	ⓑ	ⓒ	ⓓ
24.	ⓐ	ⓑ	ⓒ	ⓓ		69.	ⓐ	ⓑ	ⓒ	ⓓ		114.	ⓐ	ⓑ	ⓒ	ⓓ
25.	ⓐ	ⓑ	ⓒ	ⓓ		70.	ⓐ	ⓑ	ⓒ	ⓓ		115.	ⓐ	ⓑ	ⓒ	ⓓ
26.	ⓐ	ⓑ	ⓒ	ⓓ		71.	ⓐ	ⓑ	ⓒ	ⓓ		116.	ⓐ	ⓑ	ⓒ	ⓓ
27.	ⓐ	ⓑ	ⓒ	ⓓ		72.	ⓐ	ⓑ	ⓒ	ⓓ		117.	ⓐ	ⓑ	ⓒ	ⓓ
28.	ⓐ	ⓑ	ⓒ	ⓓ		73.	ⓐ	ⓑ	ⓒ	ⓓ		118.	ⓐ	ⓑ	ⓒ	ⓓ
29.	ⓐ	ⓑ	ⓒ	ⓓ		74.	ⓐ	ⓑ	ⓒ	ⓓ		119.	ⓐ	ⓑ	ⓒ	ⓓ
30.	ⓐ	ⓑ	ⓒ	ⓓ		75.	ⓐ	ⓑ	ⓒ	ⓓ		120.	ⓐ	ⓑ	ⓒ	ⓓ
31.	ⓐ	ⓑ	ⓒ	ⓓ		76.	ⓐ	ⓑ	ⓒ	ⓓ		121.	ⓐ	ⓑ	ⓒ	ⓓ
32.	ⓐ	ⓑ	ⓒ	ⓓ		77.	ⓐ	ⓑ	ⓒ	ⓓ		122.	ⓐ	ⓑ	ⓒ	ⓓ
33.	ⓐ	ⓑ	ⓒ	ⓓ		78.	ⓐ	ⓑ	ⓒ	ⓓ		123.	ⓐ	ⓑ	ⓒ	ⓓ
34.	ⓐ	ⓑ	ⓒ	ⓓ		79.	ⓐ	ⓑ	ⓒ	ⓓ		124.	ⓐ	ⓑ	ⓒ	ⓓ
35.	ⓐ	ⓑ	ⓒ	ⓓ		80.	ⓐ	ⓑ	ⓒ	ⓓ		125.	ⓐ	ⓑ	ⓒ	ⓓ
36.	ⓐ	ⓑ	ⓒ	ⓓ		81.	ⓐ	ⓑ	ⓒ	ⓓ						
37.	ⓐ	ⓑ	ⓒ	ⓓ		82.	ⓐ	ⓑ	ⓒ	ⓓ						
38.	ⓐ	ⓑ	ⓒ	ⓓ		83.	ⓐ	ⓑ	ⓒ	ⓓ						
39.	ⓐ	ⓑ	ⓒ	ⓓ		84.	ⓐ	ⓑ	ⓒ	ⓓ						
40.	ⓐ	ⓑ	ⓒ	ⓓ		85.	ⓐ	ⓑ	ⓒ	ⓓ						
41.	ⓐ	ⓑ	ⓒ	ⓓ		86.	ⓐ	ⓑ	ⓒ	ⓓ						
42.	ⓐ	ⓑ	ⓒ	ⓓ		87.	ⓐ	ⓑ	ⓒ	ⓓ						
43.	ⓐ	ⓑ	ⓒ	ⓓ		88.	ⓐ	ⓑ	ⓒ	ⓓ						
44.	ⓐ	ⓑ	ⓒ	ⓓ		89.	ⓐ	ⓑ	ⓒ	ⓓ						
45.	ⓐ	ⓑ	ⓒ	ⓓ		90.	ⓐ	ⓑ	ⓒ	ⓓ						

► Certified General Appraisal Practice Exam 2

1. An appraiser does not test the water supply to the subject because no evidence is found to suggest that the supply is less than adequate. This is an example of
   a. an extraordinary assumption.
   b. a hypothetical condition.
   c. an unanticipated problem.
   d. a conditional acceptance.

2. An appraiser has an assignment to value a single-family home. How far back in history must this appraiser research for prior sales of this property?
   a. one year
   b. two years
   c. three years
   d. four years

3. An appraiser who signs a real estate appraisal report prepared by another appraiser
   a. must accept full responsibility for the content of the report.
   b. must have physically inspected the subject.
   c. must have contributed to at least 50% of the work.
   d. is responsible only to the extent of the work he or she performed.

4. What language best fits an appraisal with a prospective effective date?
   a. "The market value is . . ."
   b. "The market value was . . ."
   c. "The market value may be . . ."
   d. "The market value is expected to be . . ."

5. An appraiser has accepted an assignment that requires travel to an area where the appraiser has no recent experience. If the appraiser does not spend sufficient time and effort to understand the nuances of the market related to the specific property, he or she will violate which of the following?
   a. travel provisions
   b. geographic provisions
   c. competency provisions
   d. locational provisions

6. When analyzing a parcel of land in which highest and best use is subdivision development, the appraiser should consider
   a. direct and indirect costs.
   b. the contractor's profit and overhead.
   c. entrepreneurial profit.
   d. all of the above

7. What is the least reliable tool for verifying a sale price?
   a. an appraiser's own files
   b. multiple-listing service (MLS) sale data
   c. the county property appraiser's records
   d. the contract for pending sale

8. A community is experiencing no change in the total population. A decrease in the average size of households in the community would cause
   a. a decrease in the demand for houses.
   b. an increase in the demand for houses.
   c. construction to diminish.
   d. no change.

9. What type of value conclusion ignores the value of land?
   a. insurable value
   b. market value
   c. value in use
   d. investment value

10. A real estate market has many buyers and few sellers, and it is difficult to locate homes for sale. This market may be termed a
    a. buyer's market.
    b. seller's market.
    c. broad market.
    d. heavy market.

11. What impact does an increase in the reserve requirement by the Federal Reserve System have on the availability of credit?
    a. The availability of credit increases.
    b. The availability of credit decreases.
    c. The availability of credit stabilizes.
    d. There is no impact on the availability of credit.

12. All real estate is
    a. scarce and immobile.
    b. scarce and tangible.
    c. tangible and immobile.
    d. tangible and indestructible.

13. What would yield the most reliable indication of value for commercially zoned vacant land?
    a. vacant land sales in an adjacent neighborhood
    b. abstract from improved sales in the subject neighborhood
    c. extract from improved sales in the subject neighborhood
    d. gross sale proceeds of vacant lots less development cost

14. The subject is located in an above-average neighborhood. Two comparables have been located in an adjacent neighborhood that has been judged average by the appraiser. What is the most likely adjustment required for these two comparable sales?
    a. positive adjustment for location
    b. negative adjustment for location
    c. positive adjustment for market conditions
    d. negative adjustment for market conditions

15. R values are used to measure
    a. level of mold contamination.
    b. the existence of radon gas.
    c. resistance to heat transfer.
    d. the quality of residential appraisals.

16. A point estimate of value would be least appropriate for
    a. depreciation deductions.
    b. condemnation proceedings.
    c. property tax abatement.
    d. bidding at auction.

17. An unauthorized physical intrusion into the boundary of a property owned by another is known as
    a. appurtenance.
    b. easement.
    c. encroachment.
    d. leasehold.

18. Using the following data, what depreciation percentage is suggested for the subject improvement, if each sale is equally weighted?

	Sale 1	Sale 2	Sale 3
Price	$450,000	$440,000	$475,000
Land Value	$80,000	$80,000	$90,000
Cost	$425,000	$430,000	$450,000

    a. 13%
    b. 13.5%
    c. 14%
    d. 14.5%

19. The value of observations in a sample will NOT impact the
    a. mean.
    b. median.
    c. mode.
    d. standard deviation.

20. Reasonable exposure to the market in a market value appraisal occurs
    a. prior to the effective appraisal date.
    b. after the effective appraisal date.
    c. on the effective appraisal date.
    d. none of the above. Exposure to the market is not a requirement for a market value appraisal.

21. Mortgage financing is available at an 80% loan-to-value ratio with a mortgage constant of .144451. The portion of the loan paid over the ten-year holding period is .0961, and the property is anticipated to depreciate in value by 5% over the same period. The equity yield rate is 15% and the sinking fund factor based on the equity yield rate for the holding period is .049252. What capitalization rate is indicated?
    a. .1343
    b. .1368
    c. .1418
    d. .1442

22. The subject has 80% of the total value allocated to the improvement and 20% allocated to the land. If the building capitalization rate is 11.5% and the land capitalization rate is 9.5%, what is the overall capitalization rate?
    a. .21
    b. .111
    c. .092
    d. .076

23. Land value for the subject is $60,000. The land capitalization rate is 8% and the overall capitalization rate is 9%. If net operating income is $25,000, what is the capitalization rate for the building?
    a. .083
    b. .084
    c. .093
    d. .109

24. A property generates net operating income of $50,000 and debt service is $43,264. If the mortgage constant is .1565 and the loan-to-value ratio is 75%, what is the overall capitalization rate?
    a. .1356
    b. .1327
    c. .1289
    d. .1116

25. Net operating income is projected to be $12,000 for each of the next five years in the holding period of the investment. The sixth year's income is projected to be $10,000. The terminal capitalization rate is 12%. If the appropriate discount rate is 9%, what is the present value of the reversion at the time of disposition at end of the five-year period?
    a. $31,117
    b. $37,079
    c. $54,158
    d. $83,333

26. The subject has contract rent in the amount of $35,000 annually. Market rent for the subject is judged to be $50,000. Reversionary value is projected to be $400,000. If the lease term is 15 years, and the discount rate is 10%, what is the value of the leasehold interest?
a. $95,756
b. $114,091
c. $209,848
d. $266,212

27. Highest and best use is a consideration in which of the following types of appraisal assignments?
a. market value
b. insurable value
c. value in use
d. all of the above

28. Market financing is available for a 30-year loan term with monthly payments. The annual interest rate is 7%. What is the annual loan constant?
a. .0798
b. .0823
c. .0877
d. .0912

29. A landlord has agreed to purchase dental chairs in a space rented by a dentist. The lease is for five years and the contract rent is $1,700 monthly. The landlord purchased the chairs for $15,800. If the appropriate financing rate for the chairs is 11.5% amortizing monthly, what is the effective rent payment? (Round to the nearest dollar.)
a. $1,339
b. $1,353
c. $1,398
d. $1,453

30. Carpet will require replacement in three years. The current replacement cost for the carpet is $10,000. It is anticipated that this cost will increase 4% each year. If the reserve account earns 6% annually, what contribution would have to be made at the end of each year to pay for the carpet at the scheduled time for its replacement?
a. $3,251
b. $3,432
c. $3,533
d. $3,749

31. Current net operating income is $120,000. If net operating income is projected to grow 5% annually, what is the anticipated net operating income for the fourth year of the holding period?
a. $139,990
b. $141,810
c. $145,860
d. $152,240

32. For each dollar of effective gross income collected, property value increases by a constant increment. This describes
a. a capitalization rate.
b. a gross rent multiplier.
c. an operating expense ratio.
d. a net operating ratio.

33. As part of an agreement to provide testimony as to the value of the deceased's property, a judge has asked that you provide a letter opinion of value to be entered as evidence at trial. How would you best comply with the judge's request?
  a. The letter must be written to comply with the reporting requirements of either a self-contained, summary, or restricted-use report.
  b. You must write a letter with a value conclusion as instructed by the judge.
  c. Reports written as a letter are never appropriate.
  d. Evidence must be submitted in a self-contained report.

34. An appraiser may be an advocate for
  a. assignment results.
  b. a client.
  c. himself or herself.
  d. all of the above

35. A state-certified general appraiser has been asked to estimate the market value of the leased fee of an office building. The appraiser decides that the use of discounted cash flow techniques is appropriate for the appraisal assignment. The office building has five floors and multiple tenants on each floor. Existing leases are of various terms, and during inspection, the appraiser finds that several of the leases expire during the projection period. There are several office buildings in the area similar to the subject. How should the appraiser analyze rent during the projection period in application of discounted cash flow techniques?
  a. Market rent should be analyzed and converted into value during the lease terms and following lease expiration.
  b. Contract rent should be analyzed and converted into value during lease terms and following lease expiration.
  c. Market rent should be analyzed and converted into value during lease terms; contract rent should be used after lease expiration.
  d. Contract rent should be analyzed and converted into value during lease terms; market rent should be used following lease expiration.

36. What is the probability that the subject property will fall within the range of value suggested by measuring the value of one standard deviation from the mean in a normally distributed sample?
  a. 68%
  b. 72%
  c. 88%
  d. 98%

37. The subject is being appraised in April. A similar property traded in the same market sold the prior July for $89,000 and sold again the following March for $98,000. If no other adjustments were necessary, what is the indicated monthly rate of change in this market?
   a. .0139
   b. .0132
   c. .0121
   d. .0119

38. Which of the following appraisal reports is NOT recognized in a federally related transaction?
   a. self-contained
   b. restricted use
   c. summary
   d. oral

39. Examination of prior sale of the subject would be performed to protect against
   a. refinancing.
   b. flipping.
   c. moral turpitude.
   d. gentrification.

40. The design and placement of windows, doors, and other openings in a structure is
   a. fenestration.
   b. gentrification.
   c. plottage.
   d. windage.

41. The value determined by a local taxing authority as a basis for *ad valorem* taxation is
   a. taxable value.
   b. assessed value.
   c. market value.
   d. value in use.

42. The following adjustments have been made to a comparable sale. What is the net adjustment?
+2% Property Right
−5% Location
   a. −3.1%
   b. −3%
   c. +3%
   d. +3.1%

43. The most precise method of estimating construction cost that also requires the greatest amount of expertise is
   a. segregated cost.
   b. unit in place.
   c. comparative unit.
   d. quantity survey.

44. An income property is leased for $8,200 annually. Vacancy and collection loss is estimated to be 4% of annual rent. Total annual operating expense is $3,500. Annual debt service is $4,000. What is the debt service ratio for this property?
   a. 1.09
   b. 1.2
   d. 1.25
   e. 1.3

45. Industrial buildings are measured in terms of
   a. GBA.
   b. GLA.
   c. GTA.
   d. GTO.

46. All of the following are variable operating expenses of real property EXCEPT
   a. depreciation.
   b. maintenance.
   c. management.
   d. utilities.

47. If the comparable property has a deck worth $4,000, but the subject property does not, what is the correct adjustment?
   a. Subtract $4,000 from the comparable property.
   b. Add $4,000 to the comparable property.
   c. Subtract $4,000 from the subject property.
   d. Add $4,000 to the subject property.

48. A property sold for $280,000. Replacement cost of the improvements at the time of sale was $250,000 and land value was $80,000. The difference between the sale price and the replacement cost is
   a. builder's profit.
   b. value.
   c. depreciation.
   d. realized sale price.

49. Value indications should be rounded to reflect the
   a. interest of the client.
   b. imprecision of data.
   c. location of the property.
   d. lack of valuation expertise.

50. A site contains 12,000 square feet. Using regression analysis, it is determined that the marginal contribution of an additional square foot is $1.98. Minimum value of property in the subdivision is $6,000, regardless of size. What is the indicated property value?
   a. $32,900
   b. $29,760
   c. $24,620
   d. $18,420

51. What is the annual percentage rate on a fully amortizing loan with monthly payments if the beginning balance is $150,000, the term is 30 years, the annual interest rate is 12%, and the lender charges four discount points?
   a. 12.02%
   b. 12.08%
   c. 12.12%
   d. 12.55%

52. An appraisal of a property indicates that the total property value is $100,000. A portion of the property is being condemned. The condemned portion is appraised for $20,000. If an after-appraisal indicates the property to be worth $85,000, what is the compensation due the owner?
   a. $15,000
   b. $20,000
   c. $85,000
   d. $100,000

53. For every mile measured from the lake, a corresponding decrease is found in property value. What is the indicated correlation coefficient?
   a. +1
   b. 0
   c. −1
   d. no relationship

54. The loss in property value, which may occur in a partial taking, is
   a. special damage.
   b. severance damage.
   c. remainder damage.
   d. jurisdictional damage.

55. What is the square footage of a site described by the legal description, beginning at the NW corner of Section 8, T2S, R15E, thence 2,500 feet to the POB, S 0 E 150 feet, thence N 90 E 50 feet, thence N 0 E 100 feet, thence N 45 W 70.71 feet to the POB?
   a. 9,200
   b. 6,250
   c. 5,750
   d. 5,250

56. What type of appraisal report is characterized by the use of tables of data?
   a. self-contained
   b. summary
   c. restricted use
   d. oral

57. Which of the following illustrate the applicability of appraisal standards, but are not enforceable?
   a. statements
   b. rules
   c. advisory opinions
   d. all of the above

58. What type of study focuses on specific goals of an investor to determine the optimum use for specified real estate?
   a. highest and best use
   b. feasibility
   c. marketability
   d. rent

59. An informed purchaser will pay no more for a property than the cost of acquiring an acceptable substitute describes the principle of
   a. opportunity cost.
   b. substitution.
   c. balance.
   d. competition.

60. A mortgage lender wishes to protect his or her loan origination investment. What type of value would best suit this lender's goal?
   a. liquidation value
   b. market value
   c. going-concern value
   d. cost value

61. Victorian homes in a neighborhood are being restored following the original plan, form, and style of the structures. Which of the following terms best describes this restoration?
   a. modernization
   b. remodeling
   c. rehabilitation
   d. renovation

62. Which of the following is NOT a site improvement?
   a. landscaping
   b. driveway
   c. garage
   d. irrigation system

63. The taking of public property for a private use is
   a. eminent domain.
   b. condemnation.
   c. appropriation.
   d. expropriation.

64. A home has suffered from below-average maintenance. It is located in a neighborhood where the surrounding homes have been very well maintained. The poorly maintained home is benefiting in value from its association with the surrounding homes. This is the appraisal principle of
   a. regression.
   b. progression.
   c. contribution.
   d. change.

65. Appraisal data is all of the following EXCEPT
 a. universal.
 b. logical.
 c. defensible.
 d. variable.

66. In an attempt to value a site, an appraiser located three equally comparable sales. Based on the verified sales data, what is the value of the subject on a per-acre basis if no adjustments are necessary? (Round to the nearest $1,000.)

Subject	X	60 Acres
Comparable A	$665,000	72 Acres
Comparable B	$520,00	52 Acres
Comparable C	$640,000	70 Acres

 a. $608,400
 b. $595,280
 c. $567,560
 d. $562,142

67. The existing site is below street grade and must be filled at a cost of $1,000 and public walk must be installed at a cost of $900. There are three comparable sites in the subdivision that are now ready for construction that were identical to the subject when they sold for $18,000 each. The annual inflation rate is 6%. What market value is indicated for the subject?
 a. $16,100
 b. $17,000
 c. $18,000
 d. $19,200

68. Replacement cost of a house is $42,000. The improvement is estimated to be 10% depreciated. What is the value of the house?
 a. $37,800
 b. $45,450
 c. $46,300
 d. $55,000

69. Identification of houses with three bedrooms, two bathrooms, and pools all sold in the same market within the prior six months is
 a. penetration.
 b. forecasting.
 c. segmentation.
 d. saturation.

70. Investment in real estate differs from investment in stocks and bonds in that
 a. real estate is less liquid than stocks and bonds.
 b. stocks and bonds must be managed.
 c. stocks and bonds require a larger capital outlay.
 d. real estate assets are homogeneous.

71. An appraiser finds that an energy-efficient earth home has been built in an area of conventional construction. The home is found to be virtually unmarketable because of its unique construction. What appraisal principle applies?
 a. conformity
 b. balance
 c. externalities
 d. competition

72. What depreciation is possible in an improvement that is determined to be highest and best use of land as though vacant?
 a. physical
 b. functional
 c. external
 d. none of the above

73. The starting point in measuring accrued depreciation is
 a. original cost.
 b. acquisition cost.
 c. replacement cost.
 d. direct cost.

74. An appraiser has observed a reasonable degree of similarity to the subject with respect to the architectural design, market desirability, and the influence of noise pollution from a nearby interstate highway. Which principle of value best applies?
   a. balance
   b. supply and demand
   c. consistent use
   d. conformity

75. Improvements have been made to the street, sidewalks, and sewers that have caused an increase in property value. The cost of these improvements may be paid by
   a. *ad valorem* tax.
   b. special assessment.
   c. appropriation.
   d. distribution.

76. Which of the following is NOT a governmental influence on value?
   a. census information
   b. police protection
   c. zoning
   d. building codes

77. The value conclusion reported in a self-contained report, compared to a value opinion in a restricted-use report, is
   a. equally reliable.
   b. less reliable.
   c. not reliable.
   d. more reliable.

78. A developer is marketing a subdivision consisting of 100 lots. It was originally thought that all lots could be sold within three years. There have been 26 lots sold in 24 months. What is the monthly absorption rate?
   a. 1.08%
   b. 2.6%
   c. 5.7%
   d. 6.01%

79. What window style is hinged at the top of the sash, allowing the window to open horizontally?
   a. jalousie
   b. awning
   c. double hung
   d. single pane

80. The Department of Transportation is taking a five-acre tract for highway right-of-way and leaving a remainder with a building on it. How is the value of the take and damages to the remainder determined?
   a. Value the entire tract and the five acres and then subtract it from the whole.
   b. Value the entire tract and the remainder and then subtract it from the whole.
   c. Value the five-acre tract and the building and then add the two together.
   d. Value the five-acre tract only.

81. What portion of the individual condominium or Planned Unit Development (PUD) unit form report is to be completed by the lender?
   a. cost approach
   b. estimate of defined value
   c. budget analysis
   d. loan charges to be paid by the seller

82. Potential uses are being considered for the development of a site. Based on the following information, which investment alternative is the highest and best use for the site?

	Apartment	Retail	Office	Motel
Cost to Construct	$400,000	$200,000	$350,000	$950,000
Net Operating Income	$100,000	$80,000	$95,000	$140,000
Building Cap Rate	12%	12%	12%	12%

   a. apartment
   b. retail
   c. office
   d. motel

83. Which of the following is NOT a measure of central tendency of a sample?
   a. mean
   b. median
   c. mode
   d. standard deviation

84. A structure has many super-adequacies. What appraisal principle applies?
   a. supply and demand
   b. substitution
   c. increasing returns
   d. decreasing returns

85. Appraisers in the local community are seeing an increase in rent levels for investment property. The increased rent levels have pushed prices paid for these properties higher. This increase in prices represents the impact of
   a. social value influences.
   b. economic value influences.
   c. governmental value influences.
   d. environmental value influences.

86. Why would an appraiser choose to use a market data grid in sales comparison?
   a. It is required by USPAP.
   b. It facilitates the comparison process.
   c. It justifies fees charged.
   d. Appraisers do not use market data grids in sales comparison.

87. If a discount rate of 10% is appropriate, which of the following alternatives represents the highest and best use of the site?

Use	NOI	Cost	Economic Life
Office	$175,000	$375,000	50 years
Strip Center	$169,000	$200,000	40 years
Lounge	$205,000	$400,000	30 years
Garage	$120,000	$100,000	40 years

   a. office
   b. strip center
   c. lounge
   d. garage

88. An appraiser accepts an assignment to appraise a property in an area where criminal activity has recently been publicized. The most acceptable terminology describing this activity in an appraisal report is
  a. one crime reported annually per 1,000 population.
  b. high crime area.
  c. unsafe living conditions.
  d. sporting opportunities available.

89. The subject has been judged to require a negative 5% adjustment for financing and a negative 10% adjustment for location. What is the net adjustment?
  a. –15%
  b. –14.5%
  c. –14%
  d. –13.5%

90. Value in use requires
  a. scarcity.
  b. transferability.
  c. utility.
  d. demand.

91. A comparable property sold for $50,000. Due to location, the comparable property is judged to be 5% inferior to the subject property. What adjustment should be made to the comparable property?
  a. –$2,421
  b. –$2,500
  c. +$2,500
  d. +$2,631

92. Which principle states that the value is created by the expectations of future benefits associated with ownership of the land or site?
  a. anticipation
  b. demand
  c. substitution
  d. supply

93. Which of the following is NOT part of a septic system?
  a. water meter
  b. sanitary tee
  c. absorption field
  d. distribution box

94. What income capitalization technique may be used to identify the highest and best use of land as though vacant?
  a. building residual
  b. land residual
  c. equity band of investment
  d. mortgage band of investment

95. The utility produced by the last unit of an economic good or service determines its value. This is the economic principle of
  a. supply and demand.
  b. balance.
  c. regression.
  d. marginal utility.

96. When is internal rate of return an unreliable measurement of investment performance?
  a. when no down payment is made
  b. irregular income stream
  c. when reversion at the end of the investment is zero
  d. always

97. The subject is located on a street surrounded by commercial properties. Zoning and deed restrictions for the subject require multifamily residential use for the subject. Which of the following will be the most likely highest and best use?
   a. retail
   b. single family
   c. apartment
   d. motel

98. The final profitable application of capital to a site is
   a. extensive margin.
   b. intensive margin.
   c. margin.
   d. sub-margin.

99. The appraisal for a property for the price that it would bring in a quick sale with a short marketing time assumed is found in
   a. investment value.
   b. value in use.
   c. liquidation value.
   d. insurable value.

100. Which of the following is NOT true concerning a measurement of insurable value?
   a. It ignores land value.
   b. It emphasizes replacement cost estimate.
   c. It anticipates a sale of the subject.
   d. It considers amenities in the improvement.

101. A designation of the U.S. Census Bureau for metropolitan areas with a central city having at least 50,000 people and including all counties that are economically linked is
   a. a township.
   b. a district.
   c. a metropolitan statistical area.
   d. an economic base area.

102. Which roof design would be best able to withstand the impact of hurricane force winds?
   a. salt box
   b. gambrel
   c. gable
   d. hip

103. The increment of value obtained when two or more properties are combined to achieve highest and best use is
   a. assemblage.
   b. plottage.
   c. agglomeration.
   d. gentrification.

104. What type of wiring would the market typically prefer?
   a. copper
   b. aluminum
   c. nickel
   d. steel

105. In the market, the optimum use of real property is identified in what study?
   a. market
   b. feasibility
   c. highest and best use
   d. rent comparability

106. The lower part of an interior wall that is decorated differently from the upper portion, or is separated by a molding and finished in a material different from the upper portion, is
   a. veneer.
   b. wainscot.
   c. nogging.
   d. sheathing.

107. The extent of research and analysis that is conducted in an appraisal report defines
   a. appraiser certification.
   b. hypothetical conditions.
   c. scope of work.
   d. extraordinary assumptions.

108. When an appraiser makes the decision to exclude the cost approach in an appraisal assignment, the decision is
   a. an ethics violation.
   b. a competency issue.
   c. a scope of work consideration.
   d. a limited assumption.

109. In an appraisal assignment, highest and best use of land as though vacant, and highest and best use of the property as improved, is
   a. sometimes the same.
   b. greater than as though vacant in property as improved.
   c. less than as though vacant in property as improved.
   d. never the same.

110. Interim use is best described as
   a. a preexisting use that predates a change in zoning.
   b. an improvement that enhances land value.
   c. a temporary use that results in a change in zoning.
   d. an increment of value gained during a period of transition.

111. Net operating income is $20,000. The discount rate is 10% and the remaining economic life expectancy for the improvement is 25 years. Land value at the end of the building's economic life is anticipated to be $90,000. What is the value of the property? (Round answer to the nearest thousand.)
   a. $160,000
   b. $170,000
   c. $180,000
   d. $190,000

112. In an office building, what term describes the area capable of generating income compared to the total area of the building?
   a. income ratio
   b. use ratio
   c. efficiency ratio
   d. net efficiency ratio

113. An appraiser is analyzing a hotel property for highest and best use. The appraiser determines that there is an existing lease between the hotel and an airline to house flight crews on layovers. This impacts what criteria in highest and best use analysis?
   a. legally permitted
   b. physically possible
   c. marginally acceptable
   d. appropriately financed

114. According to the following data, what is the operating expense ratio?

Sale Price	$120,000
Potential Gross Income	$12,000
Operating Expenses	$3,000
Debt Service	$6,200
Effective Gross Income	$9,000
Net Operating Income	$5,875

   a. 31.5%
   b. 33%
   c. 53.8%
   d. 57.2%

115. Which of the following is true concerning an ideal improvement?
   a. It takes maximum advantage of the site's potential.
   b. It conforms to current market standards.
   c. It contains the most suitably priced components.
   d. all of the above

116. Making adjustments in the sales comparison approach
   a. reduces reliability of the approach.
   b. improves the reliability of the approach.
   c. involves no particular sequence.
   d. all of the above

117. When is the cost approach most reliable in indicating market value?
   a. Improvements represent the highest and best use of the land as though vacant.
   b. Improvements are relatively new.
   c. Improvements are unique.
   d. It is never reliable.

118. An appraiser is estimating replacement cost of the subject improvements using a benchmark structure. The benchmark lacks a fireplace and a pool, both components in the subject. How would the appraiser estimate the cost of these components?
   a. comparative unit
   b. unit in place
   c. quantitative reduction
   d. unit in comparison

119. A property is sold for $100,000 and analysis of the transaction indicates a net operating income of $10,000, an equity investment of $25,000, and a mortgage loan in the amount of $75,000, payable in annual installments of $7,125. Leverage in this investment is
   a. positive.
   b. negative.
   c. equal.
   d. There is insufficient information.

120. Property is purchased for $460,000, five years ago. Today, the property is worth $550,000. What is the annual rate of appreciation demonstrated by this property?
   a. 3.63%
   b. 4.28%
   c. 4.65%
   d. 4.91%

121. Where would a floor's location in a building be found?
   a. on a topographic map
   b. on a flood map
   c. on a building survey
   d. in tax assessor's data

122. Which of the following factors would NOT be important in comparing properties within the sales comparison approach?
   a. difference in sale date
   b. difference in real estate taxes
   c. difference in appearance
   d. difference in original construction cost

123. In what approach is an opinion of market value developed by comparing properties similar to the subject that have recently sold, are listed for sale, or are under contract?
   a. market approach
   b. income capitalization
   c. cost approach
   d. unit in place

124. According to FNMA guidelines, the gross adjustment percentage for an ideal comparable should NOT exceed
   a. 30%.
   b. 25%.
   c. 20%.
   d. 15%.

125. A property appears to be earning above-average returns. In order to estimate future cash flows, an appraiser should perform a detailed analysis of
   a. competition.
   b. substations.
   c. conformity.
   d. surplus production.

▶ Answers

1. a. Extraordinary assumptions are made when a condition that may exist is not verified. Hypothetical conditions exist when a condition is created that does not exist.

2. c. According to USPAP Standard Rule 1–5(b), an appraiser must research at least three years for prior sales.

3. a. As required by USPAP Standard Rule 2–3, an appraiser who signs a real estate appraisal report prepared by another appraiser must accept full responsibility for the content of that report.

4. d. In an appraisal, prospective effective dates occur in the future, so the language used should be consistent.

5. c. According to the "Competency" rule in USPAP, the appraiser will be in violation of competency provisions.

6. d. Direct and indirect costs, contractor's profit and overhead, as well as entrepreneurial profit, are all considerations in the subdivision analysis technique in land valuation.

7. d. The least reliable tool for verifying a sale price is a contract for pending sale because it is unknown if that sale ever actually closes at that price.

8. b. More households are needed if there is a decrease in the average size of households in the community coupled with the community's population size remaining constant.

9. a. Insurable value considers the replacement cost of the improvement only.

10. b. When the market is undersupplied, sellers have control of the prices, and therefore, home values increase as a result.

11. b. An increase in the reserve requirement will cause lenders to keep more capital on hand, making fewer dollars available for mortgage loans.

12. c. Real estate is physical in nature, which makes it tangible and immobile (which means fixed in location).

13. a. When available, vacant land sales in an adjacent neighborhood should always be compared to measure vacant land.

14. a. Location in a different neighborhood would require a location adjustment; in this case, a positive adjustment for location.

15. c. *R* values indicate the resistance to the transfer of heat: The higher the *R* value, the greater the resistance.

16. d. An auction participant would like to know when to begin bidding and when to end. A range of value would be most appropriate.

17. c. This is the definition of an encroachment.

18. d. The math solution is as follows:
Sale Price – Land Value = Value of Improvement
Cost – Value of Improvement = Depreciation
$\frac{\text{Depreciation}}{\text{Cost}}$ = Percentage of Depreciation

19. b. Median is the positional average in a sample and is determined by the number of observations, not the value of the observations.

20. a. The subject is assumed to sell on the effective appraisal date. To accomplish this sale, it must be exposed prior to the date.

21. **d.** The math solution is as follows using the Akerson (Ellwood) Formula.

$.80 \times .144451 = .1156$

$LTV(M) \qquad R_M$

$.20 \times .15 = .03$

$1 - M \times Y_E$

$.80 \times .0961 \times .049252 = .003786$

M% loan paid SFF

$-5 \times .049252 = -.0024262$

$-\Delta o \qquad SFF$

$.1156 + .03 - .003786 = .141814$ (Basic Rate)

$.141814 - (-.0024262) = .1442$

22. **b.** The math solution is as follows using the land and building band of investment:

$.20 \times .095 = .019$ (Weighted Land Rate)

$.80 \times .115 = .092$ (Weighted Building Rate)

$.019 + .092 = .111$ (Overall Capitalization Rate)

23. **c.** The math solution is as follows using the land residual technique:

$\$60,000 \times .08 = \$4,800$ (Income to the Land)

$\$25,000 - \$4,800 = \$20,200$ (Income to the Building)

$\dfrac{\$25,000}{.09} = \$277,777$ (Value Overall)

$\$277,777 - \$60,000 = \$217,777$ (Value of the Building)

$\dfrac{\$20,200}{\$217,777} = .0927$, which rounds to .093 (Rate of the Building)

24. **a.** The math solution is as follows using the debt coverage formula:

$\dfrac{\$50,000}{\$43,264} = .11556$ (Debt Coverage Ratio)

$.11556 \times .1565 \times .75 = .1356$ (Overall Capitalization Rate)

25. **c.** The math solution is as follows using a Hewlett Packard 12c:

$\dfrac{\$10,000}{.12} = \$83,333$

Keystrokes: 5 n, 9 i, \$83,333 FV

Solve for PV = \$54,160

26. **b.** The math solution is as follows using a Hewlett Packard 12c:

$\$50,000 - \$35,000 = \$15,000$

Keystrokes: 15 n, 10 i, \$15,000 PMT

Solve for PV = \$114,091

27. **a.** Highest and best use reflects how property is traded in the marketplace. Market value assumes that a sale will occur.

28. **a.** Math solution is as follows using a Hewlett Packard 12c:

Keystrokes: 30 g n, 7 g i, 1 PV

Solve for PMT = $.006653 \times 12 = .0798$

29. **b.** Math solution is as follows using a Hewlett Packard 12c:

Keystrokes: 5 g n, 11.5 g i, \$15,800 PV

Solve for PMT = \$347.48

$\$1,700 - \$347.48 = \$1,352.52$, which rounds to \$1,353

30. **c.** Math solution is as follows using a Hewlett Packard 12c:

Keystrokes: 3 n, 4 i, \$10,000 PV

Solve for FV = \$11,248

3 n, 6 i, \$11,248 FV

Solve for PMT = \$3,533

31. **c.** Math solution is as follows using the Hewlett Packard 12c:

Keystrokes: 4 n, 5 i, \$120,000 PV

Solve for FV = \$145,860

32. **b.** Gross rent multiplier is a unit of comparison that states the value per dollar of gross income.

33. **a.** All appraisal reports must follow one of three reporting options (self-contained, summary, or restricted-use), as per the USPAP Standard Rule 2–2.

34. **a.** Appraisers must not be biased, but must be supportive of their assignment results.

35. **d.** Contract rent dictates the value of a leased fee; however, if contract rent is not available, market rent is utilized.

36. **a.** According to probabilities dictated by standard deviation, the probability is 68%.

37. **c.** The math solution is as follows using a Hewlett Packard 12c.
Keystrokes: 8 n, $89,000 CHS PV, $98,000 FV
Solve for $i = .0121$

38. **d.** Oral reports are legal; however, they are not recognized, because oral representations are difficult to support.

39. **b.** Researching prior sales gives the appraiser insight as to how the market has treated the subject previously and alerts the appraiser to suspicious sales.

40. **a.** The design and placement of windows, doors, and other openings in the structure is defined as fenestration.

41. **b.** The value determined by a local taxing authority as a basis for *ad valorem* taxation is assessed value. Taxable value (choice **a**) is not valid terminology. Market value (choice **c**) is the most likely selling price. Value in use (choice **d**) reflects utility.

42. **a.** The math solution is as follows.
$1 + .02 = 1.02$
$1.02 \times .05 = .051$
$1.02 - .051 = .969$
$1 - .969 = .031$, or -3.1%
The property right adjustment must be made prior to the location adjustment. The answer is negative because the adjusted sale price is less than the beginning sale price.

43. **d.** Quantity survey identifies the smallest possible component of construction.

44. **a.** The math solution is as follows using the debt coverage formula.
$8,200 \times .04 = 328
$8,200 - $328 = $7,872$
$7,872 - $3,500 = $4,372$
$\frac{\$4,372}{\$4,000} = 1.093$, or 1.09

45. **a.** GBA is gross building area.

46. **a.** Depreciation is not a recurring annual expenditure.

47. **a.** The comparable property must be adjusted to the subject property; here, the appraiser would subtract the market value of the deck ($4,000) from the price of the comparable property.

48. **c.** The replacement cost sets the upper limit of what a reasonable purchaser would pay. Therefore, any difference in cost and the price paid must be depreciation.

49. **b.** The less precise the data, the more rounding is required.

50. **b.** The math solution is as follows:
$1.98 \times 12,000 = $23,760$
$23,760 + $6,000 = $29,760$

51. **d.** The math solution is as follows using a Hewlett Packard 12c:
Keystrokes: 30 g n, 12 g i, $150,000 PV, PMT = $1,542
$150,000 \times .04 = $6,000$
$150,000 - $6,000 = $144,000$
Keystrokes: 30 g n, $144,000 PV, $1,542 CHS PMT
Solve for $i = 1.045505$
$1.045505 \times 12 = 12.546$, which rounds to 12.55%

52. **b.** Compensation is based on the appraisal of the condemned portion of the property ($20,000). Compensation is not offset by the increase in value of the residue.

53. **c.** This describes a direct inverse relationship. Choice **a** describes a direct positive relationship.

54. b. The loss in property value that may occur in a partial taking is defined as severance damages.

55. b. The math solution is as follows.

$100' \times 50' = 5{,}000$ square foot rectangular section

$50' \times 50' = 2{,}500$

$\frac{2{,}500}{2} = 1{,}250$ square foot triangular section

$5{,}000 + 1{,}250 = 6{,}250$

56. b. According to USPAP, the summary appraisal report is characterized by summarizing data. The best way to summarize is to place the data in a table.

57. c. Advisory opinions are used to illustrate and offer advice from the ASB.

58. b. Investor-specific goals must be considered because feasibility varies from investor to investor.

59. b. By purchasing one property, the opportunity is given up to buy another.

60. b. The lender is interested in the price the property would sell for in the event of default and subsequent foreclosure.

61. c. Following the original plan, form, and style results in the rehabilitation of the same design.

62. c. Site improvements are necessary for a site to be developed to its highest and best use. The garage is part of an improvement that could be highest and best use.

63. c. The taking of public property for a private use is defined as appropriation.

64. b. Progression is the appraisal principle that suggests that inferior properties benefit from their association with superior properties.

65. a. Data is collected for every appraisal assignment. It is not universally applicable.

66. c. The math solution is as follows:

$\frac{\$665{,}000}{72} = \$9{,}236$ per acre

$\frac{\$520{,}000}{52} = \$10{,}000$ per acre

$\frac{\$640{,}000}{70} = \$9{,}142$ per acre

$\$9{,}236 + \$10{,}000 + \$9{,}142 = \frac{\$28{,}378}{3} =$

$\$9{,}459$ per acre $\times 60 = \$567{,}560$

67. c. By direct comparison, the subject would be worth $18,000.

68. a. The math solution is as follows.

$\$42{,}000 \times .10 = \$4{,}200$

$\$42{,}000 - \$4{,}200 = \$37{,}800$

69. c. Dividing the housing market into smaller components for the purpose of analysis is market segmentation.

70. a. Real estate is unique, and as a result, there are few potential purchasers for any one property; therefore, real estate is less liquid.

71. a. Property values are maximized when improvements are in harmony with their environment. This unique home violates the appraisal principle of conformity.

72. d. Assuming the land is vacant, any improvement that is highest and best use must meet all the requirements being legally permitted, physically possible, financially feasible, and maximally productive. It is the ideal improvement.

73. c. The appraiser can use either replacement cost or reproduction cost as a beginning point.

74. d. The appraisal principle of conformity states that improvements are in harmony with their environment.

75. b. Property owners who benefit from the improvements may be asked to pay for their costs by special assessment.

76. a. Census information deals with population characteristics; therefore, it is a social value influence.

77. a. The reporting option chosen by the appraiser does not influence the reliability of the value conclusion.

78. a. $\frac{26}{24} = \frac{1.08}{100} = .0108$, or 1.08%.

79. b. A window that is hinged at the top of the sash, allowing the window to open horizontally, is known as an awning window.

80. b. By subtracting the value of the remainder from the value of the entire property, that which remains includes the value of the taking and any damages.

81. d. According to Fannie Mae guidelines, the lender is required to inform the appraiser of any concessions paid by the seller.

82. c. The math solution is as follows:

Apartment: $400,000 × .12 = $48,000;
$100,000 − $48,000 = $52,000

Retail: $290,000 × .12 = $34,800;
$80,000 − $34,800 = $45,200

Office: $350,000 × .12 = $42,000;
$95,000 − $42,000 = $53,000

Motel: $950,000 × .12 = $114,000;
$140,000 − $114,000 = $26,000

The highest and best use generates the greatest amount of residual income to land; therefore, the office (choice **c**) is the best investment.

83. d. Standard deviation is a measure of variation of a sample.

84. d. Super-adequacies cost more than what they contribute to value.

85. b. Rent and price levels are property characteristics. Property characteristics fall in the category of economic value influences.

86. b. The comparison of sales is simplified by organizing data on a market data grid.

87. c. The math solution is as follows using a Hewlett Packard 12c:

Office:
Keystrokes: 50 n, 10 i, $175,000 PMT,
PV = $1,735,092 − $375,000 = $1,360,092

Strip center:
Keystrokes: 40 n, 10 i, $169,000 PMT,
PV = $1,652,659 − $200,000 = $1,452,659

Lounge:
Keystrokes: 30 n, 10 i, $205,000 PMT,
PV = $1,932,517 − $400,000 = $1,532,517

Garage:
Keystrokes: 40 n, 10 i, $120,000 PMT,
PV = $1,173,486 − $100,000 = $1,073,486

Highest and best use generates the highest net present value, which is the lounge (choice **c**).

88. a. The appraiser should use factual data that is not subject to interpretation by the reader of the report.

89. b. The math solution is as follows.

1 − .05 = .95

.95 × .10 = .095

.95 − .095 = .855

1 − .855 = .145, or 14.5%

Percentage adjustments are made in a sequence that requires that adjustments for the characteristics of the transaction are made before adjustments for property characteristics.

90. c. Value in use measures only utility.

91. d. The math solution is as follows.

$\frac{1}{.95} = 1.052631 × $50,000$
$= $52,631 − $50,000 = $2,631$

The comparable is stated in terms of the unknown subject.

92. a. Anticipation is the perception that value is created by the expectation of financial or psychological benefits (pride of ownership, shelter, etc.) to be derived in the future.

93. a. Water meter is part of the water supply.

94. **a.** Residual techniques measure the income left over to a component of the property. The improvement that generates the greatest residual income to the land is the highest and best use of the property as though vacant.

95. **d.** Once the market is satisfied with a component, additional components contribute less to value.

96. **a.** The internal rate of return measures investment performance; if no investment is made, then the internal rate of return would not be an adequate tool.

97. **c.** The first consideration in determining highest and best use is legally possible. If the zoning requires a multifamily, then that would be the legally possible use for the property. Therefore, apartments would be the most likely highest and best use.

98. **b.** This is the principle of intensive margin. Once this point is reached, capital should be spent elsewhere.

99. **c.** Limitation on marketing time usually results in a lower sales price.

100. **c.** A sale of the subject is not necessary in insurable value, as destruction of the improvement is anticipated.

101. **c.** A function of the census is to maintain demographic and economic data. Cities and counties are linked economically as metropolitan statistical areas.

102. **d.** Hip roofs are sloped on four sides, so wind pressure actually serves to exert downward pressure regardless of wind direction.

103. **b.** Plottage is the value earned from the combination of two or more properties under a single ownership to increase value.

104. **a.** The two possible types of wiring include copper and aluminum. Aluminum has been rejected in many markets because of its poor reputation for resistance to fire damage.

105. **c.** Highest and best use is market determined. Feasibility studies are investor-specific.

106. **b.** This is the definition of wainscot.

107. **c.** The scope of work is determined by the nature of the appraisal assignment. The scope of work must be broad enough to develop credible assignment results. See the USPAP "Scope of Work" rule.

108. **c.** Eliminating an application of an appraisal approach limits the scope of the appraisal, possibly reducing the reliability of the value conclusion.

109. **a.** Based on consistent use, highest and best use categories should usually be the same in an appraisal assignment.

110. **a.** Interim uses contribute to value but do not fully explain the motivation of the buyer. Buyers are expected to anticipate the long-term prospects for the property in making a purchase decision.

111. **d.** The math solution is as follows using a Hewlett Packard 12c:
Keystrokes: 25 n, 10 i, $20,000 PMT
Solve for PV = $181,540
Keystrokes: 25 n, 10 i, $90,000 FV
Solve for PV = $8,306
$181,540 + $8,306 = $189,846

112. **c.** As it relates to the total building area, the efficiency ratio is the part of the building that is capable of generating rent. Hallways, lobbies, stairs, and elevator shafts are not included in the efficiency ratio.

113. **a.** Leases legally restrict the possibility of finding more profitable options for the property.

114. **b.** The math solution is as follows:
$\frac{\$3,000}{\$9,000} = .33$, or 33%.

115. **d.** The ideal improvement must meet all criteria of highest and best use analysis.

116. a. Having to make adjustments in sales comparison suggests that comparables do not match subject characteristics, reducing reliability of the approach.

117. a. Improvements that represent highest and best use of the land as though vacant must meet all criteria of highest and best use analysis and would be the ideal improvement with no forms of depreciation. As such, the cost of building the improvement would equal its value.

118. b. Unit in place is a cost estimating technique that considers the cost of finished units of construction.

119. a. The math solution is as follows:

$$\frac{\$10,000}{\$100,000} = .10$$

$$\frac{\$7,125}{\$75,000} = .095$$

$$\$10,000 - \$7,125 = \$2,875$$

$$\$100,000 - \$75,000 = \$25,000$$

$$\frac{\$2,875}{\$25,000} = .115$$

At any time, if the equity position is earning a higher yield than the property would earn if it were not financed, leverage is positive.

120. a. The math solution is as follows.
Keystrokes: 5 n, $460,000 PV, $550,000 CHS FV
Solve for $i = .0363$, or 3.63%

121. c. A building survey locates the components in the structure of a building. Location of floors, rooms, stairways, and elevators are illustrated in a building survey.

122. d. Sales comparison considers the characteristics in the other answer choices, but not for original construction cost.

123. a. Sales comparison is also known as the market approach.

124. b. Gross adjustments are calculated by totaling adjustments.

125. a. The principle of competition states that properties with superior characteristics should sell for a higher price.

▶ Scoring

Once again, in order to evaluate how you did on this last exam, find the number of questions you answered correctly. The passing score for this practice exam is 113 correct answers (75%), but just as on the real test, you should be aiming for something higher than that on these practice exams. If you haven't reached a passing score on both practice tests, look at the suggestions for improvement in Chapter 2. Look at the table on the following page to see what problem areas remain.

The key to success in almost any pursuit is complete preparation. By taking the practice exams in this book, you have prepared more than many other people who may be taking the exam with you. You have diagnosed where your strengths and weaknesses lie and learned how to deal with the various kinds of questions that will appear on the test. So go into the exam with confidence, knowing that you are ready and equipped to do your best!

Certified General Appraisal Practice Exam 2 for Review

Topic	Question Numbers
Influences on Real Estate Value	11, 76, 85, 119
Legal Considerations in Appraisal	12, 17, 52, 54, 63
Types of Value	9, 27, 41, 60, 90, 99, 100
Economic Principles	59, 64, 71, 74, 84, 95, 98, 125
Real Estate Markets and Analysis	8, 10, 20, 37, 58, 61, 69, 70, 78, 88, 101
Valuation Process	4, 7, 16, 49, 65, 75, 80, 81, 96
Property Description	15, 40, 45, 79, 93, 102, 104, 106, 112, 114, 121
Highest and Best Use Analysis	72, 82, 87, 94, 97, 105, 109, 110, 113, 115
Appraisal Math and Statistics	19, 28, 29, 30, 36, 51, 83, 120
Sales Comparison Approach	14, 32, 42, 47, 50, 53, 86, 89, 91, 116, 122, 123, 124
Site Value	6, 13, 55, 62, 66, 67, 103
Cost Approach	18, 43, 48, 68, 73, 117, 118
Income Approach	21, 22, 23, 24, 25, 31, 44, 46, 111
Valuation of Partial Interests	26, 35
Appraisal Standards and Ethics	1, 2, 3, 5, 33, 34, 38, 39, 56, 57, 77, 92, 107, 108

Notes

Notes

Notes

Notes

Notes

Notes

Notes